PAT DURBIN AND TERRY DOERSCHER

TAMING
CHANGE

WITH
PORTFOLIO
MANAGEMENT

Unify Your Organization,
Sharpen Your Strategy,
and Create Measurable Value

GREENLEAF
BOOK GROUP PRESS

Published by Greenleaf Book Group Press
Austin, Texas
www.gbgpress.com

Distributed by Greenleaf Book Group LLC

For ordering information or special discounts for bulk purchases, please contact Greenleaf Book Group LLC at PO Box 91869, Austin, TX 78709, 512.891.6100.

Design and composition by Greenleaf Book Group LLC
Cover design by Greenleaf Book Group LLC

Publisher's Cataloging-In-Publication Data (Prepared by The Donohue Group, Inc.)

Durbin, Pat (Patrick)
    Taming change with portfolio management : unify your organization, sharpen your strategy, and create measurable value / Pat Durbin and Terry Doerscher. -- 1st ed.

    p. : ill., charts ; cm.

    ISBN: 978-1-60832-038-7

1. Organizational change--Management.   2.Business planning.   3. Technological complexity--Psychological aspects. I. Doerscher, Terry. II. Title.

HD58.8 .D87 2010
658.4063   2010922613

Part of the Tree Neutral™ program, which offsets the number of trees consumed in the production and printing of this book by taking proactive steps, such as planting trees in direct proportion to the number of trees used: www.treeneutral.com

TreeNeutral™

Printed in the United States of America on acid-free paper

    11 12 13 14 10 9 8 7 6 5 4 3 2

First Edition

We dedicate this book to our customers.
They are the source of our knowledge, passion, and inspiration.

CONTENTS

PREFACE

TERRY AND I HAVE SPENT MOST of our business careers in *portfolio management*, although we are mature enough to remember when this discipline was called by different names and was focused on different concepts. Over the years, we have seen a number of trends become generally accepted practices and others go by the wayside. Through all of this, we have observed some universal principles that have proven their value time and again in actual practice. This book is first about sharing these core portfolio management principles with you, our reader.

We also want to explore with you the comprehensive use of portfolios to manage change events. Change is inescapable in today's world. In many ways, change defines us. We are confident that portfolio management tools and techniques can help you manage the cycle of change, from identification to analysis, execution, deployment, and retirement. You may find that some of these ideas challenge conventional thinking, but give them a chance; you might be surprised by the opportunities they offer.

This leads us to the third driver for this book—timing. We believe we are at an important juncture in the evolution of business management that is best summed up by one word—convergence. Over the last decade, improvements in processes, techniques, and supporting technology have enabled us to make significant advances in several individual fields of business management. However, the proliferation of specialized capabilities within individual functional areas is also awakening the business world to the need to unify how organizations operate. We are seeing this among industry analysts, executives in different business sectors, professional associations, supporting vendors, and practitioners in many disciplines. As the volume and pace of change increases, there is a compelling need to align and consolidate the efforts of marketing specialists, product and brand managers, strategic planners, financial analysts, PMOs, project managers, operations leaders, technologists, and others to achieve shared business objectives.

We believe this growing recognition, combined with the use of portfolio management as a common unifying mechanism, creates a perfect storm for improving how organizations perform.

This book is a reference guide to help you master portfolio management. We hope you will find "nuggets of information" that you can apply to your organization. We do not expect to revolutionize your thinking, but rather to incrementally evolve it. In fact, the journey of writing this book will be fulfilled for us if you make a place for it on your bookshelf of business guidance that you routinely reference.

This industry has offered a wonderful career to Terry and me. We hope to pass to you the techniques that will open doors to advance your own career opportunities and improve how your organization operates, now and in the future.

Patrick Durbin
Founder and CEO of Planview, Inc.

ACKNOWLEDGMENTS

WE WOULD LIKE TO THANK the people who helped us in so many ways with this endeavor.

First, to our wives, Jane and Theresa, who endured "author's widow syndrome" for so many nights and weekends and supported us through this project. Terry would also like to thank his daughter, Ali, an author in her own right, for reviewing content—I promise to return the favor.

We would like to thank the following people for their support, valuable insights, and candid feedback:

Rex D'Avilia	Rich Murphy
Dan Dudek	Mark Perry
Eric van Gemeren	Brad Rable
Greg Gilmore	Kay Redditt
Mark Hendricks	Linda Roach
Roger Hurwitz	Gunes Sahillioglu
Randy Leiser	Patrick Tickle
Jerry Manas	Jason Wright

Thanks to Flowserve, the University of Utah, and The Carphone Warehouse for allowing us to share their portfolio management success stories.

We also want to extend our sincere appreciation to the entire staff at Planview for their enthusiasm, understanding, and support of this project.

Finally, thanks to the entire team at Greenleaf Book Group for their partnership, expertise, and support. Special appreciation goes out to Bill Crawford, our developmental editor at Greenleaf, who patiently helped us approach our writing from the reader's perspective.

Section 1

THE CASE FOR ACTION

Change is coming at an increasing rate in our modern world. It affects how we plan and control work and how we manage our workforce. This section discusses how to use portfolio management to embrace and take command of change events in your organization.

CHAPTER 1

ADAPTING TO CHANGE

It is not the strongest of species that survives, nor the most intelligent.
It is the one that is the most adaptable to change.
—CHARLES DARWIN, *On the Origin of Species*

THIS BOOK IS ABOUT MANAGING CHANGE. More specifically, it is about how to apply the discipline of portfolio management to take command of change events as they flow through your organization. Whether you work in a mid-sized company, government agency, global corporation, or nonprofit institution, portfolio management can improve how you and your organization handles change.

You are probably already familiar with the concept of managing a portfolio of projects that share common resources or funding. You might also be familiar with managing change in the context of change orders within a project, enhancements to a product, or change requests to a computer system. While all of these concepts of portfolios and change are valid, we are approaching these subjects from a broader perspective—applying portfolio management to changes that impact you on an organizational level to effectively manage these change events, deliver exceptional growth, and create measurable value.

The discipline of portfolio management can be applied to manage strategies, products, markets, and more. The portfolio management tools and techniques used to plan and manage a collection of projects are equally applicable to investment analysis and operational planning. Portfolios provide a consistent way to view the information provided by these tools and techniques so you can manage change events more effectively.

In *Taming Change with Portfolio Management*, we demonstrate how you can use portfolios to link operational planning, investment analysis, and work and resource management into a unified approach for handling change, from initiation to operation. By taking a comprehensive approach to managing change, you establish an extremely powerful set of tools that helps you make informed decisions, effectively execute the work needed to achieve them, and measure the value that your decisions create.

Although portfolio management brings tremendous benefits in each functional area of your organization, its greatest value lies in its ability to align the entire organization to successfully manage change. Portfolio management unifies your organization by improving communications and breaking down functional silos. Your organization will be more effective when all staff members can see and understand the impact of their decisions.

RELENTLESS CHANGE

While some organizations manage change well, others have found it difficult to adapt. In 1942 Harvard economist Joseph Schumpeter introduced the theory of "creative destruction," which defines change as the natural consequence of our economic system. He wrote that a market economy will "incessantly revitalize itself from within by scrapping old and failing businesses and then reallocating resources to newer and more productive ones."* Our market-based system is built to cause constant change, and yet we are surprised when it occurs.

---

* Joseph A. Schumpeter, *From Capitalism, Socialism and Democracy* (New York: Harper, 1975) [orig. pub. 1942].

There are numerous examples of how the process of creative destruction led to the growth of one business and the disappearance of another. Consider the retailers Woolworth and Wal-Mart. The first F. W. Woolworth Company store opened in the late 19th century and pioneered the concept of offering customers a wide variety of low cost items in a self-serve environment. Over the next hundred years, Woolworth's adapted well enough to become one of the world's largest retail operations.

However, Woolworth's leaders eventually missed business environment changes caused by younger, more nimble and efficient competitors. Rather than refining its basic model, the company invested heavily in the acquisition of specialty retailers. By the 1980s, an over commitment to niche stores and an inability to adjust to change led to the destruction of the company. In 1997, Woolworth's closed the last of its U.S. stores and today survives only as a chain of Foot Locker shoe stores.

Creative destruction brought about Woolworth's demise and the rise of its greatest competitor—Wal-Mart. The history of Wal-Mart Stores is one of relentless change management in which the company continually refined basic retailing skills—merchandising, pricing, location, and especially, supply and distribution. The company's ability to get the right goods at the right prices in the right places on store shelves eventually overpowered Woolworth's and others. From a converted Ben Franklin five-and-dime store in Arkansas, Wal-Mart rode the wave of creative destruction to its position as the undisputed king of global retailing.

Take another look at *In Search of Excellence* (New York, Harper & Row, 1982), the classic business book by Tom Peters that profiled forty-three companies that exhibited the traits of excellence. How many of them are still leaders? Think of household names like Kmart, Digital Equipment Corporation, and Kodak. Where are they now?

Futurists agree that we are only at the doorstep of an era of intense change that will far surpass the rise of the industrial age. The technological breakthroughs that launched the digital age have already brought about such a rapid increase in change that the inner workings of most organizations are barely recognizable from just a few decades ago. While the year-over-year effects of these innovations may not have seemed very dramatic at the time, compared to the analog world of the late 1970s, the cumulative effects are significant.

Without question, our business environment will continue its rapid evolution, driven by an unrelenting stream of changes in technology and society. Are you equipped to capitalize on change or will your organization be left behind?

LEADING MODERN ORGANIZATIONS

Technological change has transformed our organizations and the business environment. We now create products and services from information and intelligence rather than steel or brick. Organizations have relocated production lines to emerging economies while they focus their attention on more innovative, intellectual endeavors. The exponential increase in our body of knowledge has led to more and more specialization in every profession.

With increased complexity and more specialization comes change in how we plan and execute our work. Dedicated project teams have become a luxury in most organizations. Instead, we now carefully orchestrate the skills of different groups of people to create and deliver complex products and services. The result is that organizations have become more collaborative.

They work with outside organizations, often treating them like employees. Product managers negotiate for the skilled individuals needed to do the work. Financial analysts often face a complex set of investment options. Brand managers are coordinating with groups throughout the organization to meet their goals. Project managers now focus more on communications and risk management. Resource managers deal with conflicting priorities from many sources with different agendas. Leaders often wonder if their organizations are actually implementing their strategic decisions. The building blocks of our business, our decision-making processes, are changing as rapidly as the economic environment.

The cumulative results of these factors can be summarized into a set of new and interrelated challenges:

- Increased levels of uncertainty that disrupt operational stability and impact long-term planning
- An increased need for innovation driven by the reduced life span of products and services
- More project-based work competing with ongoing operations for resources
- The emergence of human capacities, skills, and knowledge as the most critical assets of the organization
- Expanded reliance on expensive, specialized professionals, extended by the use of global third-party resources
- The need to have the proper information to make decisions in real time
- A more dynamic work environment that mandates planning flexibility at all levels of the organization
- The need to quickly communicate and coordinate changes in plans to maintain organizational direction, priorities, and focus

As a result, how we govern our organizations is changing as well. Governance defines expectations, grants power, and verifies performance. Portfolio management strengthens corporate governance by defining and codifying decision rights at each level of your organization, making it more agile and better equipped to manage change. Using portfolios enables you to:

- Implement appropriate decision-making methods and tools
- Provide a clear view of how individual actions fit within the big picture
- Measure and assess effectiveness and improve future performance

MANAGING CHANGE WITH THE PORTFOLIO ECOSYSTEM

In natural terms, an ecosystem is a self-contained area in which the inhabitants function together and share a common physical environment. The mutually beneficial relationships that form between its inhabitants and natural elements are what make an ecosystem unique from other areas. However, an ecosystem is not self-contained nor is it immune to change. External factors like the weather and the introduction of new species drive it to evolve and adapt. The Florida Everglades offers a good example of a natural ecosystem that is constantly responding to change.

You can think of your organization as an ecosystem to visualize its operating cycle, interrelationships, and how it is affected by change. The basic concept is applicable whether you use it to describe a product line, program, department, or the entire enterprise.

The portfolio ecosystem in figure 1-1 models how organizations operate in a continual cycle of change. Each cycle begins by understanding your current operation and the value you are deriving from it. Change events cause your current operational state to shift, driving a series of change management stages that move it to a new, future state.

Each stage in the ecosystem represents specific change management actions that move the cycle forward. We will show you how to manage the cycle of change using strategic portfolios, investment portfolios, and execution portfolios. Each type of portfolio enables you to make decisions appropriate to where you are along the continuum of change.

The portfolio ecosystem reflects the primary business functions that you use to govern your organization. Because maintaining equilibrium between demand and capacity is a universal management consideration throughout the life cycle, we have placed it in the center of the figure. We refer to this as the *portfolio balancing act*, which we develop more fully in subsequent chapters. Let's introduce the primary business functions and how the ecosystem relates to each type of portfolio.

Figure 1-1: The Portfolio Ecosystem

Operational Planning

Operational planning begins when you analyze the current performance of products, services, assets, and the organization itself. This analysis gives you the information you need to evaluate the impact of change. As changes occur, you should consider ideas and opportunities that drive your organization's strategies in order to take advantage of those changes. In turn, your analysis and brainstorming will provide you with high level guidance—in the form of organizational objectives, strategies, budgets, and staffing levels—about how to meet demand by using your organization's capacities, primarily people and money.

You can use *strategic portfolios* to establish a foundation for measuring current operational performance, which provides a mechanism for collecting and analyzing information to support ideation and operational planning. The strategic portfolios can then be used to analyze and redistribute human and financial capacities to support new organizational goals and objectives. The information you gather in strategic portfolios forms the basis of high level trade-off decisions about the best way to create value for your organization.

Investment Analysis

Investment analysis takes the high level guidance developed by operational planning and helps you determine the best way to implement it. Typically investment analysis consists of making trade-off decisions between competing opportunities. This leads to a commitment of capacities (people and money) to meet the demand expected to produce the greatest value.

Investment portfolios start with the constraints and objectives of the approved operating plan. They are used to make comparisons between competing ways to implement the plan by considering factors such as strategic balance and alignment, timing, effort, risk, cost, and benefit. Ultimately, investment portfolios allow you to identify, approve, and fund the best possible combination of investments.

Work and Resource Management

Work and resource management focuses on tactical functions including planning, execution, and delivery of the combined demands placed on the organization, whether they are ongoing operational activities or strategic investments.

Execution portfolios give managers a way to make priority and resource allocation decisions and strike a balance between the competing demands of many different tasks.

Measuring the Value Delivered

As work is accomplished and deliverables become operational, the results of the work are rolled back into strategic portfolios with other products, services, and assets. Your assessment, done as the first step in operational planning, provides the information needed to measure the value delivered from the business decisions. This change event life cycle defines how the portfolio ecosystem functions.

CASE STUDY: THE PORTFOLIO ECOSYSTEM IN A NONPROFIT FOUNDATION

We first apply the portfolio ecosystem to a small nonprofit foundation. We chose this example because it offers a simple way to illustrate our key points, and it shows how a variety of organizations can derive value from using portfolios.

This nonprofit foundation provides short-term transient housing assistance and social services to people in the homeless population who want to move to safe and secure housing and are willing to work for it.

The foundation's board of directors is made up of volunteers—people with a heart for the mission of ending homelessness. Using a third-party consultant, the organization applied portfolio management to prepare a current state analysis for its board in late 2008. Here is the organization's analysis.

Current State Analysis

Strategic Portfolio—These items encompass the current state of the foundation's programs and infrastructure:

- **Social services program**: The foundation has a client-intake process that selects homeless families that have the desire and ability to change their situation. The foundation has had a 90 percent success rate at moving clients to safe and secure housing. Over 75 percent of the time, the foundation's services have helped those clients improve their income.

- **Transient housing network program**: The foundation offered housing, food, and transportation to transient members of the community for 8 to 16 weeks while those clients stabilized their situation. The transient housing facility has a capacity of thirty thousand bed/nights per year, typically in family units.

- **Infrastructure**: The foundation's infrastructure is a combination of volunteers and paid staff. The organization was highly leveraged with the use of volunteers. Paid staff included trained social workers that offered the social services needed to "graduate" the clients to safe and secure housing.

Change Events—In 2009 some key changes occurred, they included:

- The recession caused all funding sources to drop 30 percent.
- The U.S. government moved funding away from transient housing to homelessness prevention and rapid re-housing.
- The recession left more families homeless and confused about their options.

Ideas and Opportunities—Here are a few of the ideas and opportunities that were considered in response to the change events:

- Cut costs.
- Cut services or programs.
- Raise more money.
- Evaluate the impact of the new government funding plans; consider a new program?
- Look for ways to reach out to the newly homeless.

Investment Portfolio—After the board evaluated the potential responses to the change, it authorized the following investments of time and money:

- Cut costs by 10 percent.
- Go back to contributors to raise additional funds.
- Evaluate the government program to see if the funding redirection created opportunities.

Execution Portfolio—Taking the board's direction, staff developed the following projects, ranging from immediate action items to those running 2 years in duration:

- Require staff members to pay more of their health care costs.
- Add an additional fund-raising event.
- Appeal to past donors to give again in this time of need.
- Appeal to members of the volunteer network to give their money as well as their time to the foundation.
- Hire an external consultant to write a grant request for U.S. government funds.
- If the request is successful, repurpose some social services to work in homelessness prevention and rapid re-housing.

Update to the Strategic Portfolio—After 6 months, this was the value delivered from the investments:

- All program services continue, and there were no program cuts.
- The government grant request was successful, and the program now funds a social services caseworker, which has resulted in a repurposing of staff time from transient housing to homelessness prevention and rapid re-housing.
- Operational costs are down 10 percent.

Updates will continue to be posted quarterly until investment and projects are closed.

The nonprofit organization realized an immediate benefit from using portfolios. The board of directors got a clear picture of the current state and the impact of change events that led to investment opportunities. By using portfolios, the foundation was able to communicate the changes throughout the organization and react in a positive manner instead of being driven by events.

ADAPTING TO CHANGE EVENTS

We can use the game of soccer to describe the power of using portfolios in a unified manner. Soccer may appear to the uninitiated as unstructured and random; however, every participant has a distinct perspective on the game based on the role he or she plays. Participants apply these views to analyze the action and reposition themselves according to the plays and strategies of their game plan.

So it is with your organization. If you look at every change as a single, isolated event that threatens your survival, the people in your organization might respond like five-year-olds on the soccer field, "buzzing" around the ball like a swarm of bees. Using portfolio management, you will be able to see individual changes from a broader perspective and respond with fluid adjustments to your game plan. Once you understand that change is the nature of the game, it becomes a strategic tool.

Our goal is to provide you with a comprehensive game plan for managing change with portfolio management. Your team will function more effectively and efficiently when everyone is working from a common perspective of how your business operates. No matter what role you have in your organization, you will find some area of portfolio management that speaks directly to your immediate responsibilities. You will see how your decisions affect the flow of the complex game of business and improve the overall performance of your team, even under the pressure of continuous change.

KEY POINTS IN THIS CHAPTER

☑ Change disrupts the status quo; it is relentless and coming at an ever-increasing rate.

☑ Modern organizations face a unique new set of management challenges as a result of changes brought on by the digital age and other technological advances.

☑ The concept of "creative destruction" shows us that our economic system is built on relentless change, but we are still surprised when it occurs.

☑ The discipline of portfolio management is a unified decision-making process that allows an organization to embrace change and benefit from it.

☑ Balancing demand and capacity is essential to proactive change management; portfolios offer a mechanism to maintain this balance.

☑ The portfolio ecosystem models the core business functions of an organization that are impacted by the continuum of change.

☑ The primary business disciplines that are modeled in the ecosystem are operational planning, investment analysis, and work and resource management. There are three portfolio types that apply to each of these business functions:

- *Strategic portfolios* assess the current state of the operation, create guidance for the organization, and can be used to measure the value delivery.

- *Investment portfolios* are used to manage the commitment of money and people to work.

- *Execution portfolios* assign resources to projects and operations, which is the art and the science of getting things done.

☑ Portfolio management defines an approach to unify your organization by taming the power of change to deliver maximum benefit.

CHAPTER 2

MANAGING KNOWLEDGE WORKERS

MODERN ORGANIZATIONS ARE DEFINED by how their knowledge workers use ideas and information to create value. Over the past 30 years, the business environment has been in the middle of its most radical transformation since the industrial age. The technology revolution that began in the 1980s set the stage for today's constant change and compressed time to market, which led to the rapid growth in business sectors that use knowledge workers to provide technology-based services.

These organizations can be stand-alone entities that directly develop and market technology, such as computers and related hardware, software, pharmaceuticals, medical devices, energy, transportation, automation, or telecommunications. However, you will find the same work and resource management challenges in various technology services groups, departments, or business units in virtually every large corporation. Typified by Information Technology (IT), these units also include areas such as engineering services, new product development, and research and development (R&D), to name a few. We refer to these groups that rely on knowledge workers as Technology Services Organizations (TSOs).

The unique challenges and characteristics of TSOs are driving us to rethink how we manage them. If we are to improve our management methods, we must first recognize what makes TSOs different.

CHARACTERISTICS OF TECHNICAL SERVICES ORGANIZATIONS

Regardless of their sector or makeup, TSOs share the following characteristics:

- They serve multiple internal and/or external customers with virtually unlimited needs, resulting in an opportunity-rich environment.
- They have responsibilities to simultaneously facilitate change and manage ongoing operations.
- They deal with a high volume of inbound work of different types, ranging from strategic projects to level-of-effort support requests.
- Their primary mechanism of producing deliverables is through the talents of a limited number of skilled, specialized, professional knowledge workers.
- A significant portion of this staff multi-tasks across a range of different assignments and responsibilities.
- Resources are arranged in a matrix organizational structure, with various groups dependent on one another to achieve useful results.
- Staff members function in a dynamic business environment where strategies and priorities are constantly being adjusted in response to the ever-increasing pace of business, new opportunities, and rapidly evolving technology.
- Many times projects cannot be fully planned and staffed in advance due to the iterative nature of the work or use of new technology.

- The elusive nature of knowledge-based work requires different measurement and control methods compared to creating tangible deliverables from physical materials.

These influences, and other considerations that we introduce later, shape the approaches and techniques we have developed for using portfolios to manage work and resources in TSO environments.

MATRIX ORGANIZATIONS

Dramatic increases in various bodies of knowledge over the past century have led to specialization in practically every subject area. Professional fields are becoming increasingly narrower and deeper out of necessity. Because of this, most TSOs have shaped themselves into a matrix organizational structure where employees with related skill sets are grouped into specialized teams.

For example, within an Information Technology department, you will usually find groups such as application development, data center, security, architecture, web services, and so on. Engineering support services often group electrical, mechanical, or civil disciplines together. Product development teams may reflect specialized knowledge of component types used within multiple products. Each of these examples demonstrates the compartmentalization and consolidation of specific resource skills and roles within the enterprise, which are then temporarily deployed to any number of tasks that make up many different individual projects and ongoing operational functions.

This is in sharp contrast to organizations that arrange staff in mostly self-contained units. For example, a large construction project or defense program assembles a workforce that is dedicated to one initiative and contains all the necessary skills and roles to accomplish the deliverable. Staffing is a temporary variable like any other type of capacity; project managers ramp up or release human resources as needed, with little or no concern about what these individuals were doing before or after their project assignment. Project management has traditionally approached resource management in this way.

While this approach makes sense for one very large project, it does not reflect the TSO environment. Today, we often find a multi-project environment, with hundreds or even thousands of different sized projects in the portfolio. This work is accomplished collectively, using a relatively fixed number of specialized professionals deployed across different projects at different times. In this situation, it is usually human resources and their skills that limit how much work can be done and how quickly it can be accomplished. Human resources also usually constitute the single largest expense of a TSO. As a result, it is critical that staff members have effective direction to ensure that they are accomplishing the right work at the right time and that they stay as productive as possible. This is one of the most important and complex management challenges that TSOs face.

In such a situation, a matrix environment has many advantages. It allows professionals with similar development needs, expertise, and capabilities to operate as a cohesive team, share workload, and create synergies within their focus areas. It offers greater flexibility for work assignment. A matrix structure also effectively controls the size and cost of the professional staff when compared to creating dedicated project or program teams. Needed expertise can be dispatched *just-in-time* from matrix groups to perform discreet, specialized functions across a wide spectrum of otherwise disparate activities, rather than dedicating critical skills to each project, product type, or service. When properly managed, a matrix organization maximizes utilization and provides a high degree of resource flexibility without hiring and releasing a large temporary staff.

A matrix organization also creates management complications. A by-product of a matrix arrangement is that few, if any, of these specialized teams can deliver anything of business value on their own; intricate interdependencies exist between different parts of the matrix in order to achieve a useful outcome. The end-to-end creation and delivery of complex products draws on different skill sets from multiple teams. As deliverables are developed, groups are choreographed to make incremental contributions.

Each project plan needs to be carefully coordinated with other projects and types of work to define priority and resource sequencing.

Research has shown that in modern organizations, formally managed major projects typically constitute an average of 15 percent to 30 percent of the total workload. A good portion of the workforce has ongoing operational responsibilities in addition to specific project tasks that often span multiple initiatives. Many project managers and other leaders are not trained to understand the complexities of the modern knowledge worker environment. As a result, they simply repeat the resource management practices that they have always used in more traditional single-project situations.

Multi-tasking and Disruptions

Matrix organizations are synonymous with multi-tasking. The majority of today's knowledge workers are simultaneously assigned to several different work activities of varying duration. Frequently, these project tasks and other types of work have little in common other than the fact that they are all competing for the time and attention of the staff.

Stops and starts are the bane of multi-tasking matrix organizations. With each transition from one assignment to the next, individuals lose productive time. Our experience indicates that stops and starts alone consume 15 percent or more of the total availability of people who are trying to make progress on several different unrelated tasks per day.

Added to this are the constant interruptions often present in work environments. One study suggests that on average 28 percent of working time is consumed by phone calls, new e-mail notifications, doorway conversations, and similar disruptions.* In our experience, legitimate interruptions can consume an additional 20 percent of available effort. In a very reactive and unfocused work environment, *over half* of the total available effort may be spent on unproductive activities or firefighting.

Proactive task planning is the best way to reduce multi-tasking and to counteract lost productivity. When given the opportunity to concentrate

---

* Jonathan B. Spira and Joshua B. Feintuch, *The Cost of Not Paying Attention: How Interruptions Impact Knowledge Worker Productivity* (New York: Basex, 2005).

on a single task without distraction for an hour or more, we become fully invested mentally in the work at hand. We often find ourselves asking, "Where did the day go?" as we emerge hours later from a period of highly productive behavior. To maximize results, managers should strive to limit the number of tasks simultaneously assigned.

THE ELUSIVE NATURE OF KNOWLEDGE WORK

Knowledge work is difficult to plan, estimate, and complete. Unlike physical work such as construction or component assembly, knowledge-based activities are often one-of-a-kind endeavors with no direct historical comparison for estimating purposes. Knowledge-based work also lacks discernable indicators of progress.

Every individual employs unique thinking approaches to perform knowledge-based tasks. From an external perspective, you cannot readily observe these processes or objectively measure progress on interim results. Often, you need to first begin a new knowledge-based task to accurately assess how much effort is going to be required. As a result, estimating frequently becomes a series of iterations, based on previous assumptions, versus actual progress and an ever-increasing understanding of the task itself. Knowledge work estimates have two primary components—the amount of effort that will be required and the length of time this effort will be applied. We already know from the multi-tasking discussion that these two components are not likely to be the same.

Given that the quality and completeness of the end product is often difficult to clearly define, perhaps the most challenging aspect of knowledge work is determining when it is finished. It is readily apparent when physical work such as building a bridge is complete; objective measures are compared to well-defined requirements. Whether the task is a presentation, marketing plan, product design, or writing a computer program, there comes a point when we must subjectively ascertain whether the result is *good enough*. Could you spend another hour, day, or week on the task and add meaningful value or does that time spent offer little incremental improvement?

TRAITS OF THE MODERN WORKFORCE

Our approach to work and resource management is impacted by the changes in the modern workforce itself. Over the past few decades, the relationship between employer and employee has undergone a dynamic shift. Today's professional knowledge worker is more educated, culturally diverse, motivated, and mobile. There is a mutual expectation that knowledge worker professionals will be largely self-directed. The supervisor-to-worker ratio has widened, and first-level managers spend less time on oversight and direction of their staff.

Today's workforce is far less homogenous than in the past. With specialization comes a unique combination of capabilities that each individual possesses—in technical skills and in other important considerations such as language; soft skills; roles; and specific experience with particular products, markets, or applications. People in the workforce are also becoming more nomadic; unlike their parents, today it is increasingly rare that a young professional expects to stay with any given organization longer than 3 to 5 years. In a word, today's professional knowledge workers are *individuals* in every respect.

There is also the undeniable impact of globalization on the modern workforce. A physically distributed and culturally diverse labor pool is now typical in large and small companies alike. In addition to cost considerations, a global workforce adds capacity and skills to supplement a local, direct staff. Whether you are managing direct staff, participating in virtual teams, or outsourcing work to third-party contractors your management methods and tools are impacted by a virtual workforce.

THE END RESULT

Given the characteristics of the TSO environment, it can sometimes seem difficult if not impossible to juggle various work demands and time constraints while maximizing the limited availability of resource capacities. Whether you are trying to manage several unrelated projects, a series of business applications, a portfolio of products or services, a complex technical environment, or effectively deploy a group of specialized staff, the operational aspects of modern work environments present a number of demanding conditions.

Your workload is composed of many different kinds of tasks that are often difficult to definitively plan far in advance because of their inherent ambiguity, incremental disclosure of scope and effort, or simply because it is often difficult to ascertain when deliverables are finished. Work activities rely primarily on the expertise of skilled professionals that are neither unlimited nor homogenous. Each individual offers a unique combination of capabilities and experience (and limitations) that must be considered to maximize that person's potential to contribute to objectives.

Managers often expect these workers to apply their specialized capabilities to several different tasks simultaneously, but too much multi-tasking has productivity implications. Added to all of this is the often-volatile nature of business priorities and the resulting dynamics that affect how work is assigned and accomplished. Use of portfolios combined with appropriate planning and management techniques can help you address these issues.

KEY POINTS IN THIS CHAPTER

☑ Modern organizations create value from the ideas and information created by their knowledge workers.

☑ Technology Services Organizations (TSOs) are business units or groups within an organization that have common characteristics that define how they intake and manage work.

☑ Modern resource management techniques can control excessive multi-tasking and disruptions that impact the productivity of knowledge workers.

☑ The elusive nature of knowledge-based work presents unique challenges to measuring progress and identifying when it is complete.

☑ The modern workforce is culturally diverse and globally dispersed.

CHAPTER 3

USING PROCESSES TO MANAGE CHANGE

PORTFOLIO MANAGEMENT PROCESSES play a critical role in determining how well your organization responds to change. In addition to enabling portfolio management in your organization, these processes also improve general transparency, discipline, and trustworthiness. Together, they link different business functions together to integrate change management capabilities.

We offer a framework for creating a comprehensive portfolio process model later; this chapter explores the role that processes play in allowing your most critical asset, your people, to respond to changes in their environment, individually and collectively.

EVOLUTION VERSUS REVOLUTION

During the peak of the radical corporate reengineering era of the 1990s, the dominant approach to addressing organizational change was to treat it as a one-time event. One analogy described the organization as normally existing in a stable, "frozen" state; the status quo was "melted" by a change event and then "refrozen" into a new norm. Yet another view described the impact of change and subsequent loss of familiar stability as something akin to adjusting to the loss of a loved one, with periods of denial, grief, and ultimately acceptance.

Clearly, these concepts treated change as a more or less infrequent and often jarring event, followed by a relative stable period. Because change events were considered relatively rare and unique occurrences, there was little reason to have standard policies and processes to manage them. Today, we view change as a constant reality for modern organizations; we are always in a state of change.

But let's acknowledge that there are certainly abrupt, significant events that severely disrupt or fundamentally transform your business. When faced with revolutionary change such as a merger or similar major occurrence, your organization will typically mobilize to manage the impact. And even then, the more disciplined, transparent, and trustworthy your change management processes are, the better you will handle change.

Evolution, rather than revolution, more aptly describes the relentless nature of the pressure of change on your organization. Today, incremental change is an inherent aspect of your normal operations. So it is prudent, even necessary, for you to establish polices and processes to manage change as an ongoing function. Portfolio management processes provide a disciplined approach to anticipate and manage both revolutionary and evolutionary changes in a consistent, repeatable, and transparent way.

HOW CHANGE IMPACTS PEOPLE

Change, of course, has always existed. Historically, the most successful organizations have not only accommodated change—they have used it to their advantage. But the amount of change being injected into our business lives is coming at a rate we've never seen before, and there is no apparent slowdown in sight.

But, how much change are we capable of absorbing at any given time? Just as there are limits that constrain change in the physical world, there are limitations to change in the business world. Examples of such constraints might include our ability to acquire and employ funding, analyze and act on new data, access specialized competencies, redirect corporate strategy, or leverage scientific discoveries.

The most obvious and difficult constraint to organizational change lies with people themselves. As an example, the newest generation fighter jets now have the ability to perform maneuvers that exceed the physical endurance of any pilot; the human component rather than the aircraft has become the limiting factor. In the same way, the ability of people to adapt to change may ultimately prove to be the limiting factor in the rate of business evolution.

As individuals, people routinely demonstrate great ability to change. Certainly as individuals we are remarkably resilient, adaptable, and flexible—extreme g-forces notwithstanding. When facing personal adversity, given a promotion, changing employers, or embarking on new careers, individuals routinely adapt to new situations in a matter of days or a few weeks, sometimes overcoming seemingly insurmountable challenges.

However, when grouped in an organization, people respond to change in a more complex way. Change in a socialized context takes on a whole new set of dynamics. Why can't an organization collectively change as nimbly as the individuals within it? The short answer is that change applied in an organizational setting often forces the people affected to *simultaneously* adapt and adopt new methods to deal with each other, representing the greatest challenge to the organization. When single individuals are faced with changes in a new situation, there is usually an existing foundation of operational norms and support from others around them. Such is not the case when change impacts the entire organization.

Thus, the ability of an organization to evolve is limited in large part by how well its workforce can adapt by retooling itself to work differently. Portfolio management offers the process framework to communicate changes and reestablish the rules of the new future state. It can offer the workforce the assurance that there is a plan and it is being executed for a purpose.

PROCESSES ENABLE CHANGE MANAGEMENT

People require explicit guidance to operate as an efficient unit. In our society we have guidance through behavioral norms, politics, laws, and social standards. In a business, processes establish the standards, rules, and related methods for communications and teamwork. Your organization might have written policies and processes about how to do operational planning, investment analysis, and work and resource management. However, you may not be using portfolios or applying them as an organization-wide set of processes.

A measure of the maturity of your portfolio management processes is whether your organization handles change as a normal part of business. No questions, no arguments; it just works. During periods of relatively stable operations, informal approaches to managing change often seem adequate. During these times organizations may question the need for defined business processes. It is when the storms of change strike that the value of such processes becomes more readily apparent.

A correlation between process maturity and the ability to manage change was identified in an extensive portfolio management office (PMO) survey* that we conducted, which included responses from over 450 organizations. While details are available in the survey report and additional results will be covered more fully later, findings clearly illustrate a difference in the ability to handle operational challenges between organizations with low levels of process maturity compared to organizations that followed defined and repeatable processes.

In the survey, we asked the respondents to identify the most vexing challenges they were facing from a list of 33 common issues, most of which relate to the effects of change. *More than half* of respondents rated the following 8 issues as a "Critical Problem" or "Significant Challenge":

- Departmental silos
- Interdepartmental politics
- Uncontrolled demand

---

* "2008 PMO 2.0 Survey," January 15, 2009, available through www.tamingchange.com.

- Inadequate resources

- Incomplete requirements

- Organizational maturity

- Metrics and reporting

- Business dynamics

Most of these challenges are symptomatic of inadequate or ineffective portfolio and project management processes. Figure 3-1 is a simplified depiction of the impact of the "Top 20 Operational Challenges" from the survey, organized by the process maturity level of the organization.

It is clear that low levels of process maturity reflect an organization that is ill equipped to manage change. As an organization's process maturity level increases, it is better prepared to manage change events as part of the normal course of business.

No amount of personal coaching or technological wizardry can make a bad change management process effective. Today, fewer organizations view implementation of new software as a silver bullet initiative. More likely, a new business application is expected to act as a vehicle for evolving a part of the process framework through automation, integration, or outright redesign.

The majority of organizations also now clearly recognize the distinction between acquiring new technology and securing its adoption by the organization. This shift in the general attitude of the business toward technology has emerged in less than a decade, and it has had a profound effect.

As organizations have become more process-centric, or at least process sensitive, we have seen a dizzying array of new and improved process standards, techniques, and supporting applications, each with an acronym. CRM, ERP, PPM, ITSM, BPM, and myriad others now fill the business lexicon. Almost without exception, each has dealt with process improvement by carving off a particular area and treating it as a largely autonomous function. Such specialization has led to some innovative and useful management methods within specific disciplines, but this reductionist approach has also served to unintentionally isolate the management of various process areas.

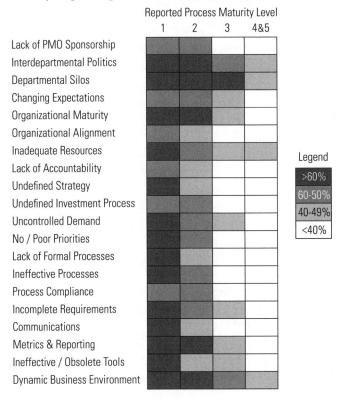

Figure 3-1: Top Change Management Challenges by Process Maturity Levels

Our approach to managing the cycle of change with portfolio management unifies related processes for operational planning, investment analysis, and work and resource management. Members of your organization may not see the benefit of change management processes when they are feeling secure and comfortable. *It is when the systems are stressed by change events that poor process definition and poor integration is exposed.* If we accept the relentless nature of change, then the question is not *if* it is going to affect you, but rather *when* and *how much.*

KEY POINTS IN THIS CHAPTER

☑ Portfolio management processes provide a disciplined approach to anticipate change events and structure the decision-making activities in a consistent, repeatable, and transparent way.

☑ Applying portfolio management processes to your business functions will mature the transparency, discipline, and trustworthiness of those functions.

☑ Change was once viewed by organizations as one-time events to be endured and ultimately accepted. We now see change as constant, both in regular evolution and in the disruptive transformational events.

☑ People have always faced change, but today it is occurring at a rate never seen in history, with no apparent slowdown in sight.

☑ Individuals have demonstrated a great ability to change but have difficulty dealing with the simultaneous nature of change within an organization.

☑ The ability of an organization to evolve is limited in large part by how well its workforce can adapt by retooling itself to work differently.

☑ Studies show that mature change management processes prepare organizations for change and help them manage its impact. Those organizations with mature portfolio management processes look at organizational change as a positive event.

☑ Portfolio management processes take a unifying view of the key business functions affected by organizational change management—operational planning, investment analysis, and work and resource management.

PRINCIPLES OF PORTFOLIO MANAGEMENT

Portfolio management is a set of disciplined processes for making smart business decisions about change events. The value of portfolio management lies in the flexible way that you can view, analyze, and act on meaningful business information. In this section we introduce the concepts of portfolio management, discuss the important information to help you back your business decisions, and focus on the core concepts of managing demand and capacity.

CHAPTER 4

PORTFOLIO MANAGEMENT CONCEPTS

A *PORTFOLIO* GETS ITS NAME from a case used for carrying documents such as maps, photographs, or drawings. In a business management context, a portfolio allows you to group a set of common subjects, like products, projects, or resources, so they can be collectively managed. Portfolios are used to make change management decisions by comparing and ranking the subjects inside them. These comparisons and rankings are based on supporting information such as priorities; risk factors; and cost, effort, and schedule estimates. Processes collect information, link decisions, and measure performance through the cycle of change.

While working with an organization faced with the challenge of managing change, one executive told us the following story:

The newly appointed CIO of a major corporation was called into the CEO's office. During the visit, the CEO was direct—"I am spending $50 million a year on IT and when I asked the last guy in your job where it was going, he couldn't tell me. Don't you make the same mistake!"

After 3 months of trying to find the answers to the CEO's questions, the new CIO realized that she needed a better approach. She had a lot of facts about operations and projects but lacked a way to explain the overall value that IT was delivering to the organization.

She needed help structuring the decisions that she and the business unit managers needed to make. She needed better information about what it was costing the company to implement technology decisions and what real impact those decisions had on company performance metrics—like revenue and profit. She wanted to improve communications throughout the organization on the value and risks associated with spending corporate resources on technology. She turned to portfolio management.

Your boss may not be quite so explicit in expecting quick and accurate answers about how you're using your organization's capacities. But, your company's long-term profitability and ultimate prosperity do depend on balancing your use of resources to achieve maximum return with acceptable risk.

USING PORTFOLIOS

Portfolio management is a set of disciplined processes that help you make smart decisions about change and efficiently execute actions stemming from those decisions to achieve your expected benefits. Implementation of portfolio management offers clarity of purpose, commitment to common goals, and consistent work execution to any organization that is under the pressure of change. Portfolios provide a way to view the information that you and your fellow executives need to make better-informed business decisions.

Given the general definition of portfolios that we offered earlier, you can apply portfolios to any number of decisions, subjects, and kinds of information in a business setting. However, to demonstrate their power and range of use, we will concentrate on the three portfolio types that we introduced in chapter 1: strategic portfolios, investment portfolios, and execution portfolios. Each type of portfolio supports a specific set of change management decisions and the needs of different users.

Sections 3 through 5 of this book describe the specific tools and techniques that you apply for each of type of portfolio. In this section, we present general portfolio management principles and concepts that are applicable to virtually any business management setting.

INFORMATION THAT SHAPES YOUR DECISIONS

The value of portfolio management lies in the flexible way that it allows you to view, analyze, and act on meaningful business information. Over the years, we have identified four broad types of management information that are pivotal to the decisions you make about change events:

- **People**, both direct staff and other resources (contractors, partners, etc.)
- **Money**
- **Work** you do (projects, operational tasks, etc.)
- **Deliverables** you produce (products and services)

People and money represent the primary *capacities* that you have. Using these capacities to perform work and create deliverables satisfies *demand*. Figure 4-1 further illustrates these information elements.

Figure 4-1: Primary Types of Portfolio Management Information

Obviously, every organization already has this kind of information in some form. Some of it may be very well defined, while other types may be less detailed or lack fully defined interrelationships.

For example, accounting requirements drive how you manage financial data, from general ledger accounts to individual expenses, so it is often contained within a detailed hierarchy. You may also have a well-defined organization structure that includes everyone and all reporting relationships. However, your organization chart probably does not reflect the contractors or partners who work with you. Not all organizations have their projects clearly associated with the strategies they support or document relationships between markets and products. It is also common to find that each type of information is stored in a different database, that a different application is used to access and manage each of those databases, and that different groups of people within the organization manage each information type.

Understanding this information, how it is structured, and how it relates to your decisions is a basic concept of portfolio management. Figure 4-2 provides an example of how you might structure information within these categories.

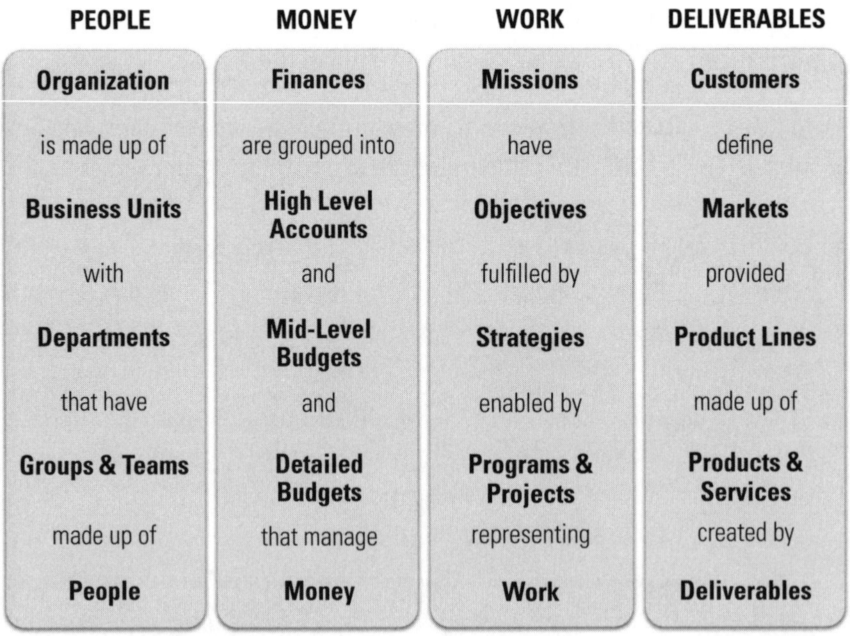

PEOPLE	MONEY	WORK	DELIVERABLES
Organization	**Finances**	**Missions**	**Customers**
is made up of	are grouped into	have	define
Business Units	**High Level Accounts**	**Objectives**	**Markets**
with	and	fulfilled by	provided
Departments	**Mid-Level Budgets**	**Strategies**	**Product Lines**
that have	and	enabled by	made up of
Groups & Teams	**Detailed Budgets**	**Programs & Projects**	**Products & Services**
made up of	that manage	representing	created by
People	**Money**	**Work**	**Deliverables**

Figure 4-2: Portfolio Management Information Structures

As we move down the information structures in figure 4-2, each level represents an increasing amount of detail and the basic relationships between them.

In addition to the relationships and levels within each type, there is also significant value in understanding how one type of information relates to another. For example, you probably budget money to the organizational unit that is responsible for managing it. As a result, you might define financial cost centers according to the different levels of the organization chart. You may also structure resource teams based on the type of work they do or the products they support.

Any change that occurs in one type of information, such as investment decisions, affects information in other areas, like the organization, projects, or products. Figure 4-3 provides an example of how the information in these structures is related.

Information Structure Interdependencies

Organization	utilizes	Finances	to achieve	Missions	for its	Customers
Business Units	utilize	High Level Accounts	to achieve	Objectives	for its	Markets
Departments	utilize	Mid-Level Budgets	to achieve	Strategies	for its	Product Lines
Groups & Teams	utilize	Detailed Budgets	to execute	Programs & Projects	to produce	Products & Services
People	consume	Money	to perform	Work	to produce	Deliverables

Figure 4-3: Relationships Between Portfolio Management Information Structures

These relationships represent the most common elements of the business that you compare and manipulate with portfolios and those that are most prone to the effects of change. Whether you proactively initiate a change or respond to one caused by external influences, it usually has a direct impact on some element in one information area that reverberates though the others.

Because of these interrelationships, it is important that you have the ability to analyze change events across all of the management information structures we have noted. Otherwise, you run the risk of not fully understanding the consequences and implications of your decisions.

Portfolio management provides a method to define, structure, and align information in such a way that you can view different types of information simultaneously, at different levels of detail. You can use portfolios to collectively analyze and act on your key management information from any number of different levels and perspectives, depending on your specific needs.

WHERE PORTFOLIOS APPLY

The first generation of business portfolio management focused on making investment decisions, and as a result, primarily employed financial tools and information. Later, portfolio management concepts were applied to control ever-expanding project lists; what we now recognize as project portfolio management. In the past several years, portfolio management concepts have evolved into a broad business discipline to manage change through strategies, initiatives, products, services, and more.

We will use three types of portfolios to demonstrate the portfolio management concepts—strategic portfolios, investment portfolios, and execution portfolios. What differentiates one type from another is the subject matter that you are making decisions about and the depth of information that you use to make those decisions. However, the unifying factor is that they always deal with the same core information structures. The following sections describe how each portfolio type uses common types of information in different ways.

Strategic Portfolios

Strategic portfolios facilitate operational planning to guide the future direction of the organization. This includes:

- Assessing the current state of operations and change influences
- Establishing the objectives and strategies of the organization
- Allocating financial and resource capacities
- Measuring the resulting value created by these decisions.

Figure 4-4 reflects the broad scope of strategic portfolios.

Strategic Portfolios	PEOPLE	MONEY	WORK	DELIVERABLES
Provide a Mechanism to Perform Operational Planning, Direct Investments and Govern People, Money Work & Deliverables:	Organization	Finances	Missions	Customers
	Business Units	High Level Accounts	Objectives	Markets
	Departments	Mid-Level Budgets	Strategies	Product Lines
	Groups & Teams	Detailed Budgets	Programs & Projects	Products & Services
	People	Expenses	Work	Deliverables

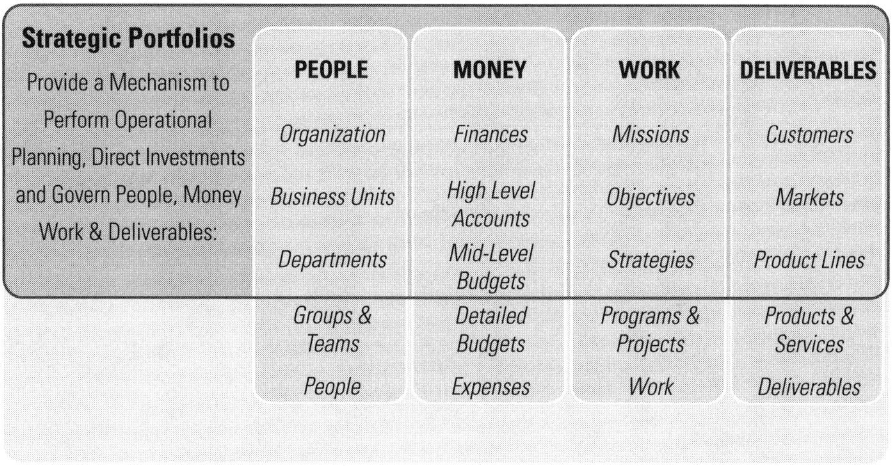

Figure 4-4: The Typical Range of Strategic Portfolios

Even though operational planning may primarily act on the upper levels of the information structures, one of the purposes of strategic portfolios is to align and communicate top-down decisions. Any portfolio is just a specialized view of information based on the type of decision you are making; it is flexible and defined according to your specific circumstances and information needs. A single strategic portfolio could be all-inclusive in smaller organizations, while larger organizations may use a strategic portfolio for each business unit and limit their information interests to higher levels. Section 3 of this book is devoted to conducting operational planning using strategic portfolios.

Investment Portfolios

Investment portfolios are specialized decision-support tools used to analyze, compare, and select potential opportunities that represent the best value, lowest risk, and greatest alignment with the strategies they support. Investment portfolios utilize the high level guidance and constraints established by strategic portfolios to make trade-off decisions between competing funding requests relative to available capacities. Figure 4-5 offers an example of how investment portfolios apply to portfolio management information structures.

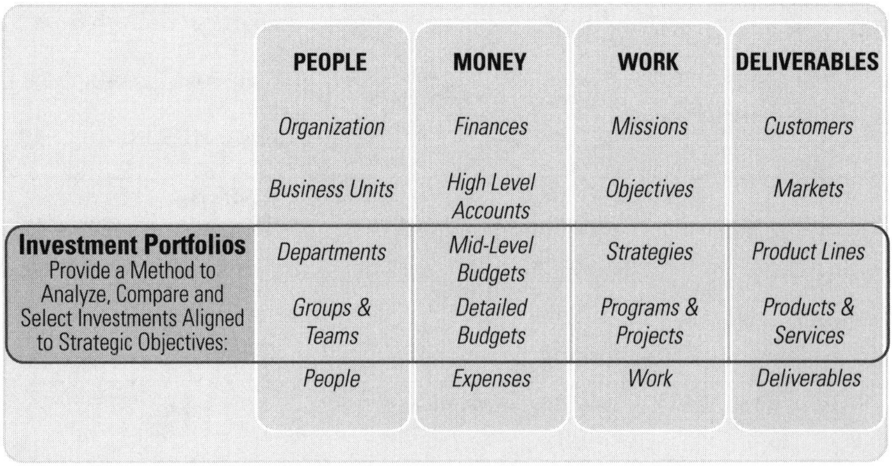

	PEOPLE	MONEY	WORK	DELIVERABLES
	Organization	Finances	Missions	Customers
	Business Units	High Level Accounts	Objectives	Markets
Investment Portfolios Provide a Method to Analyze, Compare and Select Investments Aligned to Strategic Objectives:	Departments	Mid-Level Budgets	Strategies	Product Lines
	Groups & Teams	Detailed Budgets	Programs & Projects	Products & Services
	People	Expenses	Work	Deliverables

Figure 4-5: The Typical Range of Investment Portfolios

Section 4 describes how investment portfolios are used to assess and select the work that the organization commits to pursuing and to reconcile any differences between bottom-up estimates and top-down strategic guidance.

Execution Portfolios

Execution portfolios are used to manage the tactical details of how projects, services, and the activities within them are planned and executed as well as how resources are assigned and managed. Execution portfolios give managers the opportunity to organize and view data from common information sources based on their specific decision rights and needs (figure 4-6). Managers can focus on the information and issues that are meaningful to them and coordinate their activities with other managers. Because of the relationships defined by the information structures, they can also clearly see how their actions relate to the bigger picture provided by strategic and investment portfolios. Section 5 explains how to apply execution portfolios to plan and manage work and resources.

	PEOPLE	MONEY	WORK	DELIVERABLES
	Organization	Finances	Missions	Customers
	Business Units	High Level Accounts	Objectives	Markets
	Departments	Mid-Level Budgets	Strategies	Product Lines
Execution Portfolios *Provide a Method to*	Groups & Teams	Detailed Budgets	Programs & Projects	Products & Services
Collectively Manage Work and Resources:	People	Expenses	Work	Deliverables

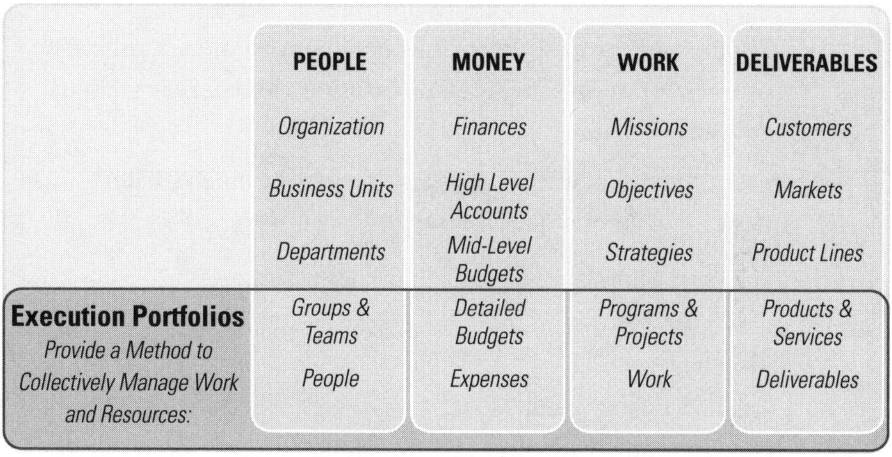

Figure 4-6: The Typical Range of Execution Portfolios

PORTFOLIO MANAGEMENT TOOLS AND TECHNIQUES

Applying portfolio types, tools, and techniques to these information structures allows you to:

- Visualize the elements competing for common resources and management attention
- Establish consistent and repeatable processes to accurately gather and compare information
- Define life cycles to address how this information is used and acted on throughout the change management cycle
- Define relationships between information structures
- Define decision rights for each level of information
- Compare and contrast alternative ways to invest money, utilize resources, establish schedules, set priorities, and perform other management actions
- Present consistent quantitative results to make objective decisions using analysis techniques such as:
  - Financial analysis
  - Risk assessment
  - Idea management
  - Capacity management
  - Planning and scheduling
  - Performance measurement
- Communicate decisions throughout the organization so they can be acted on
- Assign resources to execute the work with confidence taking into account the complete spectrum of organizational demand
- Measure performance against the expectations defined by your business decisions

HOW PORTFOLIOS UNIFY YOUR ORGANIZATION

The extension of portfolio management across an organization allows multiple users in different roles to view common information in different ways:

- **Executives** use portfolios to set goals, develop strategies, govern the organization, control capacities, and monitor performance.
- **Financial managers** use portfolios to link budgets and funding to strategy.
- **Market or brand managers** create portfolios to analyze market segments by demographics, geography, product lines, and so on.
- **Investment managers** have portfolios of investment opportunities.
- **Product managers** have portfolios of products or services.
- **Resource managers** have portfolios of staff by skill, location, or role.
- **Program/project managers** have portfolios of projects.
- **Portfolio management offices** support and facilitate alignment throughout the organization and provide common portfolio management methods and tools.

In every case, individuals are drawing on common sources of portfolio management information but are viewing and using it in different ways. They can arrange the information and pick the level of detail depending on their needs. They interact with each other and often see the real-time impact of decisions made by others.

The subject of the portfolio will vary based on the kind of decisions you are making and your role in the organization. Let's take a strategic portfolio as an example. The CFO might choose to define his view of the portfolio based on funding categories to understand how different deliverables, work, and resources are consuming capital versus noncapital expenses. The CEO might choose to arrange her portfolio view based on business objectives or product lines to see how they are performing and contributing to revenue. A business unit president may view his portfolio based on how different divisions of the organization are assigned strategic responsibilities.

While it is common for most organizations to use multiple portfolios, remember that the ultimate goal of portfolio management is to provide a unified view of change events from many different perspectives.

A CEO in a consumer products company found that he could control his strong-willed and ego-driven division managers by adding a vice president of strategy position. The new VP knew that he had to play the role of negotiator and arbitrator over a group that was generally used to getting its own way. His first step was to build an investment portfolio of all investment opportunities. Everyone was happy to add ideas to the mix.

He then built criteria to evaluate priorities and asked everyone to assess the options. The VP of strategy did not participate in the prioritization exercise; instead, the CEO provided the tie-breaking vote. The process was a dirty one, with politics and personalities often being injected in the middle of each decision, at least the first time. The investment analysis process resulted in a common investment portfolio that each business unit signed off on and that the CEO could use to track and evaluate the benefits ultimately created.

Even organizations that do not have the added obstacles of functional silos and fiefdoms will see the benefit of using portfolios to improve how information is collected, decisions are made, and initiatives are implemented. Effective portfolio management is applicable across a wide range of business process areas and organizational levels. While information collection may be mature and freely shared in some areas, that is seldom true everywhere. For example, one organization might have strong project management processes but be weak in investment analysis. A comprehensive approach to portfolio management is based on a unified, interlinked set of enabling business processes.

CREATING MEASURABLE VALUE

The vast majority of organizations struggle with measuring and analyzing the value of investment decisions once the results are operational.

This practice is often referred to as the discipline of *benefit realization*. Whether for a single project or a new strategic initiative, organizations often lack specific operational objectives, which form the basis for comparing actual value delivered. Even if you have measurable goals established, you still need a method to compare actual product and market performance with total development and operational costs.

Applying the different types of portfolios across the information structures as we have described in this chapter gives you a way to link operational planning, investment analysis, and work execution to support benefit realization measures. Each type of portfolio provides a way to track changes through their life cycle, from current state analysis to operations. The strategic portfolio enables you to make the analysis needed to make change decisions and passes those decisions to investment portfolios for refinement. Investment portfolios give you a way to select investments based on specific parameters related to business value. These investment decisions are managed to completion using execution portfolios. The actual performance of resulting project and service deliverables is then measured against original objectives using the strategic portfolio.

The ultimate benefit of portfolio management to your organization is that it helps you create measurable value. It takes time, commitment, and perseverance; however, it is such a powerful capability that it is worth the effort to truly know the value that your decisions deliver to your organization.

BENEFITS OF PORTFOLIO MANAGEMENT

The ultimate objective of portfolio management is to tame change by providing a proven discipline for delivering value through informed decision making.

We would like to focus on three critical characteristics of the portfolio management discipline that leverage its power in taming change:

- **Transparency**: The goals and methods of reaching decisions are available for all participants to see. While individuals may not always agree with them, business objectives are clearly documented and communicated. Communicating decisions and inviting opinion from others is a high priority in portfolio management.

- **Discipline**: Strict adherence to consistent and proven methods that apply a systematic, quantified analysis approach avoids venturing into personality-driven dead ends and alerts decision makers to opportunities that might otherwise go unnoticed.

- **Trustworthiness**: Each person involved in the process understands how decisions are made. Trusting the process becomes a critical component in each person's proactive commitment to implement the decisions. Performance toward goals is communicated to everyone. It creates a mechanism for personal accountability through clearly articulated goals, achievable plans, and defined responsibilities.

When a decision incorporates these three traits, the result is greater collaboration in setting goals, improved decision-support information, and better execution.

Job security weighs in as a personal rather than organizational concern. Yet portfolio management also addresses this issue, as illustrated by the experience of the CIO whose story began this chapter. Through the use of portfolio management, the CIO was able to explain to the CEO the total cost of supplying IT products and services to the business units. Technology investments became an open discussion that included the business units as equal partners rather than something imposed by IT. The CEO was better informed and, as a result, he set about expanding the portfolio management concepts to the rest of the organization. In short, unlike her predecessor, the new CIO kept her job—and maybe a little more.

KEY POINTS IN THIS CHAPTER

☑ Portfolio management is a set of disciplined processes for making smart business decisions and effectively executing them to drive positive change.

☑ Four core portfolio management information structures help you gather what you need to make decisions about change events:

- People
- Money
- Work
- Deliverables

☑ Operational planning is how executives offer guidance to the organization.

☑ Strategic portfolios allow you to define and communicate organizational goals and objectives to the organization.

☑ Investment portfolios give you a way to compare and select the best opportunities to commit the capacities of the organization.

☑ Work and resource managers use execution portfolios to make work and resource trade-off decisions. Work in a knowledge-based organization is a blend of projects, operations, work orders, and functional work.

☑ Portfolio management enhances how you deliver value by linking together operational planning, investment analysis, and execution (work and resource) management to let you measure the value created.

☑ These are the critical characteristics of portfolio management:

- Portfolios result in trustworthy decisions that are understood throughout the organization.
- Portfolios are transparent throughout the process.
- Portfolios offer a disciplined process for decision making.

CHAPTER 5

BUILDING PORTFOLIO INFORMATION

THE CONCEPT OF BUILDING COMPLEX INFORMATION using a hierarchical structure is certainly nothing new. Most organizations already have organizational charts, accounting information, product breakdown structures, and work breakdown structures (WBSs). Although this information may have been initially established for a singular purpose, over time a natural alignment developed. For example, most operating budgets are developed based on how the organization is structured.

Portfolio management offers you the framework to formalize the relationship between your information structures and to organize them in a useful manner to manage change events.

PORTFOLIO INFORMATION STRUCTURES

There are a few universal principles for developing portfolio information. One is to ensure that each information structure is complete and contiguous, from the highest level to the most detailed information. For example, work information can range from a high level view of business objectives to individual projects and the activities within those projects. Some organizations only have the work breakdown structures of their projects to reflect work information. That is useful for a manager with project-level decision rights, but not for someone who is planning across the organization. Think broader and deeper in structuring your information to create greater flexibility.

Focus on the interdependencies between the information structures as you build them. Each information structure does not need to contain the same number of levels, but you should have enough detailed information in each area to make informed decisions. A strong accounting department might have detailed accounting information, but that still won't give you much information about your products or markets. Reevaluate any proposed information structures that are obviously out of balance with the number of levels or degree of detail identified for others. Clear relationships will emerge between different levels of information structures as they are identified.

Primary and Secondary Information

We refer to people, money, work, and deliverables as the *primary information* you use to make decisions. In each case, the information elements that populate these structures have supporting attributes that further describe their characteristics. For example, a given strategy or project within the work structure can be classified using any number of additional attributes, such as by type, priority, status, funding category, risk level, and so on. A product can be similarly described, as can a resource or budget. These supporting descriptive elements are contained in their own information groupings, often referred to as *secondary information.*

When building primary information structures, keep them as simple and purposeful as possible, almost minimalist in structure and elegant in design. These structures provide basic content selection for defining portfolios and reporting at different levels. They also offer a method to set different levels of access rights. Use secondary information to further condition and describe portfolio contents as needed.

Identifying Information Relationships

As primary information is defined, you will identify relationships between levels as either one-to-one or one-to-many. In some cases there is one and only one match for an element. For example, a person works in one department at a time or an invoice is posted to only one code of accounts. Generally, capacity information about people and money has a one-to-one relationship, but there are exceptions; you might split an invoice between multiple accounts.

Demand information often has a one-to-many relationship. A product subassembly may be used in a number of products addressing different markets. A project may build infrastructure that supports multiple strategic initiatives. While portfolio information structures are often a little more complex than the simple examples we provide, they are pivotal in having the right information to make decisions and measure performance.

ORGANIZING PEOPLE

The typical organization chart offers a simple and effective view of reporting lines and how resources are arranged throughout the business. However, we need a more flexible and dynamic method to define these relationships for portfolio management purposes.

Portfolio management techniques are quite useful when it comes to understanding resources, their capabilities, utilization, and costs. Resource-based portfolios provide managers with many different views of staff and their workload. To ensure the staff is fully utilized but not overcommitted, you can create a portfolio based on the resource information where subjects include the staff, and measures reflect the task assignments and total effort needed from each individual. Unlike a work portfolio view for a group, a resource portfolio will include any task assignment to work that is within the group's responsibility. This gives managers a complete perspective of all staff commitments, regardless of the type of work or its point of ownership. In a matrix environment where multiple managers need to collaborate and coordinate their activities outside of their own work or resource groups, having this degree of visibility into the work and workforce becomes essential to manage work on a departmental level.

Creating an Organization Breakdown Structure

You can arrange your primary resource information by creating what is commonly referred to as an organization breakdown structure (OBS). The OBS usually reflects levels similar to your organization chart, such as shown in the following example:

Enterprise:
> Business Unit:
>> Division:
>>> Department:
>>>> Group:
>>>>> Resource:

Besides allowing you to summarize resource information, establish responsibilities, and define access rights, the OBS allows you to easily choose the resource information that you want to include in your portfolio by selecting the level most appropriate to your needs.

Classifying Resources

Several basic resource attributes support common portfolio management needs and provide reporting and analysis flexibility, including type, role, skill, cost rate, and location. Each example reflects secondary information that is applied to resources within the OBS.

Resource Type

Resource type denotes the source and basic nature of your staff. Some examples of resource type attributes include:

- Direct professional
- Direct hourly
- Direct part time
- Contractor
- Consultant
- Intern

Resource type options such as these establish basic differences in how you manage resources, how they can be used, and provide a general indicator of relative costs—all of which are important when making capacity management decisions or resource selections for work assignments.

Role and Skill Attributes

The capabilities of individual resources are reflected through the use of two related but distinctly different attributes: role and skill. Role establishes the general functions an individual performs, while skill denotes the specialized capabilities that an individual has in order to fulfill those functions.

Information about how to establish the attributes within these categories is one of our more common resource portfolio requests. The best way to balance providing enough options while keeping the number of selections manageable is different for every organization. However, we will provide some general guidelines that you can consider. In all cases, it is better to start simply and let necessity drive additional refinements.

Role options are more likely to have some basis in existing job descriptions and/or cost rate structures. Compared with the skills listing, the list of roles should be relatively high level and general in nature. A few common examples include project manager, business analyst, product manager, and marketing specialist. Often, rating indicators are added to the description to further designate relative seniority or capability levels, such as Project Manager I, II, or III.

Developing a skill library is a case of compromise, with the outcome best characterized as an "imperfect but functional" solution. The number of discrete skills available within the organization can represent seemingly endless possibilities, but a skill catalog containing hundreds of options can become impractical to maintain and use. It is important to remember that the objective of a skill catalog is to establish some measure of consistency and provide an indicator of general needs or qualifications. There is no replacement for the level of intimate knowledge that a resource manager has about individual worker capabilities to select the best assignment matches. The skills catalog offers a starting point for managers when identifying resource needs and selecting resources to assign.

Using a multi-tier menu to simplify navigation when defining a skill listing is often helpful. List individual options under several general categories, such as administrative skills, business skills, technical skills, and so on. Use separate categories and option lists to denote related attributes such as staff familiarity with specific product lines, components, applications, or similar specializations rather than trying to cover every variation or possibility in the skills list.

When making role and skill selections, most knowledge workers will have multiple options that are applicable and should be included. However, it is beneficial to designate one role and skill per individual as his or her primary attribute for capacity management purposes.

Resource Rate Attributes

To enable resource information to be employed for cost estimating purposes, it is useful to associate a cost rate with members of the workforce. Blended cost rates associated with a role, type, or some other general category is the preferred approach for portfolio use, given that the intent of this information is to support high level cost comparisons rather than to be the official cost accounting record. While it is often tempting to use specific cost rates for each individual to improve reporting accuracy, consider that this adds a significant amount of complexity and maintenance overhead and often results in other unintended consequences.

For example, if actual pay rates were used, a simple project or resource utilization report would expose compensation differences.

Some organizations add an additional level of sophistication to their resource rates by designating a different rate for each role and then calculating different costs depending on the role that an individual fulfills in a given assignment. This is useful when effort and role rate information is used to establish cost recovery or billing calculations. To elaborate, consider an individual who is multi-tasking on three different assignments for different customers, acting as a project manager for one, a business analyst on another, and an implementation consultant on the third. The role selected for each assignment will define the rate that is applied.

Other Resource Attributes

Other resource attributes can also prove useful. For example, designating the primary work location of staff in physically different offices can be valuable. In global organizations, information such as the time zone and the language skills of each individual are essential resource management considerations.

Bear in mind that gathering and using information about individual resource skills, roles, and any personal performance data (such as competency levels) may have legal implications in different countries. Laws about what personal information you can disclose in your portfolio management system and how you can use it to make work assignment decisions are quite different in the United States versus most European countries (each with unique requirements). There are also differences in how you manage and disclose information to employees versus third-party resources. Always consult your Human Resources organization and legal counsel when designing any resource information system.

INFORMATION ABOUT MONEY

Financial information is one of the most common and important portfolio attributes. No matter how you characterize your portfolio objectives, almost all portfolios include some form of financial data as one or more of the parameters used for analysis. Aligning financial information to the demand-related information structures offers you a way to improve the quality and visibility of information about money, the most ubiquitous portfolio characteristic.

As a basic accounting practice, every organization has a mechanism to allocate and track money based on how it is distributed to the organization. While this organizational view of financial expenditures shows you *how* money is spent, it does not show you *why*.

Taking a broader approach to financial planning, using strategic, investment, and execution portfolios, gives you an additional perspective about how money flows through your organization relative to your work and deliverables.

One of the most powerful tools that portfolios can offer your organization is the ability to relate financial data with your missions, objectives, strategies, and tactics. We explore this concept in more detail in section 3. Likewise, improving how you link financials to your products and markets offers real metrics on time to market and time to profitability. By analyzing financial information relative to this demand-based information, you can better understand the costs and revenue associated with those products and markets. This will provide additional insights and management levers to supplement your current financial planning practices.

Extending your financial management capabilities by developing demand-based portfolio views is an exercise in convergence. You already have an operational financial planning structure, system, and process in place to meet rigorous accounting and reporting requirements. As a result, it is probably the least flexible in terms of how existing structures can be modified. Because of this, your approach to establishing other primary planning structures often begins with understanding how your financial information is structured.

Consistency in the terminology and definitions associated with different approaches is important. Key functional considerations to allow information about work and deliverables to be aligned with current financial planning methods include financial planning cycles and periods, investment and spending categories, and how shared service centers and transfer pricing works.

Shared service center/transfer pricing refers to how funds are moved internally between providers and consumers; for example, how you use charge backs for internal services or how the cost of material inventory goes from manufacturing to finished goods distribution. Ultimately, you can think of extending your financial management views as a form of transfer pricing on an informational level, rather than actually moving funding. We reserve additional discussion about how to use financial information in portfolios for the next section.

STRUCTURING WORK INFORMATION

Surprisingly, many organizations do not have a formally defined work structure that aligns strategic intent with the programs and services that they provide. A defined structure that links work to business objectives allows you to realize the substantial benefits that portfolios offer.

Portfolio management adapts to almost any work planning approach, including the popular MOST approach adapted from the Hoshin Kanri method. The acronym stands for missions, objectives, strategies, and tactics. We endorse the MOST approach because it is simple and effective. Its flexibility makes it adaptable to almost any operating scenario, and it establishes and aligns the key elements necessary to achieve operational planning success.

The MOST concept facilitates the flow of operating principles and goals into a logical hierarchy of supporting strategies and tactics. Figure 5-1 offers an example work structure based on the MOST approach.

Using the MOST approach, operational planning begins by articulating the missions and objectives of the organization based on your current state and the change influences acting on that state. An enterprise may have multiple broad missions encompassing values such as excellent customer service, increasing shareholder value, or environmental stewardship.

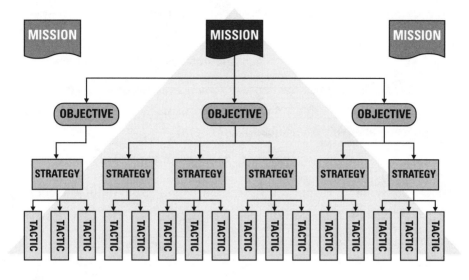

Figure 5-1: Strategic Planning Structure Using the MOST Hierarchy

Each mission has one or more enabling objectives that further refine and quantify the goals of the mission with respect to the operating horizon; for example, "Improve Customer Satisfaction Survey Results by 10% by the end of 2011." A single objective can have multiple strategies for how to accomplish that objective. These strategies can then be further expressed using underlying tactical levels depending on the depth of planning employed, for example, initiatives and programs. These tactical layers ultimately translate into actionable work as projects or service-related activities.

Organizing Strategies

The work that you do should clearly align with your strategies. Work information should be organized in a hierarchy for purposes of depicting strategic relationships, funding and resource distribution, reporting and other management functions. A typical structure for strategic information might be:

Enterprise> Mission> Objective> Strategy> Initiative> Project

You should organize the depth and naming convention of your strategic information to suit the needs of your organization. For example, the model for a relatively small organization could be

Company> Goal> Strategy> Project

A larger, more complex organization might add additional tactical levels; for example

Enterprise> Mission> Objective> Strategy> Initiative> Program> Service> Project

Nomenclature aside, the most important consideration is that the information is meaningful for your organization and that it strikes a practical balance. As with any data structure, more levels provide additional capacity and flexibility but always at a cost of more complexity and maintenance.

You should factor in the total expected volume of work that you plan to manage to determine the proper depth of your strategic information hierarchy. One example of typical groupings and resulting capacities might be as follows:

- 4 to 8 missions
- 4 to 8 objectives per mission (16 to 64 total objectives)
- 3 to 6 strategies per objective (48 to 384 total strategies)
- 1 to 4 initiatives per strategy (48 to 1,536 total initiatives), and so on

With this planning depth and distribution, each initiative could contain 4 to 10 programs or services, resulting in a planning model with ample capacity for managing over 15,000 projects in the planning period. By adding more volume per level, additional tactical levels (i.e., subprograms), or increasing the volume of programs or services per initiative, additional scalability is readily available by orders of magnitude.

UNDERSTANDING PRODUCTS AND MARKETS

Product and market information is perhaps the most challenging of the four types to capture and manage. There is an immense range of variability about the volume and nature of this information, depending on the specific products and services you offer. As a result, there is no single general approach to structuring it. Yet, establishing a balanced view of product and market information is as important as the other three information types we have discussed. Establishing this balance is where we focus our discussion next.

All organizations have a culture or style of behavior that affects how they organize information about markets and products, whether they recognize it or not. One way to understand the culture of an organization is to look at how it views markets and products. On one hand, engineering and technology-driven cultures are very product oriented, with little focus on markets. On the other hand, consumer goods cultures tend to see markets very clearly, while products are considered "packaging exercises." This marketing view of products has expanded as organizations have moved engineering and manufacturing to offshore facilities or third-party vendors.

Structuring how products deliver value to markets links product road maps with the voice of the customer. The best approach is one that balances the two areas and brings them together. The *Wall Street Journal* published an article about product development and marketing called "Playing Well with Others."* The article speaks to the cultural gap between

---

* Philip Kotler, Robert C. Wolcott, and Suj Chandrasekhar, "Playing Well with Others," *Wall Street Journal*, June 22, 2009.

groups rooted in different ways of thinking and a lack of understanding or appreciation of the other.

The most positive market change is one that you create through innovation in your technical and product development. Think of the impact Apple had on music distribution with iTunes and the iPod. The company was introducing innovation through new products every few months as the technology developed. As a result Apple grew a new music distribution model into a major business that created long-term value for the organization.

The ultimate objective of managing change is to produce value by fulfilling product demand from markets with capacity. You do that when you see a market trend and become the first to move with a new product. You also do it when you make a move to gain capacity by acquiring a competitor in a growth market.

Over the years, portfolios have established a position in product development. This could be due to more engineering, the scientific orientation of product development, or the heavier technology component in business-to-business products and services. Because there is often a strong body of knowledge about portfolio management in product development, we can build on that to manage markets where applying portfolios is less common.

There is often confusion about the role of marketing. Some people focus on advertising and public relations, and while those areas are important, they are not the focus of the market information that is meaningful in portfolio management. Our focus is on marketing as the voice of the customer in the direction of the organization.

Markets are the only place we can understand the trends in buyers' preferences, see the competitive position of a product, compared to the alternatives, and get a chance to listen to the customer. Brand and market information is a valuable decision-making tool, but it is most useful when it can be defined and presented so that it relates with information about your people, money, and work.

CASE STUDY: PORTFOLIO MANAGEMENT AT FLOWSERVE

Flowserve is a global supplier of fluid motion and control products and services. With over 15,000 employees in 55 countries, it serves industries  such as oil and gas, power generation, chemical, and water. The company has grown over the years by combining many successful independent companies. It is moving from a historically decentralized model to a unified business. The core to operating as a single global business is looking at products and solutions across business units with a view to improving global reach while leveraging existing local assets.

Portfolio management offered Flowserve the tools and techniques to identify and structure individual product and technology development efforts into an integrated plan across all units. A rationalized and more focused set of product and technology projects was driven by the integrated plan, and underscored by the clear definition of priorities, functional budgets, and resource assignments. Engineering, marketing, purchasing, and operations worked with the portfolio information to align their individual deliverables.

"We were convinced that process maturity had a direct correlation to the productivity of our research and development efforts" said Eric van Gemeren, Vice President of Business and Product Development, Flowserve. "By linking our engineering and marketing information across units, we are able to build product road maps that directly tied to our markets."

Flowserve used core metrics when implementing portfolio management. They included:

- Time to market
- Time to profitability
- Schedule slip
- Cost variance
- Performance to goals

"The rate and volume of our new product introductions can have a direct effect on overall company growth," said Mr. van Gemeren. "Delays in a product launch can have a significant impact on market share, and in industries like ours, can ultimately impact revenue and profit."

"Meeting schedule commitments in an organization is all about matching available resources with scheduling priorities," said Tom Pajonas, president of the Flowserve Flow Control Division. "The more efficient an organization is in this process of resource utilization, the more project deliverables are obtainable. Also, project deliverables change over time so an integrated resource loading and scheduling process allows one to adjust to these changes."

KEY POINTS IN THIS CHAPTER

☑ Portfolio information about your people, money, work, and deliverables allows you to make effective decisions.

☑ Primary portfolio information structures are built to accommodate the full range and depth of information:

- Clear relationships will emerge between the levels of different information structures.
- Primary information structures should be as simple and purposeful as possible; use secondary information to further characterize elements within them.

☑ Organize your people through an organizational breakdown structure and further describe that structure using various resource attributes from secondary structures.

☑ Your existing financial information will likely be a key consideration in the development of other information structures.

☑ Work information can be effectively structured using the MOST approach, describing:

- Missions
- Objectives
- Strategies
- Tactics

☑ The metrics associated with delivering products to markets typically define the value added through portfolio management. Product road maps developed by engineering should align with the customer voice presented by marketing.

CHAPTER 6

MANAGING DEMAND AND CAPACITY

THE ABILITY OF YOUR ORGANIZATION TO ANALYZE, select, and fulfill demand goes to the very essence of its mission. The decisions you make about which demands to pursue often depend initially on their potential to deliver value. However, whether you can ultimately convert demand into profit, advantage, reduced risk, operational continuity, or some other form of value depends on your organizational capacities.

In addition to simply having the necessary capacities available to fulfill demand, you also have to apply them in a cost effective, efficient manner. No matter how important these elements may be, the ultimate objective of managing change is not just to balance demand and capacity. The goal of portfolio management is much more outcome oriented—to use demand and capacity to produce value. Producing value means that the value of the delivered benefits outweighs the cost of creating them.

As a result, just about every business decision you make about demand should take into consideration whether it represents the best opportunity to create value, given your capacities and their associated costs.

Thus, the objective of this chapter is to establish the driving principles for managing demand and capacity as an integrated set of capabilities to deliver the most benefit at the lowest cost. We apply these principles throughout the ecosystem as a core concept of portfolio management by:

- Using the "portfolio balancing act" to understand the inherent relationships between demand, capacity, cost, and benefit
- Managing the complete spectrum of demand using a comprehensive approach to maintain the balance between demand and capacity
- Understanding demand and capacity management relationships throughout the continuum of change
- Gauging how uncertainties factor into the level of detail you use when planning demand and capacity
- Recognizing the unique relationship between money and people in knowledge-driven organizations

THE PORTFOLIO BALANCING ACT

We mentioned in chapter 1 that balancing demand and capacity is a universal consideration in the discipline of portfolio management. We reflect this in the center of the portfolio ecosystem diagram to illustrate how balancing demand and capacity is a pervasive part of decision making throughout the cycle of change.

Change will always disrupt the balance of demand and capacity, even though you may not recognize it. For example, a shift in the rate of inflation or sales volume affects your financial capacity, which influences how much demand you can address. Any new request, opportunity, or market fluctuation affects how you deploy capacities. Significant changes in profit or loss might eventually translate into changes in available capital and human resources.

The introduction of the Toyota Prius Hybrid offers a good example of how market changes disrupt the balance of demand and capacity. In early 2008, interest in fuel-efficient automobiles soared along with gas prices; the new Prius quickly hummed its way to the front of the pack. As oil prices peaked, wildly enthusiastic consumer response to the diminutive gas-sipper caught Toyota unprepared to fill the booming demand.

U.S. sales of the Prius fell 26 percent as dealers ran out of inventory. Facing a 6-month wait, potential Prius customers turned to alternatives. One such model, the Honda Fit, a conventionally powered subcompact, saw its sales increase as those of the Prius dropped. In short, Toyota failed to achieve its maximum value because of an imbalance in capacity and demand. Fortunately for Toyota, the Prius has since gone on to become one of the most popular and successful vehicles in the company's lineup, despite its rocky launch—capacity is back in balance with demand.

Countless organizations replicate Toyota's experience with the Prius by failing to fully coordinate marketing, manufacturing, and the other functions needed to keep demand and capacity in balance. Sometimes demand outstrips capacity, as in Toyota's case, but organizations are just as likely to overfund initiatives that the market rejects.

While demand and capacity imbalances are inevitable, these imbalances are not always negative. For example, consider the potential positive imbalance that results when you proactively create a dramatic increase in demand by introducing a new product or entering a new market area. In fact, the Prius represents just such an event.

The important thing to recognize is that regardless of whether a disruption in demand and capacity balance is reactive or proactive, it is the organization's responsibility to resolve imbalances as soon as possible to maximize potential value. Otherwise, some demands will go unmet for lack of capacity or excess capacities will no longer be engaged in value creation.

With this in mind, you can see how demand, capacity, cost, and benefit are all interrelated. Demand always seeks some form of benefit as an outcome. The consumption of capacity to satisfy demand always incurs a cost. Balancing the elements of demand, capacity, cost, and benefit should be the primary factors in every business decision you make. In almost every case, the relative cost versus benefit of competing options drives demand and capacity trade-off decisions. The "portfolio balancing act" refers to how you weigh these four elements as an essential aspect of managing change. These considerations are the critical axis points that establish the equilibrium of business. We illustrate the basic relationship between these four elements in figure 6-1.

Figure 6-1: Pivotal Business Decision Factors

Demand can come from external sources such as consumers, regulators, or shareholders, or it may come from within, such as the need for accounting, IT, or HR services. Demand always seeks some beneficial result in terms of market share, net revenue, productivity, public opinion, reduced risk, or some other form of tangible or intangible value. Ultimately, fulfillment of demand creates some combination of products, services, or other assets.

Producing these deliverables always consumes some form of capacity. We focus primarily on two forms of capacity: people and money. Obviously, there are other capacities that the organization may also depend on, such as infrastructure and tools, but they can take on infinite variations. Money and people are universally understood necessities. There is no doubt that cash is king; with enough money (and time), you can buy all other forms of capacity. However, no matter how much money you have, you also need people to produce value. In knowledge-based organizations, people and money are also usually the most limiting factors.

In addition to spending money directly, use of any capacity also incurs indirect costs. For example, labor, time, the use of infrastructure and tools, management overhead, and logistics are all indirect costs associated with fulfilling demand. Risk is another secondary form of cost, in terms of the cost of mitigating actions or insurance, and the potential for costs to exceed original estimates or not meet benefit expectations.

We can summarize these interactions with four basic relationships:

1. Demand always seeks a benefit.
2. Fulfillment of demand consumes capacity.
3. Capacity always has a cost.
4. Benefit replenishes capacity.

These relationships place an important perspective on effectively managing demand and capacity; mastering the portfolio balancing act is a fundamental requirement if you are to manage change so that it delivers value.

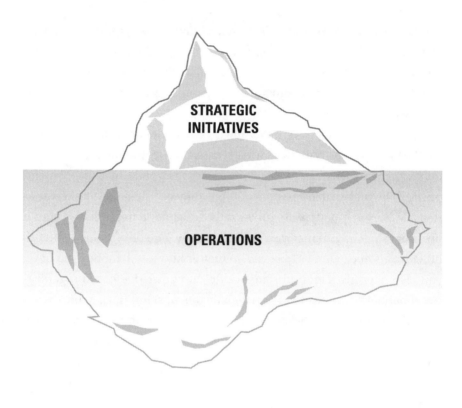

Figure 6-2: The Competing Demands of the Organization

MANAGING THE COMPLETE SPECTRUM OF DEMAND

Demand management often falls victim to the "80-20" rule; 80 percent of management attention is directed to only 20 percent of the total demands placed on the organization (figure 6-2).

Like the portion of an iceberg that sticks out of the water, high value projects and new initiatives tend to receive a great deal of organizational visibility, and rightly so. However, organizations increasingly use a common pool of capacities to fulfill strategic initiatives and to accomplish operational work. Whenever this situation exists, it is important to address all of the competing demands placed on the organization in a comprehensive manner if you are to strike a successful balance between them.

To illustrate this point, imagine trying to budget your monthly household expenses but only considering your home mortgage and car payment. Even though these two demands might constitute your two largest single expenditures, you have many other costs that you need to take into account. Food, clothing, entertainment, utilities, school loans, and myriad other expenses are likely to collectively exceed the house and car payments. All of them are competing for the same amount of income.

We can extend this personal example to the basic demand-capacity decisions you make at work every week. Managing money is relatively straightforward; for example, we understand the need to allocate the total organizational budget between operating and capital expenses. However, managing competing demands becomes more of an imperative when the resource in question is your multi-tasking staff. If you and your boss only think about the needs of a single big project that you are working on when planning how to allocate your people, you will have constant priority conflicts with all the other activities that also require attention. It is almost impossible to successfully manage that big project without knowing the total demand on the staff assigned to it.

While this basic relationship between demand and capacity seems inherently obvious, many organizations tend to segregate them into separate and distinct initiatives: "We are interested in improving visibility into our resource utilization" or "our objective is to do a better job managing our projects." However, as we have shown, to address one element effectively you must involve the other. All parts of the iceberg in figure 6-2 eventually melt into water, and all forms of demand eventually boil down to a multitude of individual actions, regardless of their origin. Each one is competing for the same resource availability. Before we can manage these competing demands, we first must better understand them.

Categorizing Demand

We can generally describe the overall spectrum of demand using three broad categories:

- **Base services** represent the continuum of level-of-effort work needed to deliver existing products and services at current production and quality levels and to generally maintain the supporting assets and operations of your organization. Base services include back-office functions, management overhead, and other general "lights on" activities.

- **Strategic initiatives** are major changes of operational significance. Typically, this class of demand constitutes the portfolio of formally managed capital investments and other large projects, including new product development.

- **Other planned work** constitutes the organizational demands that fall in between base services and strategic initiatives. This includes shorter-term activities that are beyond level-of-effort operations such as noncapital maintenance and enhancement projects; emerging major break-fix activities; and making incremental, evolutionary improvements.

As a general rule, organizations find that about half of their demand consists of base services, with the remaining amount roughly split between strategic initiatives and other planned work. The percentage distribution across the spectrum of demand for your organization will understandably differ depending on factors such as your industry sector, average product life expectancy, and economic factors. Whether the demand for your particular organization varies significantly compared to average distribution is less important than knowing what your actual percentages are; once you are able to measure demand, you can then track and manage it.

Almost every enterprise has a grasp on its strategic work. As the visible part of the demand iceberg, even the most basic and informally managed organization usually has a defined project list and a governing body to manage it. They are also likely to have some form of tools and processes established to assist in managing them.

Most organizations also have a good understanding of what is required to maintain base services as a part of day-to-day operations. Often, dedicated staff members fulfill the majority of operational work, so they are less susceptible to assignment conflicts with other forms of demand. Finally, base services usually represent a series of ongoing routine functions that require less sophisticated management processes and tools.

What is less certain is whether most organizations can see and clearly understand other planned work in measurable terms. A large volume of informal assignments and requests constantly pass between managers and staff that are seldom seen or understood outside of individual work groups. If you cannot see or measure these activities, then you cannot manage and control them as part of the overall workload.

This is when demand and capacity management in many organizations runs into trouble. Other planned work activities are left up to individual managers to handle informally (and inconsistently), even though they usually constitute over a quarter of total demand. The nature of other planned work also means it is more likely to create serious resource conflicts with strategic initiatives. Other planned work requires similar skills and roles, is often just as important as large discretionary projects, and makes up a large volume of individual short-term requests.

THE IMPACT OF THE INNOVATION: OPERATION MISMATCH

Gaining insight into how much demand constitutes innovative, entrepreneurial opportunities versus run-the-business functions can have a significant impact on your overall approach to demand and capacity management.

In addition to level-of-effort activities, a portion of your projects and other planned work are also necessary to maintain the business. Regulatory requirements, expansion due to growth, obsolescence, or necessary infrastructure investments drive some percentage of capital investments that are not related to innovation.

As a result, it is not surprising to find that over 75 percent of total demand (and capacity utilization) relates to maintaining ongoing operations, leaving little in the way of truly discretionary, innovative endeavors.

This mismatch means that if you can redirect even relatively small efficiency gains to ongoing operations you can increase your ability to innovate by a considerable amount. For example, using the 80-20 imbalance in figure 6-3, a 5 percent reduction in the capacity needed to run the business translates into a potential 20 percent increase in capacity available for innovation. Because the money and effort invested in innovative initiatives can yield value that is many multiples of the cost of the investment, transferring even small amounts of capacity between these two forms of demand offers significant potential to improve the enterprise's bottom-line performance.

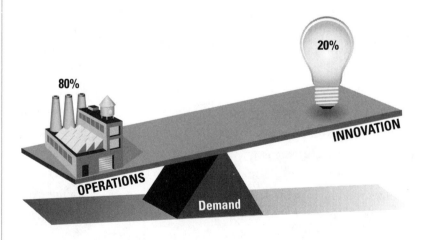

Figure 6-3: The Demand Imbalance Between Operations and Innovation

Demand Cycle Time

Understanding how cycle times differ for each kind of work is an important aspect of avoiding demand-capacity imbalances. Each type of demand in your organization has an average cycle time associated with it (see figure 6-4). Large strategic initiatives are more likely to have long lead times from the point of initiation to approval and take even longer (ranging from months to years) to plan and execute. In contrast, base services represent a continuum of resource commitments that are assumed to be relatively constant, unless major operational changes occur.

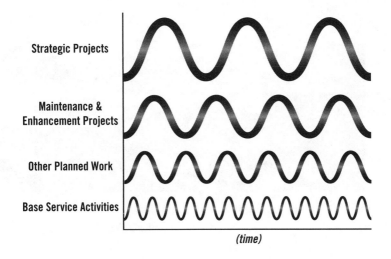

Figure 6-4: Comparing the Relative Cycle Times of Different Types of Demand

Maintenance and enhancement projects, along with less formal kinds of other planned work, have their own cycle times as well. Other planned work requests are more numerous and have a faster life cycle from the time of initiation to completion. Once this type of demand is captured and analyzed, you may find that hundreds of these activities flow through the organization each month. As a general category, other

planned work usually represents a relatively consistent volume of ongoing demand; once its average throughput is measured, you can accurately
predict future demand for it.

In addition to the effect these cycle times have on forecasting demand,
each type of demand also consumes capacity at different rates.

Because of these different cycle times, long-range demand forecasting
must address how each category of work flows into and out of the organization over time in order to adequately plan for the expected throughput
(figure 6-5).

Figure 6-5: Forecasting the Volume of Demand and Capacity

It is important to estimate the capacity needed to completely address
all types of future work in order to understand true capacity availability
for new and existing strategic initiatives. Figure 6-5 illustrates how capacity is consumed by both existing and forecasted demand over time. We
cover operational capacity planning in more detail in section 3.

MANAGING THE PLANNING HORIZON

Tracking Demand and Capacity Through the Ecosystem

As you move through the portfolio ecosystem continuum, demand and capacity management challenges are always present although business considerations may shift along the way. Capital funding distribution becomes a monthly budget analysis of planned versus actual spending—perhaps at first for a project, and later, as a measure of production costs. High level head count allocation of staff capacity translates into making individual resource assignments; long-range demand projections turn into managing the endless variety of work activities that occur on a daily basis.

Figure 6-6 illustrates how demand and capacity management perspectives change depending on the type of portfolio and your point in the portfolio ecosystem.

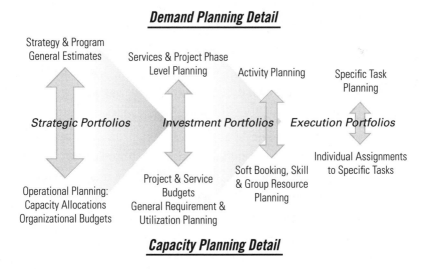

Figure 6-6: Tracking Demand and Capacity Planning

As figure 6-6 indicates, there are interdependencies between demand and capacity planning along the continuum. Each stage of planning adds additional detail and accuracy to earlier estimates, sharpening your understanding of what resources will be necessary.

Regardless of the level of detail, there is a symbiotic relationship between demand and capacity planning in terms of accuracy. Each variable is dependent on information from the other in order to improve planning precision. We can use a project plan as an example. No matter how detailed the work breakdown structure, accurately scheduling activities and tasks depends on knowing related resource information. The individuals assigned and their availability ultimately drives the dates and durations of planned tasks. Conversely, you can only reliably plan capacity to the extent that you know the details of the work. Both demand and capacity planning are subject to the planning horizon and the uncertainties that accompany it.

Applying the 50-50 Planning Rule

Management of the planning horizon relates to how far forward and to what degree you are able to reliably plan. It is a fundamental planning principle that dictates the level of demand and capacity detail that you should apply relative to how far forward you are trying to plan.

The concept is applicable to any kind of planning, whether you are defining strategic objectives, creating a budget, planning work, or managing resources. Understanding the limits of the horizon relative to the type of planning you are doing is key to efficient and effective forecasting.

As a practical example, consider the varying levels of certainty that you may have about different aspects of your life:

- A target age for your retirement
- A general plan for how you will meet retirement goals

- A working idea of the rate of return you can expect on your savings this year
- A 2-week vacation planned in the next quarter (... but still undecided about where to go)
- Clear knowledge of your monthly income and expenses
- You know you must leave the office today by 5:30 if you are to meet friends at Alfredo's for dinner at 6:00

These examples illustrate the idea that the farther forward we look in our personal lives, the fuzzier our level of certainty becomes; we naturally adjust the level of planning detail as a result.

The same approach is equally applicable to our professional lives. We define the practical working limit of the planning horizon as the point where you have at least 50-50 confidence in the plan (figure 6-7). In other words, the plan as defined is more likely to be correct than not. Attempting to plan beyond that tipping point is, in fact, no longer planning—it enters the realm of guessing, and probably guessing wrong.

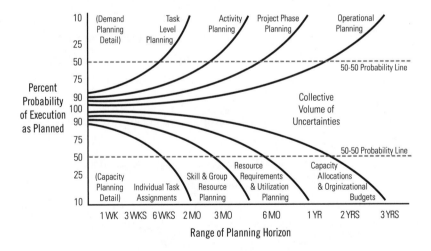

Figure 6-7: The Planning Horizon Concept

The working limit of the planning horizon shifts with the subject of the plan and its level of detail along with other influences and variables. You are probably familiar with the phrase "If we take a look at this from 10,000 feet . . ." Figure 6-7 illustrates how you can extend your view of the horizon by increasing your *planning elevation.* This works like your view from an airplane window—when the plane goes higher, your view of details on the ground is reduced but your visual range is increased.

Thus, you can extend the limits of the planning horizon by either reducing the level of detail employed in your plan or by reducing the potential influences that can act on it.

For instance, if you are planning a relatively low risk project to produce a deliverable that you have experience with, you might be comfortable defining its tasks a few months in advance. However, naming resource assignments to those tasks may have a planning horizon of only 3 to 4 weeks. Historically, you know that if you attempt to plan at that level of detail too far in advance, emerging changes in work priorities or availability will likely cause staff reassignments.

To counter this, you can reduce the level of resource detail in the plan; even though you may not be ready to name individuals to assignments, you can reliably specify the roles, skills, and estimated effort needed for each activity. This gives others a view of the capacities that will be required so they can plan for resource allocations as those activities draw nearer.

It is important to recognize the impacts of attempting to plan beyond the limits of the planning horizon. At the very least, it will likely require you to revise plan details repeatedly. Of greater concern is the effect of posting inaccurate information. Others may make important decisions based on the details of a questionable plan, further amplifying the mistake. Regardless, the net result of overextending the planning horizon is that it instills doubt about the veracity of planning information in general.

In later chapters we explain how to manage the planning horizon for demand and capacity management by taking an iterative planning approach to work and resources. This just-in-time method of planning is a proven technique for effectively directing activities in a dynamic business environment.

Changing the Planning Paradigm

For many, especially those in project management, some of the concepts we present will challenge traditionally accepted conventions. However, the effects of change are increasing and unavoidable. They disrupt the stability required to reliably establish a complete detailed plan in advance of execution. Expecting to rigorously follow an initial plan without deviation is becoming more unrealistic, and interestingly enough, less desirable.

A plan is nothing more than a point-in-time projection of intent, based on a certain set of facts, assumptions, and unknowns. While some may perceive these unknowns as threats, to the nimble they also represent undiscovered opportunities and emerging options. Perhaps this is why agile planning approaches are quickly gaining popularity well beyond their software development roots. Using portfolios to increase transparency and open communications helps an organization accept the realities of operational dynamics, while creating new levels of flexibility and responsiveness to change. Recognizing this as a shared organizational value opens up the potential for continual improvement of your plans as better information and changing circumstances warrant.

Adopting such an approach also suggests that you rethink your methods of establishing accountability. For example, the benefits of using highly structured variance measures such as *earned value analysis* become more questionable when faced with a highly dynamic planning environment. When you incrementally plan each phase based on previous progress or are constantly redirecting resources between multiple initiatives, flexibility becomes a benefit rather than a problem.

Specific yet reasonable performance expectations need to be set by appropriate levels of management. Business objectives need to be clear.

Milestones and decision gates should be included at each major planning juncture. Managers should agree on weekly goals with their staff. At each level of the organization, the goal is to establish consistent expectations while leaving how to best accomplish those expectations flexible and in the hands of those people directly responsible for their achievement.

THE RELATIONSHIP BETWEEN PEOPLE AND MONEY

We indicated earlier that we are going to focus primarily on people and money when discussing capacity management. Although these two capacities have nothing physically in common, they share an important relationship that is so obvious that it is completely missed by most organizations.

Everyone understands the need to rigorously manage financial resources—organizations often go to great lengths and levels of detail to be sure they do so. The CFO and accounting organization dedicate themselves to managing the general ledger, balance sheets, credits and debits, accounts receivable, and various budgets. Other executives spend a good portion of their energy on financial governance. The entire management team usually participates in the budgeting process. Money is also comparatively easy to measure, which is a good thing because accounting requirements and management policies dictate that you track and report how every cent, peso, or yen is spent.

The imperative for applying meticulous financial controls is due in part to the fungible nature of money; it is highly transportable, a universally accepted commodity, and convertible to practically anything else, including other forms of capacity.

However, people perform work. In knowledge-driven organizations, people represent the primary raw material used to create value. As a result, a significant percentage of financial capacity goes to acquiring, paying, and enabling staff and contracted resources. If you are in an organization that relies on its highly skilled group of professionals as the prime means of creating products and services, chances are that over half of your operating expenses relate somehow to your resources. In addition to the direct cost of staff itself in the form of salary, bonuses, and benefits, many indirect costs, such as IT, office space and supplies, training, travel expenses, and management overhead are all related to staff head count. Because of this unique relationship between money and people, it is critical to manage people and money with commensurate levels of attention if you are to manage both capacities successfully.

Yet, despite these relationships, one compelling difference between people and money elevates the priority of effective resource management—effort cannot be banked. You can put excess money in the safe or suspend payments, but the effort of your people cannot be stored or put on hold. Like water over a dam, every hour of effort passes through your organization in a constant flow. Whether you direct it productively or not, once it has passed, it is irretrievable. If a change event disrupts your organization and creates confusion among the staff, you cannot simply turn off the flow of effort until you figure it out.

With all of this in mind, it does not make much sense to go to great lengths to manage money unless you apply a similar level of diligence to manage the effort of your organization. Yet, this is often a common situation in organizations large and small.

Consider a jewelry company that spends half its operating funds just to acquire precious metals for its creations. Once the material is received, there is no doubt that a significant amount of time and effort will be spent to carefully protect that inventory, control its use, and prevent waste.

It should be the same with knowledge worker organizations—protect the utilization of your knowledge workers the same way that jewelers guard their gold. If you aren't putting at least half as much time, energy, and executive governance into managing your resource capacity as you are your financial interests, then you may have a management imbalance between your two most precious commodities—your people and your money.

APPLYING PORTFOLIOS TO MANAGE DEMAND AND CAPACITY

The fundamental advantage of portfolio management lies in how it enables you to address the demands placed on your organization so that you can produce the greatest value with the capacities that you have available. This is a universal business consideration regardless of your role, what point you are at on the ecosystem, or the type of portfolio you are using. It begins at a high level with strategic portfolios, which allow you to select the right ideas and opportunities, while taking into account the competing demands from base services, strategic initiatives, and other planned work. This makes it possible for you to allocate people and money in a manner that adequately addresses ongoing operational requirements and innovation. You can have greater confidence that objectives and strategies are achievable when you base them on a realistic assessment of organizational capacities.

Investment portfolios give you the capability to further refine demand management decisions, carefully considering the interrelated elements of cost and benefit, in addition to capacity. The outcome is less risk for your investment commitments, which are more likely to represent prudent business decisions that include adequate resources to achieve intended outcomes.

When these investments become a part of all the other demands placed on your organization, execution portfolios provide a method to make sure that budgets and resources are not overextended. You leverage the planning horizon to ensure that emerging uncertainties do not repeatedly compromise work and resource plan details that were created too far in advance. This gives you maximum flexibility to make adjustments while allowing the organization to methodically execute work in a highly efficient manner. It also ensures that your most critical commodity, the efforts of your knowledge workers, is managed at a level that is commensurate with the value of those efforts.

KEY POINTS IN THIS CHAPTER

☑ Demand and capacity are interdependent elements; to be effective, you must manage them collectively.

☑ Imbalances between demand and capacity create inefficiencies.

☑ The portfolio balancing act demonstrates that demand, capacity, cost, and benefit are all interrelated:

- Demand always seeks a benefit.
- Fulfillment of demand consumes capacity.
- Capacity always has a cost.
- Benefit replenishes capacity.

☑ The overall spectrum of demand can be categorized into three broad categories: base services, strategic initiatives, and other planned work.

☑ In situations where resources must multi-task across different types of demand, all of the demand must be commonly managed.

☑ Each type of demand has different cycle times and rates of capacity consumption; as a result, demand planning must take into account future expected capacity requirements for each type of demand.

☑ Most organizations have a large mismatch between how much capacity is used to fulfill operations versus innovation; because of this disparity, small efficiency gains in operational capacity that are redirected to innovation can have significant bottom-line impacts.

☑ The level of planning detail increases as you move around the portfolio ecosystem.

☑ Demand planning and capacity planning are co-dependent; each relies on the other for information in order to improve planning precision.

☑ Our level of planning stability is affected by the dynamics of our modern business environment.

☑ The 50-50 rule of the planning horizon states that it is counterproductive to plan beyond the point where you have less than a 50 percent probability of being correct.

☑ You can extend the working limit of the planning horizon by either reducing the amount of planning detail or by removing uncertainties.

☑ It is important for organizations to recognize that any plan represents nothing more than a point-in-time best estimate of future events based on a certain set of assumptions and unknowns; be open to continually improving plans as new information arises.

☑ Organizations should employ a level of management focus on resource management commensurate with the percentage that total staff costs contribute to the total operating budget.

Section 3

OPERATIONAL PLANNING

Operational planning is how the leadership team shapes the future direction and goals of the organization. This includes assessing current conditions, measuring performance, analyzing emerging change influences, setting strategy, allocating people and money, and developing ideas into actionable opportunities.

Section 3 consists of four chapters on operational planning. Chapter 7 discusses general concepts. Chapter 8 provides an overview of the operational planning process. Chapters 9 and 10 focus on high level capacity planning for allocating finances and human resources.

CHAPTER 7

OPERATIONAL PLANNING CONCEPTS

OPERATIONAL PLANNING ENCOMPASSES the executive-level guidance that defines, controls, and enables the future direction of your organization. You are already conducting operational planning in some manner as evidenced by the budgets, product road maps, and staffing plans that you develop. Introducing portfolio management into the process will enhance the good business practices that you are already using by adding more consistency, transparency, reliability, and alignment. Portfolios allow you to better integrate operational planning across different subjects and perspectives to deliver more cohesive results.

Operational planning includes setting organizational objectives and strategies, financial budgeting, and resource capacity planning. Integral to the process is the analysis of current operations and change influences that affect the organization and its missions. Ultimately, these changes drive you to revise or create new objectives and strategies and to develop ideas into potential investment opportunities that you evaluate, select, and execute.

Figure 7-1 illustrates the typical span of operational planning relative to the information structures introduced in section 2. Operational planning uses strategic portfolios to provide executives with the tools they can use to exercise their authority over operational direction and measure resulting performance. Operational planning utilizes a number of portfolio management tools and techniques to sharpen the organization's focus on your business objectives, including:

- Balancing supply and demand

- Governing with portfolios

- Applying portfolio processes

- Utilizing performance measurements

Strategic Portfolios Provide a Mechanism to Perform Operational Planning, Direct Investments and Govern People, Money Work & Deliverables:	PEOPLE	WORK	MONEY	DELIVERABLES
	Organization	Missions	Finances	Customers
	Business Units	Objectives	High Level Accounts	Markets
	Departments	Strategies	Mid-Level Budgets	Product Lines
	Groups & Teams	Programs & Projects	Detailed Budgets	Products & Services
	People	Work	Expenses	Deliverables

Figure 7-1: Operational Planning Using Strategic Portfolios

The information structures shown in figure 7-1 provide the portfolio management framework to define relationships, create a chain of custody for management responsibilities, and establish decision rights. The portfolio management governance board has direct decision rights and responsibility for the overall guidance of the organization. They grant execution authority to others and verify their performance through the use of strategic portfolios.

Operational planning provides high-level guidance to the organization about the products and services you offer to your markets. In order to implement your strategies, financial and resource capacities are allocated based on relative needs and competing priorities. Strategic portfolios enable operational planning by providing powerful tools and techniques to collectively analyze work, deliverables, finances, and resource capacity. We use this chapter to introduce operational planning concepts, and the subsequent chapters in this section will provide additional details.

SCOPE OF OPERATIONAL PLANNING

The scope of operational planning is a relative call, based on the needs of each organization, type of business, culture, and other factors. This affects the depth of planning and the makeup of the governance board, level of organizational involvement, roles, and responsibilities. Regardless of whether you are planning across a large enterprise or your decision rights are for a division or business unit, we all relate to a larger world in some way.

The intended span of operational planning fits within the model as shown in figure 7-2:

- **Span of control**: Elements that you can control (e.g., the enterprise or retail products division).

- **Span of influence**: Elements outside of your direct control that you can most likely influence to some degree (e.g., collaboration with business partners).

- **External factors**: Elements that have an impact on the intended scope of the strategic plan but are outside your control or influence (e.g., federal regulatory mandates, competitors, or overarching corporate goals).

Using this information, you can determine how span of control, span of influence, and external factors might relate to the structure and scope

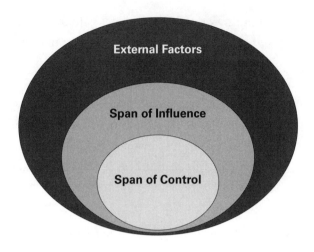

Figure 7-2: Span of Control Model

of your operational planning. This defines how you organize your port-folios and establish an appropriate decision-making framework through the portfolio governance model. It also influences the business rules, terminology, and unique attributes that you will use to support portfolio decision making.

The need to manage total demand and capacity was established earlier. Accordingly, your scope of operational planning should encom-pass all of the demands and capacities within your span of control. This ensures that you maintain balance between new initiatives and ongoing operations in your overall strategy and resource allocations.

The Range of Operational Planning

Operational planning is designed to guide an organization along a con-tinuum, rather than represent a single event—there have been past strate-gies, there are current strategies, and there will be new or revised strategies in the future. Think of operational planning as an ongoing steering func-tion for the organization provided by executive guidance. This helps you recognize that operational planning needs to be flexible and responsive, providing adjustments as conditions warrant to keep the organization on track to fulfill its missions.

Portfolios offer the framework for the operational planning team to build scenarios around different assumptions and to prepare alternative approaches. The teams can simulate alternatives with portfolio tools and techniques to build confidence in the decisions that are made. Portfolios also offer the information chain of custody that led to a decision so that you can validate expectations against the actual value created by the deliverable.

Wholesale change in overall corporate direction is relatively rare in the life of a business. While major mergers, entry into new markets, or similar impacts might cause the executive team to fundamentally redefine strategic direction, a more likely scenario is that each planning cycle results in refinements or course corrections along a chosen path.

An operating organization moves along some strategic trajectory, and like any physical body in motion, it also possesses momentum. As a result, it is impractical and unrealistic to expect it to instantaneously stop or radically change course. However, given enough advance notice, an organization can adjust its path. Like an onboard navigation system, operational planning gives you the capability to identify your current position, read how external forces are influencing your direction, and then make guidance corrections to ensure that the organization continues toward its target. While a business cycle might include a specific planning period, the resulting plan must be actively managed. To support this, most organizations typically conduct annual operational planning sessions and use quarterly reviews to make periodic adjustments.

Business objectives are likely to span multiple planning cycles, and they do not all start or finish simultaneously. Referencing figure 7-3, any given planning cycle will likely include a mix of objectives near completion, those well underway, some just getting traction, and new ones being added to the operating plan. Similarly, underlying strategies have their own relationships, dependencies, and durations, if for no other reason than to manage cash flow and resource capacity.

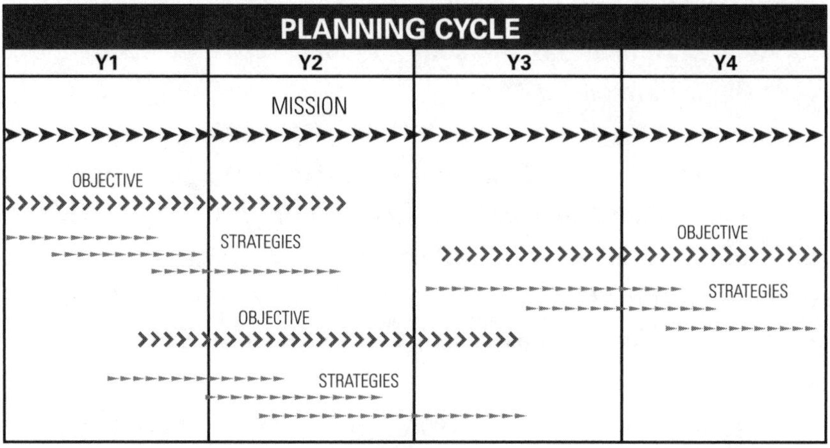

Figure 7-3: Operational Planning Continuum

The Planning Cycle

While operational planning should be thought of as a continuous process, time frames are typically broken into major cycles to support annual budgeting or other requirements.

Each organization defines its own appropriate operational planning cycle, but considerations include:

- Natural business and fiscal cycles
- Scope and complexity of the operational plan
- Depth of the planning process
- Business dynamics and environment
- Process and organizational maturity

Natural business rhythms play into the cycle duration and timing decision. Almost all modern corporations have an annual financial planning cycle to consider, but that does not automatically mean that the operational planning cycle must align on an annual basis. For example, a quarterly cycle might be more appropriate in a dynamic business environment. Releasing funds on a quarterly basis and making your investments in short-term, controllable time frames further aligns with the concept of just-in-time planning and managing the planning horizon.

Scope and complexity of the strategic plans, along with the stability of the business environment also influences planning cycle duration. A large enterprise that needs to integrate a broad operational plan across multiple lines of business may not be able to handle more than an annual strategic cycle. Conversely, organizations dealing with a volatile business environment will be driven to reassess strategic plans with more frequency. Some may need to adopt an essentially continuous operational planning approach, with appropriate staffing and infrastructure dedicated to managing such a fluid environment.

OPERATIONAL PLANNING GOVERNANCE

Governance is the process of defining expectations, granting power, and verifying performance. As such, it is an inherent aspect of operational planning. Portfolio management provides a mechanism to define and control the governance of change events. It also offers effective techniques for seizing opportunities while mitigating the risks that they contain. The most radical and positive change event is the one that you create by anticipating new opportunities and using them to your advantage.

Portfolios provide organizations with a framework to rationalize the governance process, integrate decision making, and effectively manage change. You can use portfolio management to establish the governance policies, define processes, set decision rights, and allocate organizational resources.

The Portfolio Governance Model

Central to portfolio management governance is how portfolio processes integrate into your business to manage change and its associated roles and responsibilities. These relationships are the backbone of the portfolio ecosystem process.

When you define management controls and business rules, you address the inputs utilized and outputs expected to help bound the process. Inputs include summary-level general business intelligence, such as current status and performance of in-progress initiatives, risk factors, general financial performance, and other internal and external influences. Analysis and decision making results in the following outcomes:

- Definition and documentation of the general hierarchy and relationships of the operational plan within the strategic portfolio, including the supporting basis for all decisions
- Specific tactical guidance through investment and execution portfolios that considers deliverables, priorities, time frames, and budgetary and organizational capacity parameters
- Pertinent communications to the organization
- Performance measures and mechanisms for monitoring and managing the strategies and investments and executing the work
- Continued adjustments to operational plans and guidance to the organization as business dynamics warrant

Portfolio Governance Roles and Responsibilities

A portfolio management governance board is a standing working group of executives that acts as the highest controlling authority for the operational planning process. Typically the board works directly with strategic and investment portfolios and reviews performance metrics from execution portfolios. Its responsibilities include:

- Defining and maintaining the operational planning process and its associated planning cycle
- Setting product and service standards and expectations
- Defining key performance indicators
- Gathering and analyzing necessary inputs to the planning process

- Defining the missions and objectives in alignment with overarching organizational goals—typically resulting in a strategic plan
- Recommending or apportioning funding and capacity across objectives depending on the level of authority of the senior executive on the board
- Identifying, assigning, and directing investment owners
- Owning and/or approving the business plans associated with investments
- Overseeing the strategic, investment, and execution performance
- Adjusting to strategy as required based on performance, changes in influences, or other shifts in business requirements

The senior executive with direct authority for the scope of the operational plan chairs the portfolio management governance board. Board members should consist of senior executives of the service provider (i.e., major department heads), major customer stakeholders that receive the services, and representatives from the financial office. This places the board in a position to gain insight into external driving influences, ensures a balanced customer-provider perspective, and provides ample authority to set a collaborative posture. To ensure a balance of representation with practical considerations, a typical board will include six to ten permanent members, and invite additional representatives on an ad hoc basis as needed. Boards also typically have a support group, such as the portfolio management office (PMO).

One industrial products company had hundreds of products in inventory organized by line of business. Each year the business units established their plans for revenues and operational costs. They competed for reinvestment of enterprise profits in expanding their businesses through the operational planning process in their strategic portfolios. The operational plan led to funding decisions and the assignment of engineering staff through investment portfolios. The PMO was responsible for taking the direction of the portfolio management governance board and building a plan in the strategic portfolio.

The PMO started by building the baseline in the strategic portfolio by line of business. (It takes time and effort when you have hundreds of products, but the benefits are worth the effort.) Operational planning in the strategic portfolios defined the strategies that the organization intended to implement and a broad plan to back those strategies. Next, the individual lines of business established investment portfolios where they documented the funding, business plan, and the benefit expected from the investment. Each investment had an investment owner based on the size of the investment and the time frame of the payback. (Larger paybacks that take a longer time need the attention of senior executives.) Finally, the proposed funding of new investments was linked to the strategic portfolios so that each investment was tied to an existing product or a future one.

People with the appropriate power to make decisions analyzed the investment portfolios and made the funding commitments to the work. The portfolio management governance board in this case delegated the specific investment decisions to the line of business division managers within the funding level and with the oversight of the PMO. The work was then executed through the divisions, and the investment owner was involved over the life cycle of the initiative that created the investment and the projects that it funded. As products were delivered by engineering, they were linked back into the strategic portfolios for measurement by the PMO.

Each element in the operating plan should be aligned with respective owners to establish accountability and delegate responsibilities. While the portfolio management board as a whole owns strategy collectively, each objective, strategy, or initiative should be aligned to a single individual who is responsible for developing underlying aspects and meeting the intent of the activity. In smaller organizations, an individual such as a department head may be a member of the board, own multiple objectives, and directly manage the underlying strategies and tactics. Larger operations may have a much more distributed approach, with responsibilities spread across hundreds of individuals.

MANAGING RISK

A primary function of governance is to identify and manage organizational risks. Risk can take many forms, including uncertainties about the business climate or market need, process risk associated with overextending functional capabilities, cultural risk associated with transforming the organization, technical risks, and so on. For the purposes of portfolio management, the key elements that may be subjected to risk impacts typically include: time to market, time to profitability (or return), cost, and performance.

Risk is identified at two basic levels: corporate and performance. Corporate or enterprise risk is the concern that the organization is not performing within the charter defined by its industry and/or government regulations. There have been many examples over the past few years of poor corporate governance that led to disaster, including financial ruin and prison. Portfolio management offers a valuable level of detail to support corporate risk management through strategic and investment portfolios.

The second level of risk is performance risk. Much has been written on the subject of managing performance risk from a variety of perspectives. In the weakest organizational cultures, risk plans identify every possible thing that could go wrong and take responsibility for none of it. That obviously is not helpful for the organization. There are much more productive ways to handle risk.

The first step in risk management is to identify potential risks. Identifying risk is a component in all three portfolio types—strategic, investment, and execution. Each portfolio has a different level of decision rights and differences in how to identify and handle risk. In the context of a portfolio, risk is defined as a potential impact that adds uncertainty to the planning, execution, delivery, or results achieved by the decision.

In strategic portfolios, the risks are typically strategic and have an impact on the overall performance of the organization. These are corporate governance risks that can have ramifications to government regulators, stockholders, lenders, and other external stakeholders. Investment and execution portfolios tend to focus more on the risk of not accomplishing the goals of the investment or the project. These portfolios should use financial and project-oriented risk management techniques.

Risk management identifies and quantifies risks so they can be measured, assessed, and controlled. You can think of risk management as an insurance policy to increase the certainty of a successful outcome. Ideally, all potential impacts to the scope, time, cost, and benefit of a given investment or project should be known and controlled ahead of time, creating a high certainty of the outcome. Because the ideal is seldom achievable, you must determine what a reasonable level of uncertainty is, and balance that with how much insurance constitutes a prudent investment.

Anytime you are faced with change events, you will evaluate the risk profile and react accordingly. While portfolios at every level of the organization deal with risk, the governance board typically considers risk that will have the greatest overall impact on the organization. Balancing opportunity and risk is a key to successful governance and successful portfolio management.

One larger international enterprise found itself under federal investigation about what its senior executives knew and when they knew it. The question was one of corporate governance and honest communication to stakeholders. Because the company had a strategic portfolio with a current state assessment and the history of the decisions that had been made, there was an audit trail through the portfolio.

Even better for the executives, they could track the basis for the investments they made, the projects that were authorized, and the results that they achieved. Armed with this information the corporate general counsel was able to answer all of the investigator's questions and close the inquiry.

MEASURING THE VALUE DELIVERED

Measuring the value delivered by your decisions takes patience and commitment. You are striving to answer some basic questions, such as:

- What *future state*, in terms of measurable value, were my strategies intended to create?
- Does the actual value and time frame of the results match the proposed value in the investment?
- What lessons can the organization learn from this decision?

A defined portfolio management technique called *benefit realization* provides the process for measuring value. Benefit realization adds discipline to the life cycle of your change decisions. The benefit realization process begins early in the change cycle when you clearly define and quantify the expected outcomes of your investment. These results then become the point of focus during design, development, and delivery.

Sometimes it could take years to validate that cost reductions are real or that revenue has improved as expected. Other changes continue to occur, which might raise questions about whether the results of a strategy are really attributable to future performance. The actual performance of resulting project and service deliverables can be measured by using the strategic portfolio against original objectives, as shown in figure 7-4.

To trace the value created by the investment you have to unify information from a variety of sources. Each of these sources collects information at different times in the life cycle of the change event. Portfolios provide a consistent way to link together the different types of information needed to define, manage, and measure benefits over the life of the investment.

A large international media organization adopted benefit realization as a mechanism to link actual value created to its portfolios of investments. While the company had mature operational planning and project execution processes, it could not prove that investments actually delivered promised returns. In particular, company executives realized that they often lost sight of the initial reasons for starting large infrastructure projects that went on for an extended length of time. To address this shortcoming, the PMO selected some specific investments to track and prove the value and practicality of a benefit realization program.

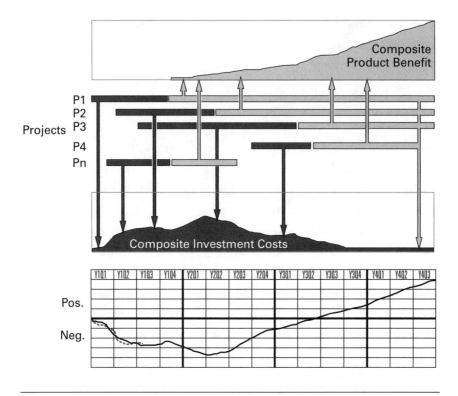

Figure 7-4: Creating Measurable Value

Results were encouraging. For example, they found that they were able to more quickly identify when products were not delivering as expected, analyze why, and take corrective actions. In another case, they realized that a project that was already in progress did not hold sufficient promise of delivering business value, and it was immediately scrapped.

They also discovered that by taking the time to document expected benefits and put that information in front of the project team, members stayed more focused on outcomes. Better project continuity was also realized as team members came and went—the project purpose always remained in the forefront. Finally, not only did the process prove useful for tracking and comparing planned versus actual benefits, but it also became an important corporate learning mechanism that fostered a more mature approach and greater accountability in how future portfolio investment decisions were made.

Operational planning with strategic portfolios is an iterative process that requires you to be mindful of past performance, clearly understand your current situation, and continually assess potential influences that can affect future plans.

COMMUNICATING THE PLAN

As operational planning information is developed and refined, it is important to consider how you will communicate the results. After all, a major benefit of formalizing the operational planning process is establishing alignment, which means that information is shared. Conversely, such information also represents the vital interests of the organization, so some control over how it is managed is equally important. Some questions that you should ask yourself about sharing this information with others include: With whom? How much? When? In what format? What about sensitive strategies?

Given a general approach for communications management, each objective should be evaluated for its unique needs, depending on its intent, span of involvement, and other attributes. For example, the communications needs for a merger with a former competitor is quite different from an objective to update certain internal business functions.

You can apply a layered approach depending on the sensitivity of certain elements of your plan. For example, simple measures can be taken to enhance security and control, such using a non-descriptive name and increasing the access security on content or storing it in a unique manner. Another notch up the list of control options is to create and use separate sections of the information structures to limit access to a more discreet population. If warranted, a completely separate plan can be developed specifically to isolate those initiatives that must be held to the highest level of security and access.

CASE STUDY: OPERATIONAL PLANNING AT THE UNIVERSITY OF UTAH

The University of Utah is the state's oldest and largest institution of higher education and is a major research university. It offers more than 100 undergraduate and more than 90 graduate degree programs to over 28,000 students. The University of Utah is one of the state's largest employers and is ranked as one of the top public research universities in the nation.

When performing a current state analysis of the information technology (IT) organization, the university identified that it was managing over 1,700 technology projects. The number surprised not only the technology executives but also the key stakeholders in multiple business units. They decided to implement operational planning using strategic portfolios to improve work prioritization and reporting. The IT Project and Portfolio Office (IT PPO) was given the lead in facilitating the initiative with the sponsorship of the president of the university and the chief information officer. "Our goal was to get the right people, at the right time, working on the right initiatives, and have them communicate with each other," explains Rene Eborn, the assistant director of the IT PPO.

The operational planning team developed strategic objectives and values and regularly discussed initiatives, prioritized projects, ranked investments, and made integrated informed decisions on defining and adjusting strategies. After over 18 months of aggressive effort, the university was able to cut the project workload by 95 percent or from 1,700 projects to 76. The change was due primarily to a disciplined prioritization process and identification of redundant efforts.

When asked about the dramatic results of their planning and control efforts, Eborn concluded "As an institution of higher education, we are responsible for not only teaching accountability but, we need to also demonstrate our commitment in striving to do better within our own organization and accurately reporting to our constituents."

BENEFITS OF AN OPERATIONAL PLANNING PROCESS

There are many benefits to basing your operational planning on portfolio management concepts. Establishing the overall direction for an organization represents the highest form of corporate governance and stewardship. It is most effective when it occurs in a transparent fashion that builds widespread ownership and acceptance for the organization's future direction. Using portfolio management techniques to develop and manage your operational planning establishes this fundamental transparency.

In addition to bringing operational planning into the open with a defined approach, the use of portfolios formalizes associated processes, roles, and responsibilities. This helps the entire organization come together with a common understanding of strategic direction and stay focused on delivering results with tangible business value. It also establishes a purpose-driven foundation for financial and resource capacity planning.

Developing a portfolio-based approach to operational planning drives efficient operations for a number of compelling reasons:

- **Consistency**: A formal operational planning process establishes a methodical, consistent planning approach at the highest levels of the organization, with clearly defined roles and responsibilities. More than simply good business, such an approach provides the transparency necessary to meet the requirements of auditors, stockholders, accountants, and regulators. It also sets the standard for planning rigor as an example for the rest of the organization to follow.

- **Alignment**: Managers are more likely to direct resources to tasks that fulfill operational direction when the organization understands and supports the plan. Achieving this alignment requires a shared vision and approach. Strategic portfolios align work with defined operational objectives and provide a common point of reference.

- **Extended planning horizon**: A defined operational planning process extends your horizon to facilitate meaningful long-range planning. This enables proactive capacity management and improves your ability to leverage emerging technology and other opportunities. The protracted nature of some strategic initiatives can span multiple years. A defined operational planning process involves a broad cross-section of your organization to provide consistent guidance and focus on long-term efforts rather than relying solely on the vision of a single executive.

- **Collaboration**: By applying a collaborative model for strategy development, executives in both supplier- and customer-facing roles become active participants in planning, rather than simply downstream recipients of operational requirements. Benefits extend beyond the internal organization. Implementing a defined operational planning approach improves collaboration with suppliers, customers, and business partners. This is an important consideration if you are to extract the highest possible return on your investments. When business units and provider groups work together to define a cohesive and balanced strategy, you can align expectations well in advance of committing significant resources, thus increasing the potential for mutual success.

- **Communication**: All staff members can grasp the basic reasons for their daily assignments when a defined, consistent operational plan is visible to all organizational levels. This "chain of custody" helps individuals understand the importance of their efforts. They are better able to relate how their personal work links to that of other groups and departments. This instills confidence in the leadership. The process also enables timely and accurate communications and ensures continuous alignment, even when business priorities change.

- **Control and flexibility**: The operational planning process is a dynamic, continuous loop function that includes long-range planning, near-term monitoring, and ongoing management and decision making based on actual results and changing operational considerations. A defined approach to operational planning establishes the necessary infrastructure for organizational agility. Organizations sometimes resist clearly defining their strategies because of the misperception that a rigid plan will reduce flexibility. In actual practice, a defined approach to operational planning increases agility and responsiveness. If everyone clearly understands the current direction of the organization, it becomes much easier to rapidly identify, communicate, and execute revisions to it. People find it easier to understand change when they have a known point of comparison.

- **Organizational efficiency**: The biggest detractor to efficient operations is lack of planning. Too often organizations are simply "taken by the current" in the absence of consistent, purpose-driven guidance. You can easily relate to this concept on an individual level. Consider the inefficiencies created when unfocused resources react to conflicting or inconsistent guidance, constantly stopping and starting as they jump from one activity to the next. This same effect translates up through the entire organization if strategic direction is inconsistent, ambiguous, or nonexistent.

If the executive team can establish a comprehensive, balanced, and consistent plan for meeting market demands, leveraging resources, and managing products, the organization can collectively focus on those priorities and proactively plan execution in the most efficient manner possible.

KEY POINTS IN THIS CHAPTER

☑ Strategic portfolios enhance how you build operational plans by
- Developing guidance for your organization
- Identifying funding opportunities
- Developing financial plans
- Developing capacity plans
- Identifying benefit goals

☑ Participants in operational planning include
- Senior business and financial executives
- Product and brand managers
- Investment and portfolio managers
- The portfolio management office
- Managers responsible for implementing decisions

☑ Governance is how you define expectations, grant power, and verify performance. Portfolios offer a set of governance processes within your existing business functions.

☑ The portfolio management governance board should be chaired by a senior executive and have six to ten permanent members.

☑ The governance board owns the overall planning process, but individuals own components.

☑ The general planning cycle should correspond to the natural rhythms of your organization, but you should conduct periodic reviews according to your operational realities.

☑ Risk management is an inherent part of operational planning and portfolio management.

☑ Risk can take many forms; it must be identified before it can be managed or mitigated.

☑ Once you have identified and measured risk, you need to determine your tolerance to the risk and take action.

☑ Develop a communications plan that spells out how you will share operational planning results to support your organization's missions and objectives.

CHAPTER 8

THE OPERATIONAL PLANNING PROCESS

FIGURE 8-1 IS A HIGH LEVEL PROCESS MAP of operational planning. The functions in bold represent those that are accomplished using strategic portfolios, with major related supporting functions included as other process elements. The references in the diagram related to investment and execution portfolios are covered in more depth in later sections of the book. This chapter provides an introduction to the operational planning functions highlighted in figure 8-1.

CURRENT STATE ANALYSIS

There is an old saying—"A map does you no good if you are lost to begin with." Determining the future for your organization begins with assessing its current state.

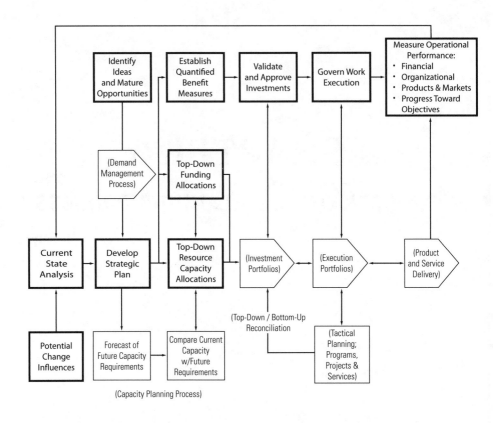

Figure 8-1: The Operational Planning Process: Strategic Portfolio Functions

Building a strategic portfolio that reflects the overall performance of your enterprise can help you accomplish a current state analysis. This current state is usually described relative to the types of information shown in figure 7-1 on page 88. For example, strategic portfolios should help you answer the following questions for your organization:

- How are we performing against the existing organizational missions, objectives, and strategies?

- What markets are we engaged in, and how are we performing in them?

- Who are our customers and stakeholders?
- What products and services are we offering to them?
- How are doing competitively?
- How are we doing financially?
- How is the organization itself performing, in human terms?
- What human capacities do we have, and how are they currently being utilized?

Any given view of your strategic portfolio (or any business portfolio) will identify one type of information as the subject and include other information for comparison. Often the portfolio subject relates to how you deliver value, which includes elements from the deliverable information structure. For instance, if you sell products to a market, the subjects in the portfolio could be your products. The metrics would include the market characteristics of those products, such as revenue, development cost, market share, market trend, competitive strength, and so on.

As another example, you may analyze a portfolio of services for a nonprofit or internal service provider with measurements that reflect customer satisfaction levels, callback rate, average response time, how many constituents are receiving each service per quarter, the total costs of services, cost per user, and the number of staff delivering them. The target values for these measures ultimately reflect the objectives, strategies, and benefits you set out to achieve. Regardless of the type of product or service, it is important that you document the goals, basis, and sources for your measurements.

A strategic portfolio designated to specifically track current state information should be routinely updated to capture measurement data and track trends. You should also periodically save and store an "as of" version of the portfolio to record a baseline of information for future comparison. When combined, these trends and baselines offer both a fixed point of reference as decisions are made and a running assessment to track whether those decisions are adding value to your ongoing operations and delivering the intended results.

Assess Potential Change Influences

The analysis of existing or potential change events that may affect your organization going forward is an integral aspect of current state assessment. These changes can be difficult to see and understand. Most of your answers will come from asking the right types of questions:

- What stands in the way of our ability to achieve our goals?
- Are the needs of our markets and customers changing?
- What is going on around us economically, politically, internally, and externally that is shaping our destiny?
- What can we anticipate about our suppliers and other resources?

There are several well-documented and established methods of assessing influences on operational planning, including:

- **SWOT Analysis** (strengths, weaknesses, opportunities, and threats)
- **Porter's Five Forces** (competitive and industry analysis technique)
- **PEST Analysis** (political, economic, social, and technological)

Each method takes different approaches to analyzing internal and/or external influences that shape business objectives. SWOT analysis is a widely used approach to categorizing internal (strengths and weaknesses) and external (opportunities and threats) influences. Porter's Five Forces approach is more oriented toward analysis of competitive environments by assessing supplier power, barriers to market entry, threat of substitutes, buyer power, and degree of rivalry. PEST analysis (political, economic, social, and technological, sometimes reordered as STEP) is also primarily an external analysis technique on a macro level.

These are a few examples of the techniques that you can use to understand the potential impact of change events. Additional information about these and other strategic analysis techniques is readily available from a variety of sources. Our goal is to help you organize and structure your strategies rather than define your strategic thinking.

Regardless of which approach you choose to employ, the objective remains the same: assess the future state of organizational requirements, evaluate the impact of change events on your current state, gain a clear understanding of what needs to change and why, and determine what actions must be set in motion to effect change. Put another way, your goal is to answer these questions:

- Where are we?
- Where do we want to go?
- Why do we want to go there?
- When do we need to be there?

As a natural by-product of this analysis, planners will begin to understand what assets and resources are necessary to execute the missions.

DEVELOPING A STRATEGIC PLAN

In chapter 5, we described how to structure strategic and work information using the MOST (missions, objectives, strategies and tactics) approach, which gives you a method to define the actions that will be taken to tame change and reshape the future of your organization. The MOST structure also provides a common rallying point to align other types of information in support of these actions within portfolios. This part of the chapter provides guidance and examples of how to develop missions, objectives, strategies, and tactical elements.

Establishing Missions

Missions represent the core values of the organization and tend to reflect long-term, even timeless, qualities. As such, they are oriented toward qualitative, visionary goals rather than specific time targets or quantified results.

Many organizations already have missions established and prominently posted. If this is not the case in your organization, or if existing mission statements do not adequately lend themselves to this purpose, then you need to create them. Consider approaching mission development using the balanced scorecard approach, expressing missions as elements related to demand, capacities, cost, and benefit, or correlating them to markets, products, and resources.

An organization's missions should adequately incorporate all aspects of its charter and purpose. If mission development falls short in accomplishing this, there may be a gap when developing and linking downstream elements of the hierarchy. Ultimately, this should be a self-correcting scenario when valid needs arise that cannot be aligned with organizational missions, but it is still worthwhile to strive to be as complete as possible in the initial definition process.

The following example is one of several missions that an information technology department might establish:

> **Mission:** *IS will manage technology and deliver services in a manner that maximizes shareholder equity and value (SV).*

Developing Objectives

Once missions establish a reasonably complete view of the purpose of the organization, you can develop objectives for each one. While missions act as touchstones that represent a balanced perspective of the values and goals of your organization, changing business priorities may shift the emphasis that you place on some missions versus others in any given planning period. This dynamic sets the stage for how you propose objectives.

Objectives breathe life into sometimes lofty or abstract missions, giving them shape and meaning. They bring your conceptual vision into realistic focus, determining how aggressively or conservatively your organization will maneuver the planning period. Objectives define specific and quantifiable goals within explicit operational windows to advance their associated mission and are the leading elements that define the priorities of overall operational planning processes. They establish the planning horizon and risk-reward posture for everything that follows. Objectives also form the initial point for top-down distribution of funding and resource capacity.

Ongoing evaluation of progress toward meeting each mission, combined with an analysis of change influences, results in a decision whether to continue to existing objectives or to modify, close out, or define new ones.

Objectives establish measurable goals over a specific time frame for a given mission. Using the earlier mission example, one of its objectives might be:

> **Mission**: *IS will manage technology and deliver services in a manner that maximizes shareholder equity and value (SV).*

> **Objective SV-2-11**: *IS will improve fiscal performance associated with efficient delivery of business applications by reducing the associated annual cost of application delivery (cost area 734) by 35 percent, from $51.6 million in fiscal year 2010 to $33.54 million for fiscal year 2013.*

The objective establishes a specific achievement target within a given time frame. This is critical in establishing measures for tracking performance and progress. *Note*: the objective does not identify *how* you will accomplish it; subsequent strategies and tactics will further refine those aspects.

The most difficult aspect of objective development is managing the scope of work, cost, and capacity that those objectives will ultimately represent. Initially, operational planning will differentiate between *approved* objectives versus those that may be initially *proposed*. Identifying potential objectives is relatively easy. Deciding which objectives to actually pursue relative to everything that has been suggested can be very frustrating without some clear approach to assessing relative priorities.

The portfolio management governance board is responsible for developing the proposed population of objectives and for further refining them into a cohesive portfolio with proper balance. Balance considerations include appropriate attention to missions most in need of focus, high level assumptions about funding and resource distribution, customer-facing versus internal-facing needs, line-of-business balance, cumulative risk, and net value.

Bear in mind that the portfolio of objectives is subject to further adjustment as the planning process moves forward. Additional information may change your initial assumptions, especially during the first pass of reconciling top-down plans with bottom-up estimates.

Building Strategies

Missions establish the *why;* objectives define *what* and *when.* Strategies shift the emphasis to *how* to accomplish objectives and add additional performance details. This is an example strategy for the mission and objective we discussed earlier:

> **Mission**: *IS will manage technology and deliver services in a manner that maximizes shareholder equity and value (SV).*

> **Objective SV-2-11**: *IS will improve fiscal performance associated with efficient delivery of business applications, reducing the associated annual cost of application delivery (cost area 734) by 35 percent from $51.6 million in fiscal year 2010 to $33.54 million for fiscal year 2013.*

Owner:	CIO		
Allocations:	2011	2012	2013
Funding:	$1.2M	$1.8M	$2.3M
Resources:	6 FTE	7 FTE	8 FTE

> **Strategy SV-2-11-2**: *Audit current business applications. Determine business applicability, value, usage, number of*

active users, and future projections of existing software appli-cations. Identify total cost of ownership, and relative cost per transaction and user. Identify high cost, low value applica-tions, and recommend subsequent improvements.

Owner:　　　　Director, IS Operations

Target date:　　Complete initial audit and
　　　　　　　　recommendations by end of Q3 2011

Target savings: 2011—$0   2012—$2.5M 2013—$2.5M

2011 capacity allocations (preliminary): Funding: $500K
　　　　　　　　　　　　　　　　　　　　　　Effort: 4 FTE

The first thing worth noting in this example is that tentative time frames and estimated cost savings targets are identified for the strategy along with 2011 funding and resource allocations. The bottom-up plan-ning of underlying tactical details (supporting programs, services, and project portfolios), and investment analysis will further refine the dura-tions, dates, and expected savings. After final estimates are approved, baselines are established and used to measure actual strategic benefit and performance.

As the example shows, the development of objectives and strategies allows you to apportion top-down capacities in the form of total available funding and resources. The intended result of strategies and tactics is to build a logical framework for achieving objectives, while defining specific guidance, parameters, and constraints that bound implementing portfo-lios of work (services and projects).

In actual practice, funding and tactical planning functions are final-ized in parallel; executives making top-down funding decisions often rely on emerging tactical details in order to understand how money and human resources should be allocated.

Note the planning horizon associated with the objective (3 years), compared to the expected shorter time frame of this initial strategy. All strategies do not have to be defined up front to fully achieve the objective. In this example, strategies represent initial actions undertaken during the 2011 planning period, as the opening gambit toward achieving the long-term objective.

The estimated savings of initial strategies does not need to fully meet objective targets. You can easily imagine how the results of the listed strategy could trigger additional actions that continue the progression toward the objective. Additional strategies will be added in future planning cycles based on initial strategy outcomes. For example, hardware and software consolidation may result in reducing the number of staff needed to maintain them, or further reduce total software maintenance and licensing costs.

Finally, recognize that this is a limited example; a complete operating plan would include other strategies and additional fields, such as originator, date, classification, and so on.

To aid in balancing and refining strategies and tactics, they should be classified to distinguish between those that are mandatory, discretionary, or associated with maintaining ongoing operations. Here are the strategy classifications to use:

- **Mandatory**: Activities that must be accomplished to meet mission-critical functions, either due to business criticality, regulatory necessity, or corporate mandate.

- **Discretionary**: Unique opportunities that should be accomplished to further missions based on relative priority and/or business value. As individual items, these activities do not fundamentally impact the ability to do business or accomplish parent goals if they are not pursued.

- **Base services**: These activities are necessary to maintain the organization as a viable operation, such as ongoing delivery of products, infrastructure maintenance, and general organizational overhead (management, staffing, training, etc.).

You may choose to further refine these basic classifications to address unique requirements, naming conventions, or to add additional levels of detail; however, these three categories represent the fundamental consid-erations to assist with assessing the overall balance of your strategy. Note that each individual element is classified on its own merit. For example, an objective defined as mandatory may contain some underlying strategies that are not essential to its accomplishment, which are flagged as discre-tionary. Conversely, a discretionary strategy may have certain underlying elements that are mandatory if you are to accomplish the parent result.

Developing Tactical Plans

Tactical planning continues the iterations necessary to link the goals expressed by missions, objectives, and strategies in actionable form as initiatives, programs, services, and projects. Tactical planning may con-sist of multiple levels depending on how you define the strategic hierar-chy. Regardless of the number of interim levels, the lowest levels of the work plan will correspond to programs you've enabled and their associ-ated projects or services.

Tactical plans should define and refine the following:

- Outcomes and actionable work that creates deliverables
- Guidance on methods, approaches, and technology to be applied
- Who is to achieve the results, including ownership/responsibility, sponsorship, in-house versus outsourced or contracted, and so on
- Timing of results, including milestones, incremental phases, and so on
- Budget and capacity limitations

The strategy manager is responsible for assigning tactical owners and coordinating with them to establish underlying approaches that meet goals within the constraints identified.

Building on the earlier examples, let's explore how tactics might be developed for *Strategy SV-2-11-2: Audit current business applications.* To achieve this strategy, the director of IS Operations works with the PMO and one of his managers to propose an Application Portfolio Manage-ment (APM) program, which will:

- Identify and catalog business applications
- Perform a functional and usage assessment
- Conduct a financial assessment
- Perform analysis of business and technical alignment, risks, and so on
- Identify opportunities and recommendations

Tactical planning uses this initial outline to formulate a more complete description of how the strategy will be achieved and provides guidelines to investment owners to help further portfolio development. The APM program may create a new service and initiate several different projects to implement it.

Using Milestones

You need to establish milestones for objectives and strategies based on target dates. In addition to establishing a target overall completion date, you can also use milestones to develop interim targets to manage performance and keep the overall plan on track. They are equally important to tactical planning.

IDENTIFYING IDEAS AND MATURING OPPORTUNITIES

The essence of positive change in an organization is innovation through new ideas. Ideas are basic to the progress of mankind and form the lifeblood of any organization. Few organizations can survive without new ideas. Even though hugely important to the organization, the capture and analysis of ideas is often one of the most underserved forms of demand. Many organizations lack a structured mechanism for taking in and managing ideas.

Ideas and opportunities refer to demand that is still in its formative stages. A proposed business venture, exploratory discussions about a new marketing initiative, or an idea about how an internal process can be improved are all examples of demand that must be further matured and articulated into tangible and explicit requests for work. It is also important to evaluate the way ideas align with the objectives and strategies of the organization.

Ideas are relatively easy to think up and promote but more difficult to put into action. A 2001 survey suggests that 75 percent of ideas submitted by employees are cost reductions; yet other studies suggest that only 2 percent to 3 percent of ideas submitted ever mature to create a positive impact on an organization. The knowledge and creativity of the workforce and customer base can represent the greatest intellectual capital that an organization has at its disposal, but it will remain an elusive and untapped asset until processes and tools are put in place to harness it.

We have all heard stories of the typical idea management initiative launched in response to a change event. The campaign starts with a big announcement for employees, customers, partners, and suppliers, inviting them all to contribute ideas. If it is well publicized, the organization might get hundreds or thousands of ideas. But, if the contributors don't hear back about their submission they begin to wonder if anything is happening and they lose interest. In time, the campaign fades away.

Successful organizations are not only open to new ideas; they also make a formal commitment to an effective and sustainable idea nurturing process. They throw open the widest net to capture ideas using methods from automation to customer surveys. Ideas are formulated, developed, and given life. Portfolio management is a perfect fit for idea management. It provides the tools for intake, analysis, and modification and matures the best ideas into opportunities that can be considered for action. Your organization will only get value from an idea after it is structured, funded, and implemented.

The most valuable ideas are those that align with your organizational strategies. Authorizing idea campaigns based on specific business objectives helps you gather the right ideas at the right phase in the change life cycle.

Most ideas need further refinement to move them from being an interesting concept to a desirable investment for the organization. Your organization can use portfolio management to collect and mature valuable ideas into structured opportunities (figure 8-2).

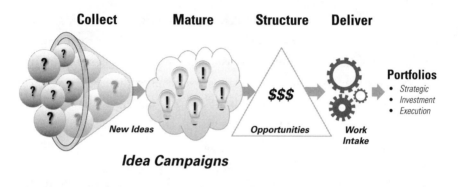

Collect   **Mature**   **Structure**   **Deliver**

New Ideas   *Opportunities*   *Work Intake*

Portfolios
- *Strategic*
- *Investment*
- *Execution*

Idea Campaigns

Figure 8-2: Developing Ideas with Portfolios

Collecting Ideas

Finding successful ideas starts with engaging a wide audience. There is some evidence that online idea-generating events offer better idea quality than face-to-face brainstorming. Some people are reluctant to speak up in front of their peers or are not very good at defending their ideas in public. The privacy of an online submission process gives contributors time to fine-tune their positions so that they can prepare well thought-out submissions. Today, social networks have become a powerful set of tools to collect and organize ideas, but any method that collects and organizes information will begin the process.

What makes an idea good? Is it based on how well the idea fits your business or the clarity of the idea? Is it based on how well written the idea is or the uniqueness of the thought? *Good* ideas are easy to understand, clearly identify the main concepts, and answer the most obvious questions posed by the reviewers. However, sometimes vague or mediocre ideas can be combined to create a single high quality concept. That is why a structured idea collection and review process is so pivotal to the success of an idea campaign.

Maturing Opportunities

Once ideas are collected, the challenge is to filter them, pick the winners, and develop them into meaningful products and services. As with any good project, idea-generating projects involve formal time lines, costs, and quality targets. Project deliverables are mature ideas, actionable steps, and fundable opportunities.

Once you choose the most promising ideas and refine them, the process of structuring them into opportunities can begin. You can determine where the ideas fit in your organization, what resources you need to implement them, and the benefits they offer.

Ideas identified as having plausible value proceed through the portfolio management workflow. The portfolio management process further categorizes, filters, scopes, and estimates the costs and benefits.

You should divide ideas into several categories depending on whether the idea has current or future value and which division is best suited to develop the idea. Some ideas may go into storage to be brought out at a later time when costs are more reasonable or the market more mature. Other ideas may offer an excellent partnering opportunity with another organization that has the specific capabilities needed for implementation. Eventually, your portfolio will contain a number of viable idea candidates for near-term funding.

During the filtering process or critical analysis of the idea, the review team needs to be realistic in exploring the different aspects of the concept while continuing to nurture it. As this process advances, the core kernel of the idea is expanded to meet a broader purpose. The team should also scope and estimate the idea to define the resources that are necessary to implement the idea. Further development of the ideas into structured opportunities with defined deliverables takes place within the portfolio management work intake process.

Structuring Opportunities

A key benefit of portfolio management is the ability to structure the work intake process so that an organization can develop opportunities depending on where those opportunities are in the life cycle of a change event. Maybe the change event is the loss of market share to a smaller competitor in a market segment; the strategic opportunity might be to "buy our competitor." The project team may identify the feasibility of the opportunity, but senior executives will make the final decision.

You may decide to enhance your product in some way. That is an opportunity that will go through the normal investment analysis process. Finally, there could be an idea to promote some features of your product not emphasized in the past, which might mean activity-level inputs to a marketing project that has already been authorized.

CASE STUDY: TURNING IDEAS INTO VALUE

One large industrial goods company grew by acquisition over the years. A recession that impacted the company's industry led management leaders to focus on increasing revenue from their existing customer base. One revenue generation strategy was to "increase the value of each transaction sold to our customer base."

They decided to authorize an idea campaign. A project team was assembled, and team members posed the question to the target contributors about how to increase the value of the average transaction. Among a number of responses was one idea—"Have customer engineers specify our full product line when they design their projects." The team found the idea interesting, but each division was dealing with different buyers, so how could that work?

Many of their customers specified the largest component of the company's products when designing projects, but the rest of the company's product line was often subject to competitive bids, resulting in several small transactions with the customer at different times. There were logical relationships between the company's products but the customer and even the company's own staff did not know much about them. One of the subject matter experts asked—"Could we offer some price incentive to have the customer buy the full product line when they buy the first, largest component?"

The idea passed the early review stage so the project team started to scope out what it would take to implement it, including an enhanced product catalog offering product combinations, a new pricing package, and new product marketing materials. The divisions would need to support the discounted pricing ideas, but the project team believed it could increase average transaction price by up to 50 percent. Even more important, the team thought the idea could virtually eliminate competitive bids by some customers, so the sponsor actively promoted the opportunity to the divisions.

The project team defined the idea as a formal investment initiative and forwarded it for consideration. Because the initiative carried a pricing and strategic impact, the team presented it to the portfolio governance board for approval before going through the investment analysis process. The initiative was approved and the work done in execution projects. Early feedback from the field shows that the strategy is working and the average selling price has improved.

In this case study, company executives understood the power of actively encouraging new ideas that aligned with their strategies, and they were willing to invest in an idea campaign. The project team members encouraged and enhanced the idea submitted to them and ran the project in a professional manner. The project sponsor understood his role of working with the division managers on the pricing issues. The work intake process led to an approved investment that coordinated pricing, marketing, and engineering to build value for the organization. A higher average transaction price leveraged the sales group and helped the organization generate revenue. The company used portfolio management to run a successful idea campaign.

ESTABLISHING QUANTIFIED BENEFIT MEASURES

Many groups and departments within an organization generate ideas for new initiatives and products. To ensure that only the best ideas are selected to proceed requires an evaluation process based on business need and benefit. To increase the chances of an idea's success, the benefits that the idea will generate should be fully articulated. A multidisciplinary review team adds value to the sponsor's proposal by sharpening the definition of the benefits. Early buy-in of key stakeholders increases the chances of later success.

The Role of Benefit Owner

The planning, development, and delivery phases of large programs could take years to complete. This is typically beyond the point at which the project team is maintained, and key players such as the project managers and program managers may be reassigned to new tasks.

Because benefit realization extends the boundaries of traditional project and program management, it requires a new role: the benefit owner. The benefit owner is responsible for executing the entire benefit realization process from definition to monitoring and reporting until benefits are delivered by maintaining custody and visibility of the business value over the life of the endeavor. This ensures that value is the critical parameter and guiding interest in decision-making processes from inception to retirement. One of the designated benefit owner's early responsibilities is to identify, quantify, and validate the forecasted value of a particular initiative.

Documenting Benefits

As a standard, expected benefits are documented in the proposed investment business case. However, they do not always appear in a standard format or in a specific section of the document. Including a defined section in the proposal template where benefits are clearly stated makes it much easier to retrieve them during later phases of the program. This will also make it easier to report post completion benefits because more time will have elapsed at that point.

To objectively measure business value, expected benefits must first be described in quantifiable terms. The benefits can be categorized by their nature (tangible, intangible) and by the period of measurement (one-time, progressive over time). All combinations of these dimensions are possible. Business value is usually expressed in tangible, monetary terms such as increased revenue or cost savings, which are linked to financial calculations that define the time span for key milestones such as the "break-even point." Efficiency improvements are also in the category of tangible benefits.

Less tangible benefits such as "customer satisfaction" or "brand recognition" are harder to quantify and measure. They may require special data collection systems or more subjective measures derived through surveys or polls. Regardless, expected benefit must represent measurable results and be clearly identified and quantified.

The target values for the benefits should include a timetable that specifies when those targets will be achieved. Generally, a phased approach is taken for benefits that accumulate over time. For instance, if the benefit were linked to sales of a new product, the monthly sales would be expected to have a steeper curve after the first three months as sales campaigns start to have an effect.

Some benefits materialize at specific points in time, or only once. If the benefit of a modular approach to software development is to reduce time to market by reusing the modules, every time this is achieved the initial project generates benefits. If the benefit is to reduce costs by replacing and retiring a legacy system, the benefits of decommissioning systems and reducing maintenance and staff for the legacy system are accumulated as each event occurs.

Often, benefits such as cost savings or revenue increases are presented in percentage terms compared to a baseline. Although you can also represent changes in percentage terms, benefit reporting has to work with units such as hours and dollars and convert those to percentages. Therefore it is useful to have benefit targets stated in real terms.

The benefit owner determines how often benefits are to be measured and reported. Practical considerations and data usefulness are factors that determine reporting frequency. It may not be possible to extract the benefit data from all the systems at the same time during the reporting period. The reporter will need to be mindful of the natural reporting rhythm of the system that supplies the benefit data.

It is important to distinguish between the most significant benefits and the rest. The benefit owner and the PMO should analyze the contribution of individual benefits to decide which ones are to be included in the monitoring and reporting phases. Best practice calls for you to establish a ranking between the benefits and aim for the top three to five that contribute the most expected benefit for detailed tracking. This approach maintains clarity and focus on the key returns from the initiative, without creating the expensive administrative overhead that comes from time-consuming data collection and analysis tasks.

TOP-DOWN FUNDING AND RESOURCE CAPACITY ALLOCATIONS

At any given time, a significant amount of your future organizational and financial capacity is committed to ongoing activities and in-progress initiatives. But, as we can see from the preceding discussions, these activities are nothing more than past ideas, opportunities, strategies, and investments that are at a higher level of maturity, which further reinforces why operational planning must consider the total capacities of the organization and how they are currently being utilized as an integral part of setting strategy.

As we introduced in section 2, chapter 6, "Managing Demand and Capacity," a significant part of operational planning includes determining how you will apply available money and resources to new strategic investments. Ultimately, operational planning must enable future changes by allocating capacities across the full spectrum of different investment types. Because these considerations are such an important part of operational planning, we have dedicated two chapters in this section—one relating to resource capacity planning and the other describing how operational planning facilitates funding decisions—to explain in detail how this is accomplished.

VALIDATING AND APPROVING INVESTMENTS

So far, we have focused on using strategic portfolios to establish top-down guidance for the future direction of the organization. However, operational plans rely on the support of investment and execution portfolios to evaluate, plan, and manage the completion of change initiatives.

Validating Investment Plans

One major benefit of using portfolio management across the ecosystem is that it gives you the ability to reconcile top-down strategy with the realities of the bottom-up information gathered about potential investments. As a business-driven effort, operational plans are initially developed with only limited information about the true requirements and capacities needed to deliver them. As potential investments are defined and analyzed in more detail, resulting estimates can differ significantly from strategic assumptions. Any differences between operational planning allocations and bottom-up estimates must be resolved to arrive at a mutually agreeable go-forward investment decision. This gives top executives confidence that their strategies can be successfully implemented, and provides work and resource managers an opportunity to provide input into the planning process.

Without a doubt, navigating this particular junction is the most complex aspect of bringing strategies to fruition. Anyone can ask for too much just as easily as someone else can respond, "I can't do that." Lack of mutual flexibility, communications, and partnership during the reconciliation process can be the business equivalent of "immovable object meets irresistible force." Working-level staff often respond to unreasonable mandates with half hearted attempts, or they simply ignore targets they believe are impossible to achieve, which results in unmet expectations, mutual frustration, and a degraded leadership posture. Conversely, it is both the right and responsibility of the executive team to direct resources toward agreed-on business priorities and to hold the staff accountable to meeting reasonable, even challenging, expectations.

When approached as a true team effort, the portfolio reconciliation process becomes an asset rather than a point of friction. Each level of the organization has an equally important role to play in the process. Certainly the senior executives are responsible for guiding the business direction and, indeed, are the most qualified to do so. Rarely, however, do they also have all the working-level expertise (or time) necessary to identify and assess the details of carrying out their plans.

Consider an auto racing team as an example—the driver always pushes the limit, demanding more speed, traction, and handling to gain an advantage on the track. The crew must do everything it can to increase performance, but it must also advise the driver about the limitations of the car, track, and laws of physics. A short-lived racing career is predictable for the driver who fails to listen. Only by combining the two skill sets will the race be won.

Validating Proposed Benefits

Investment validation also ensures that the expectations and objectives set forth during operational planning are practically achievable as a result of the individual initiatives put forth in investment portfolios. Once investment portfolios are determined to be functionally viable, technically sound, and achievable within the constraints of allocated capacities, they can be approved for execution. We explore the portfolio reconciliation and approval process in more detail in chapter 13 "Developing Investment Portfolios."

The validation of expected benefits by key departments during investment analysis improves the chances of success for the program. It is generally easier for people in vertically integrated lines of business to evaluate the benefits that they seek and to assess the impact of the projects. People in horizontal, shared service groups, such as customer service, administration, finance, procurement, or training, often find it harder to assess the impact of a program on their capabilities. It is very important that the representatives of both vertical and horizontal groups examine the benefits in the light of their capabilities and milestones before confirming that they will be in a position to deliver them.

These are the key questions to ask during benefit validation:

- Are the benefits achievable within the normal operating rhythm of the enterprise or do they require operational changes?
- Are the milestones to generate the benefits realistic?
- Can the resources sustain the realization of benefits as part of ongoing operations?
- Are the risks to the benefits manageable?
- Can supporting departments sign off on the benefits and commit to their realization?
- Can a consensus be reached between parties with conflicting views about the benefits?
- Are the benefits measurable?
- Is the effort required to measure them reasonable?

GOVERNING WORK EXECUTION

Operational planning acts as a governance and oversight function as work is planned, executed, and placed into operation. Because execution portfolios link to the strategies they support, the executive team can monitor whether planned costs and results are tracking with original expectations. While the project manager focuses on delivering a project that conforms to time, cost, and quality requirements, senior managers focus on whether the project remains a worthwhile investment. Emerging issues, changes in scope, or shifting business requirements can all affect the assumptions and expected value that led to the initial approval of a new program or product.

Projects today take place in increasingly volatile environments with regular changes in external factors and market conditions. As companies try to run more projects simultaneously, complex interdependencies also cause changes. As long as the changes are managed within the discipline of project management, they should not cause major disruption or disappointment. However, some changes can have a very serious impact on benefits.

Major changes should be referred to the portfolio governance board and the project sponsor, where the impact on strategic milestones, budget, risks, performance, capacity, and contingencies can be examined. In addition, major change requests should be examined from the viewpoint of their impact on benefits. Changes involving large increases in costs must be referred back to the sponsor and the benefit owner to avoid situations that could upset the fundamental cost-benefit balance and operational planning assumptions. Corresponding benefit increases should be agreed to and secured before a new baseline is determined.

By definition, uncontrolled changes run counter to project management good practices. Poorly managed changes waste resources and time and contain the seeds of long-term benefit failures. They are often the product of hastily arranged project recovery attempts or ill-conceived specifications. In all cases, they spell trouble. Therefore, the PMO and governance team should be on the lookout for such cases because they usually signal deeper problems. They should also revalidate all benefits to ensure that they are not diminished as a result of rogue changes. Changes that involve significant shifts in milestones can push the program beyond the market opportunity window, impacting benefit forecasts.

Regardless of what causes deviations, anyone charged with managing operational strategy should recognize whether a particular initiative continues to be a good investment.

MEASURING OPERATIONAL PERFORMANCE

Earlier we defined governance as a method to set expectations, grant decision rights, and verify performance. Performance measurement sets the parameters that define the success of your strategies, investments, programs, and projects.

There are many types of measurements. We encounter them in school, sports, music, dance, and every phase of our lives. In business, you can measure sales performance, customer satisfaction, financial ratios, or other benchmarks. Here, we focus on using portfolio management to measure the impact of business decisions within change events.

The modern business world generates vast quantities of data. It is easy to get overpowered without understanding what that data means to your decision making. General Colin Powell once observed that the hallmark of a good general is in knowing when you have enough information to act. Conversely, you must also recognize when you do not. In the Civil War, General Ulysses Grant was awakened in the middle of the night with news of enemy troop movements. He thought for a moment and said, "It is not possible" and went back to sleep. As it turned out, his decision not to act was correct.

The traditional control-oriented performance measurements that were developed for industrial age organizations are losing their relevance in today's world. Many organizations are reshaping themselves into flat, global operations. Managers are dealing with increasingly complex geography, teams, and business models. We need to think differently about how we measure performance. While financial measurements remain meaningful, we need more timely information about the "why" behind the numbers.

The purpose of portfolio management is to organize information in support of your decision making regarding change events. With credible information you make informed decisions, implement them, and then verify the performance of your organization. Most of the business decisions that you make impact your organization in one of the following ways:

- **Operational efficiency**: Global competition requires your organization to constantly assess and improve efficiency. Today, both your competition and your resource pool could be located anywhere in the world. Your decisions must ensure that you gain the greatest value from available capacities, whether they are your own or those of your suppliers.

- **Strategic transformation**: There was a time when a well thought-out strategy might sustain an organization for decades, but that is no longer our reality. Mergers and acquisitions, changes in markets, or retiring a cash-cow product are all transforming events. You need to be proactive in identifying and driving change, particularly when it is transformational.

- **Improved agility and scale**: You have to determine what needs to be done today to develop more agility in responding to future challenges. Decisions made in search of greater flexibility and the ability to grow larger and faster should look beyond the financial results for this quarter or this year.

All of these decisions are about a change in demand or capacity or both. Portfolio management offers you information to prepare for and make effective decisions.

Using Key Performance Indicators

Key performance indicators (KPIs) refer to the set of core metrics that are primary measure of an organization's health and performance. Some use the popular Balanced Scorecard approach or SEI CMM measures, while others develop their own system of unique metrics. Regardless of the measures used, KPIs are the subset of metrics that your organization has chosen as core to the decisions of the portfolio governance board. These metrics benchmark current status, compare that status to historical performance or related measures, enable analysis of the results, and measure the success of actions taken to control and manage performance within acceptable ranges.

KPIs are a communication tool for your entire organization. While each person has measurements that are important to his or her job, there is a core set of KPIs that everyone cares about. All employees should have the opportunity to see and understand organizational performance so that they can internalize their personal stake in the people they influence, share in the success of performance gains, and better understand when and why improvements or changes are made. Posting KPIs where people can review organizational performance fosters useful conversations about performance issues from different perspectives.

Here are some best practices when building core performance metrics for your portfolio governance board:

- Ensure that metrics are simple to understand and unambiguous.
- Measure the process, not the people:
  - Define and label measures directly related to core business objectives.
  - Use leading metrics to support performance management.
  - Use lagging metrics to demonstrate outcomes.
- Select a balanced set of metrics that present a holistic view of business objectives.
- If you cannot directly measure outcomes, measure the behaviors that should contribute to achieving those outcomes.
- Recognize that metrics will drive behavior:
  - Select actionable metrics.
  - Be aware of unintended consequences.
- Identify a small set of actionable metrics meaningful to the business, rather than large, unquantifiable metrics.
- Certify that each measurement has its personal ownership defined.
- Ensure that each measure has predefined action limits that, if exceeded, invoke specific corrective responses.
- Review regularly the alignment of metrics with changing business objectives.
- Adjust upper and lower control limits as performance improves and variability is driven out of the processes being managed.
- Treat out-of-tolerance metrics as formal issues that must be managed to closure.
- Create guided metrics to ensure organizational adoption.

Overall, an organization's performance can be monitored with a surprisingly small number of well thought-out KPIs. It is preferable to have only a handful of clearly defined and relevant metrics rather than to overwhelm the organization with a dozen that are not reviewed, studied, or understood.

CASE STUDY: PERFORMANCE MEASUREMENT AT THE CARPHONE WAREHOUSE

The Carphone Warehouse was founded in 1989 to bring mobile communication services to consumers. The market was always complex, and the company's aim from the very beginning was to offer its customers simple, impartial advice and outstanding value. As a result, it grew from a handful of stores operating exclusively in the UK selling mobile handsets and contracts, to a European-wide platform of over 1,500 stores in ten countries, providing a wide range of mobile and residential telecom services.

This company's experience illustrates how portfolios can improve the quality of performance measurement in a complex, progressive organization operating in a highly competitive sector. During a period of several months, the company implemented a flexible performance measurement approach to replace an older report generation method that was proving to be inadequate.

In the past, the organization responded to management information needs by accessing the raw data generated by its portfolio management system. When a manager requested a certain report, IT staff would respond to the request by generating a report and delivering it to the manager. In part because of mismatches and miscommunications between IT staff and the original requester, as often as not the manager would then have to adjust the report to meet his or her real needs.

Among changes that were stressing the old system was the increased importance of outsourced and offshore vendors. These vendors offered The Carphone Warehouse attractive opportunities to reduce costs, but those opportunities added complexity and rigidity. For instance, the vendors wanted to be guaranteed a certain minimum level of work and, to get the best prices, asked that The Carphone Warehouse provide them with a certain lead time between issuing contracts and requiring deliverables.

Their executive team members decided on a product road map within their operational planning. They wanted to forecast products a year in the future to give their staff and vendors more visibility. The road map was to include financial data, product deliverables, and cost and resource informa-tion by product line.

The Carphone Warehouse established key metrics that supported the creation of the product road map. The company then offered its managers access to automation that would let them build the information that they needed as they needed it. Figure 8-3 is an example of an interactive chart that offered their managers access to backup information through the tabs at the top of the pages with drill-down capabilities to more detail behind each page.

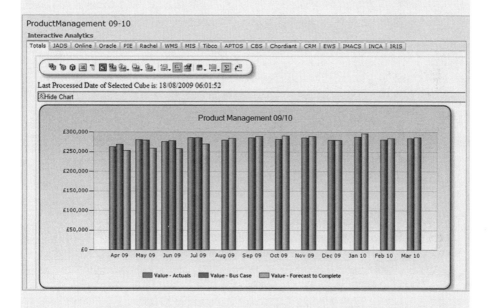

Figure 8-3: Product Investment Information

They informed managers about the data that was available to them and provided training on the best way to access it; the gains were worth the added effort.

Today, The Carphone Warehouse can provide appropriate decision mak-ers with a detailed breakdown of supplier costs; identify areas where the company has gaps in its performance; and target specific business units, teams, or departments. Drilldowns are available by model, period, account type, and subaccount type, among other options. When needed, decision makers can identify a high level anomaly and then drill down to the indi-vidual project manager for an explanation.

KEY POINTS IN THIS CHAPTER

☑ A current state analysis shows how your organization currently delivers value.

☑ You can understand the impact of change events by asking the right questions.

☑ Your decisions can add value to your organization through

- operational efficiency,
- strategic transformation, and
- improved agility and scale.

☑ Strategic portfolios give you a consistent basis to

- assess the current state,
- evaluate change events,
- prepare an operational plan,
- link investments and execution to that plan, and
- update the operational plan with measurable value delivered.

☑ New ideas on innovation and cost savings are the lifeblood of your organization.

☑ Defining idea management policies and processes nurtures new ideas.

☑ Successful idea campaigns support your strategies.

☑ Ideas are matured into opportunities that are candidates for funding and staffing.

☑ Some ideas and opportunities that are not funded can be stored for future consideration or offered to partners.

☑ Portfolio management supports decision makers by supplying relevant, timely, accurate, and suitably sliced-and-diced metrics.

☑ Portfolio management offers performance information for your key business areas that are impacted by change events.

☑ For decision making, financial metrics are always lagging indicators and management information is generally a leading indicator. Portfolio management helps reconcile these differences.

CHAPTER 9
FINANCIAL CAPACITY PLANNING

FINANCIAL MANAGEMENT CAN GENERALLY BE DEFINED as the processes used to maximize the value of an enterprise's money. In the same way that managing demand and resource capacity takes different forms along the portfolio ecosystem, managing money is also an ongoing activity that functionally shifts depending on where you are on the continuum of change.

Operational planning uses strategic portfolios to make high level funding allocations to various organizational spending categories and divisions. In turn, these allocations drive operating budgets and investment portfolio decisions. Execution portfolios are used to develop and manage additional tactical budgets for specific programs, services, and projects.

In addition to providing your executive team with a method to conduct operational planning, strategic portfolios add a new conceptual dimension for financial executives who are responsible for preparing and managing budgets. By supplementing the typical organizational view of funding distribution with a strategic view, executives can link financial planning with objectives and strategies to get a better sense of how to allocate money. The same is true for product and brand managers, who can clearly associate the revenue and costs of customer products and markets to the objectives and strategies of the organization. Investment managers can also gain better insight into how their responsibilities relate to the bigger picture.

The following exchange helps to illustrate a common situation within many organizations:

The chief operating officer of a rapidly growing mid-sized business finished presenting a summary of the upcoming annual budget at the quarterly board meeting. One of the board members asked a relatively simple question: "What percentage of the expenditures in this budget relate to the three major operating objectives that have been set for this fiscal year?"

Lacking an immediate answer, the COO looked to the chief financial officer, hoping she was preparing to respond. She was flipping through a multi-page listing of the 85 projects that were included for funding, but it provided no answer. Both were reaching the same conclusion— while they had many supporting details and a good view of where money was going organizationally speaking, they were unprepared for such a simple, big-picture question.

The project list reflected the sponsoring department but it didn't indicate how projects aligned and contributed to strategy. Even if it had, that provided only half the answer; incremental growth was also driving a lot of organizational and service consolidation that wasn't even reflected in the project list. After looking at each other, the COO turned and said, "We'll have to take a follow-up action and get that data to you . . ."

After the meeting, the COO and CFO discussed the question posed by the board member. The CFO explained that she saw her role as a financial adviser, rather than as an active participant in deciding how to allocate money. She saw her foremost responsibility as meeting accounting and regulatory reporting requirements by factually presenting financial data in an objective manner.

The COO thought about the CFO's comments for a moment and replied, "All that may be true, but you still hold the keys to all of our financial information; what we need is a way to look at it differently. We—both of us—should have been able to answer that question. Quite frankly, now I am wondering if we really do have the right balance between our ongoing expenses and these new initiatives. When we defined our operating plan, did we establish a budget that properly enables its strategies?"

To help you understand better the value of extending your existing financial management capabilities, it is useful to first review the typical accounting practices that most organizations employ. This will provide a foundation for comparing and contrasting how strategic financial management relates to operational approaches and what it offers.

OPERATIONAL FINANCIAL MANAGEMENT

Accounting requirements and regulations form the basis for how most organizations approach operational financial planning. At an enterprise level, operational accounting for publicly traded organizations (and most private enterprises) focuses on four primary accounting instruments: the balance sheet, income statement, cash flow, and shareholder equity. Management and external parties use the resulting financial accounting information for reporting and management. This information must be objective, precise, verifiable, and conform to appropriate accounting guidelines and requirements specified by Generally Accepted Accounting Principles (GAAP), the Securities and Exchange Commission (SEC), Financial Accounting Standards Board (FASB), and International Accounting Standards Board (IASB).

The veracity of the cost elements in these financial instruments is determined by underlying budgetary details that refer to a defined financial management hierarchy and a chart of accounts. Traditionally, accounting practices are structured around how money is apportioned to each cost center across the organizational hierarchy, as shown in figure 9-1.

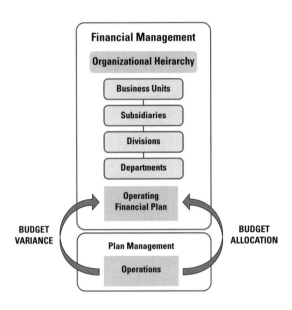

Figure 9-1: Organizational-based Hierarchy Approach to Financial Management

Tracking the flow of money through the organizational structure aligns different levels of the hierarchy with defined responsibilities. This supports the concept of *agency doctrine*, which establishes the individual lines of responsibility for the finances of the organization. The vice president, director, or manager of each cost center acts as an agent for governing financials within his or her span of control, driving vertical accountability for spending.

In addition to meeting accounting requirements, this general approach to financial management also offers managerial benefits. It provides a clear understanding of "who" by tracking how money goes to different parts of the organization. It also provides a clear understanding of "what," by virtue of the chart of accounts. You know how much money is budgeted and spent by category, such as labor, travel, hardware, software, and so on. It even provides information about "where" money is being spent; you can easily see from accounting information which service providers, suppliers, and so on are receiving payments.

What the operational financial plan does not do very well is tell you "why." Although project and program budgets give you limited tactical insights into why money is spent, organizational-based budgets do not have inherent provisions for understanding how money is distributed and consumed from a strategic perspective.

CREATING A STRATEGIC VIEW OF YOUR FINANCIAL PLAN

Your organizational financial management methodology, combined with a defined strategic plan, provides the foundation to create a strategic view of financial management. Strategic-based financial management leverages the chart of accounts and other features of your existing accounting structure, but it follows *how* money flows through the strategic work hierarchy.

This gives you the ability to see how financial capacities align to objectives and strategies and how you allocate the money to accomplish them across organizational boundaries. For example, a particular business objective and its underlying strategies may involve multiple business units and departments.

Even though these two approaches often rely on the same underlying financial data, they have different objectives. Strategic-based financial management offers an additional approach to accounting for managerial purposes, unencumbered by regulatory accounting requirements. It has a strong emphasis on future orientation, relevance, and timeliness, and as a supplemental technique, it is not mandatory that it conform to GAAP.

Rather than being a tool primarily intended for the chief financial officer, strategic financial management offers a financial tool that other executives can apply during the operational planning process. It offers a way to "twist the cube" of operational financial data to better understand the balance of funding between various planning imperatives.

Of course, the CFO and accounting staff can also benefit from this information. As the story about the board meeting points out, in addition to meeting accounting requirements, your finance team also has to serve the management needs of your organization. Anything that improves financial visibility and transparency is a welcome addition to your current arsenal of tools. Furthermore, because this strategic view of money is so closely tied to operational accounting information, it is essential that the CFO and financial staff be involved as full partners in developing this capability.

IMPLEMENTING STRATEGIC FINANCIAL PLANNING

Organizational and strategic-based financial management methodologies are interrelated and work in parallel. Yet, different technology applications often support each approach. Your general ledger platform is usually the system of record for financial operations, but it is probably not designed or equipped to enable broad operational planning as we define it.

A full-featured portfolio management system gives you the capabilities to not only define your strategic plan, but also to distribute money and people across it. Different types of raw data originate in either the financial or portfolio management application, with information shared between the two using appropriate process controls and interfaces.

The goal of strategic financial planning is to provide decision-support capabilities by supplying financial information for strategic portfolios. It offers a method to make financial allocations across objectives and strategies, to analyze the financial risk of these allocations, and to track financial performance of the operating plan.

Figure 9-2 shows how the two financial management processes interrelate and converge. Mapping programs, projects, and services (work) to the strategic hierarchy makes this possible. Once you are able to align tactical work to the strategies and objectives it supports, then the assigned responsibility and budgets for these activities and the resources engaged in performing them, provide the linkage for information to flow between the organizational and strategic hierarchies.

Figure 9-2: Convergence of the Financial Management Approaches

APPLYING THE STRATEGIC VIEW OF FINANCIAL INFORMATION

Governance of the strategic financial plan is an additional tool for the leadership team to use in operational planning.

In our story, if the COO and CFO had been able to look at the operational budget using a strategic perspective, they would have readily seen how funding distribution related to the objectives of their organization. In such a case, the strategic perspective of financial information serves as a check function; if you do not like the distribution balance, you can adjust the operational budget until it aligns with strategic intent.

Earlier, we indicated that it is sometimes desirable to disrupt the equilibrium of demand and capacity intentionally in order to effect proactive change. For organizations that want to take a more outcome-oriented, top-down approach, you can use a strategic view of financial information as the leading method to drive organizational budgets.

The previous version of the operating budget is commonly used as the basis for the next cycle of financial planning. While this incorporates historical spending, it also tends to propagate past spending patterns. By starting with the future strategic focus of the organization instead, you establish a much stronger, forward-looking position that intentionally disrupts past patterns. Funding is allocated to objectives and strategies to emphasize and drive priorities. By doing that, you redefine the funding distribution in line with the overall strategic direction. Operating budgets are then established based on their relative ability to accomplish defined objectives.

USING FINANCIAL PLANNING TO MANAGE RESOURCES

Operational planning involves more than just money. Controlling staff distribution is almost as powerful a lever as funding. Typically, high level budgets use a summary-level chart of accounts; by defining direct and contracted labor types as budget line items, you effectively control head count distribution and manage what types of resources are used. You can apply this technique in conjunction with strategic financial planning to redistribute head count between objectives and strategies and to balance staffing between programs and services on the tactical level.

Using financials to direct resource utilization provides for gross adjustments, but ultimately, you need to manage human capacity using more refined methods, as we describe in the next chapter.

The following Monday, the COO and CFO called a meeting with the lead financial analyst and PMO director. They explained what they needed and put them in charge of working together to figure it out. It took some time for each group to understand how the other worked, but once they identified the points of commonality, they were able to produce a strategic view of the budget. By the next quarterly board meeting, the COO was ready to discuss how funding related to the objectives and strategies of the company, including updates to the budget that were made to put more emphasis on key initiatives.

KEY POINTS IN THIS CHAPTER

☑ All organizations already have an established financial management method based on regulatory requirements and accounting standards; typically this is designed to follow the organizational structure and budget responsibilities.

☑ These operational financial plans provide a mechanism for fiduciary governance and some managerial information but do not provide much insight into how budgets and spending align with the strategic direction of the organization.

☑ A strategic view of financial management leverages the MOST structure to supplement existing financial management practices and provide a strategic perspective of how money is distributed.

☑ Strategic financial planning aligns with existing operational accounting processes, information, and tools to share information and operate in parallel as a decision-support tool for the leadership team.

☑ The strategic view of financial information supports operational planning by providing financial information to strategic portfolios.

☑ Strategic financial planning can also be used to proactively drive change in the way money is distributed throughout the organization so that it proactively emphasizes and enables strategic priorities and intent.

CHAPTER 10

RESOURCE CAPACITY PLANNING

CHAPTER 6 USED THE PORTFOLIO BALANCING ACT to describe how any portfolio must balance demand with capacity to arrive at a feasible planning scenario. In that chapter, we also described the three basic forms of demand: *base services, strategic initiatives,* and *other planned work*. We discussed how each of these demands has different cycle times and demonstrated how to apply the planning horizon to develop appropriate demand and capacity forecasts. In this chapter, we build on those concepts to establish the process and techniques for resource capacity planning as part of developing strategic portfolios.

Most organizations create a capacity plan based on the limitations of existing direct staff. The plan might include incremental expansion or contraction of head count, or perhaps the limited use of contracted resources. However, among the many changes in today's business environment are new opportunities for sourcing the skills you need to accomplish your objectives. Whether you leverage third-party service partners, search the web to find individuals with unique skills for temporary assignment, or use globally dispersed staff to create virtual teams, there are new alternatives to consider. Organizations are steadily becoming more open to exploring resourcing opportunities and finding creative ways to provide more staffing flexibility to extend their capabilities.

Thus, the intent of resource capacity planning is not simply to incrementally change or redistribute current state capacity. The objective is to proactively manage capacity to meet anticipated needs, rather than miss opportunities because of the false barrier of existing head count. When properly executed, operational planning gives you ample time to anticipate and adjust resource needs as part of your overall strategy.

Resource capacity planning establishes a capacity allocation plan that takes into account the following inputs:

- Ongoing operational demands of the organization (base services)
- Current in-progress projects and initiatives and their future capacity needs
- Additional strategic initiatives proposed by operational planning
- Other anticipated demands over the planning horizon (future emerging initiatives and other planned work)
- Relative timing of these demands and their capacity consumption rates
- Current resource capacity and utilization
- Capacity sourcing options and the cost of capacity

The capacity allocation plan provides inputs into each of the three portfolio types as follows:

- Strategic portfolios, as estimated resource capacity costs for operational planning
- Investment portfolios, as initial estimates and available capacity allocations
- Execution portfolios, in the form of a capacity sourcing plan and resource utilization plan

THE RESOURCE CAPACITY PLANNING PROCESS

Figure 10-1 is the process map for resource capacity planning. The blocks outlined in bold lines indicate the functions directly associated with capacity planning, accompanied by related operational planning, investment analysis, and execution planning functions to indicate critical interrelationships.

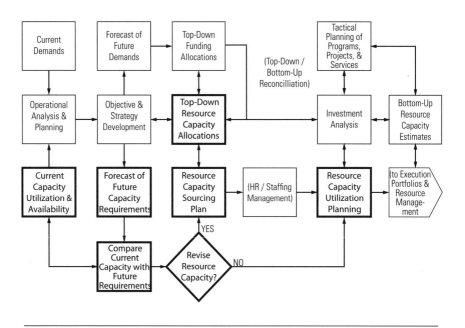

Figure 10-1: Basic Resource Capacity Planning Process Map

Several bi-directional arrows in the process map reflect the iterative nature of capacity planning. While initial operational planning establishes high level estimates and proposed top-down capacity distribution; bottom-up plans and estimates for programs, projects, and services add additional information to consider and reconcile before you can finalize the resource capacity allocation plan. This chapter reviews the bolded functions in figure 10-1. We address the details of bottom-up planning in later sections.

ANALYZING CURRENT CAPACITY UTILIZATION AND AVAILABILITY

We discussed earlier that operational planning begins with a clear assessment of your current state. Information about current and future resource capacity and utilization should form some of the key data inputs into your analysis. A historical baseline of current resource usage, along with knowledge of the capacity needed to execute in-progress work, establishes the basis for future capacity planning.

Obviously, developing a historical baseline presumes that you are regularly collecting such information. Every organization should be able to obtain total head count easily from HR information and organization charts. You can identify the capacity utilized from nondirect staff through contract information. However, head count needs to be refined to reflect how much capacity you are using to fulfill strategic initiatives, base services, and other planned work. For capacity planning purposes, information should, at a minimum, provide a full-time equivalent (FTE) level of detail consumed by each type of demand. However, the more detail that you have available about capacity usage and planning, the more accurate future planning will be.

The ideal mechanism for gathering historical capacity information is to report effort expended on individual work activities. Time reporting provides the summary level information needed for capacity planning. The detailed historical records provided by time reporting are also indispensable for developing accurate work estimates and general resource management purposes.

In lieu of reporting time for specific work activities, many organizations capture time at a high level for accounting purposes; for example, time is submitted on a monthly basis by product or customer for billing purposes. These records are typically less detailed and accurate than time reported for work management purposes, but they may be useful to establish high level capacity utilization information.

If no form of time reporting information is available, you may have to rely on some other form of non-labor information to extrapolate an estimate of capacity utilization. Examples of this include converting the labor line items from historical budget data to FTE utilization or using management judgment to assess the relative percentage that each group in the organization applies to each form of demand.

The remaining data elements needed to complete the profile of current state capacity are determined by estimating future availability based on the current demand scenario. For people who are already performing resource planning across the entire spectrum of demand, it is a simple matter to roll up the total effort planned for the current workload. Referring back to our demand iceberg in chapter 6, organizations that only focus on work above the waterline might have information readily available for their existing project portfolio, but they may not have effort data specifically planned for base services and other planned work. In these cases, you can carry forward the FTE estimates extrapolated for historical utilization into future planning periods for capacity planning purposes.

Regardless of the data sources employed, assembling this information should result in a chart that resembles figure 10-2.

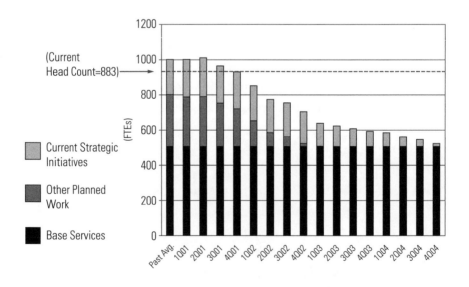

Figure 10-2: Capacity Utilization and Availability Based on Current Demand

In this example, the chart reflects the recent historical average for capacity utilization (the first stacked bar) and a 4-year projection of capacity requirements based on the existing total demands of the organization. This baseline of current state capacity utilization and availability becomes a key input to operational planning.

FORECASTING FUTURE CAPACITY REQUIREMENTS

As you formulate objectives and strategies during the operational planning process, related estimates begin to emerge for resource capacity and funding. Each strategy should include an estimate of the number of FTEs required over a defined period. This information creates the inputs to the proposed go-forward capacity profile.

Figure 10-3 builds on the previous current state capacity utilization and availability projections by forecasting capacity needed to support operational planning.

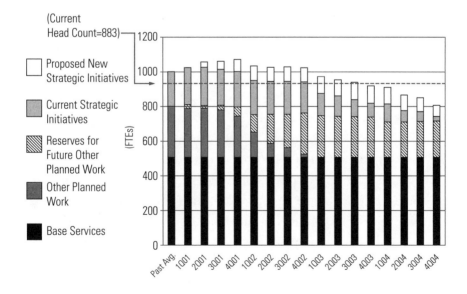

Figure 10-3: Forecast of Total Capacity Requirements

This forecast reflects the addition of new objectives and strategies, modifications to the effort allocated for the portfolio of existing initiatives, the anticipated future demands of other planned work, and adjustments to the FTEs that will be required in the future for base services. The cumulative total of anticipated future demands provides a comprehensive resource profile of proposed capacity requirements.

RESOURCE CAPACITY COMPARISON AND REVISION

At a minimum, the proposed capacity scenario allows an initial analysis of whether future capacity needs will be level, expanding, or contracting. Bear in mind that three interrelated operational planning activities are happening simultaneously; objectives and strategies are being proposed, resulting capacity requirements are being analyzed, and high level budgets are being developed. The full implication of the portfolio balancing act becomes readily apparent as the leadership team works to reconcile the competing considerations of demand, capacity, cost, and benefit.

From a capacity management perspective, the operational planning process exercises a number of control levers to arrive at a go-forward scenario. Among those levers is a reassessment of planned and in-progress initiatives from previous planning cycles to determine whether they should continue. To the extent that operational planning is an ongoing, dynamic function, the value and business alignment of previously approved initiatives should be under continued scrutiny. Even if their original basis for approval remains valid, capacity constraints and the greater priority or value of new proposals might force existing initiatives to be cancelled, rescheduled, or put on hold.

While the operating plan needs to accommodate changing conditions and organizational needs, it is equally important to avoid routinely replacing existing initiatives just to make room for "the next best thing." Such practices make for costly scenarios, given that the costs sunk into these displaced initiatives yield no business value. If this practice becomes habitual, it is just as unlikely that new additions will mature to completion; the next round of planning will simply put them in jeopardy as well. The decision to halt an in-progress initiative should receive the same level of diligence and scrutiny that it took to approve it initially.

This is where the value of the MOST (missions, objectives, strategies, and tactics) approach becomes evident. Each cycle of planning consistently asks the same basic questions as a starting point: Are our objectives still valid for our operating conditions? Do our strategies still represent the best way to achieve them? Do the programs, services, and projects that we have in our portfolio still reflect the best value to accomplish our strategies? This steady focus on your business objectives helps to ensure that decisions are not erratic from one cycle to the next.

When proposing new strategic work in the planning cycle, it is important that you factor in capacity for expected future initiatives. For example, note that in the scenario in figure 10-3, proposed strategic initiatives combined with other demand projections will exceed current resource availability through quarter 2 of year 3. This infers that the organization will add no additional initiatives in the next few years unless capacity is significantly increased or the proposed commitments are reduced. While it is appropriate to plan for 100 percent utilization in the current year, total planned capacity utilization for future years should be consciously tapered off to allow availability for inevitable additions in future planning cycles.

Leadership has another lever at its disposal to manage capacity—timing. As new objectives or strategies are identified, the natural tendency is, "Hurry up! Let's get this done as soon as possible!" However, near-term availability is often scarce or nonexistent. Operational planning may need to consider slowing down, spreading out, or rearranging how the total portfolio of initiatives is slated for execution.

Deciding to pursue certain initiatives with external resources or service providers is yet another capacity management lever. If a strategy represents work that is outside the capabilities of existing staff, then the "build versus buy" discussion might conclude that it is faster, less expensive, and less risky to contract that work out rather than perform it in-house. In addition to offering human resource flexibility, contracting out new capabilities often makes economic sense as well. A growing number of organizations are opting to contract out back office and routine transactional services to external providers so that the organization can free up its own resources to concentrate on proprietary, business-critical functions.

While we have used examples that reflect a scenario where demand exceeds capacity, situations where capacity planning must contend with excess staff also arise. Market downturns, creative destruction, product obsolescence, automation, consolidation, or restructuring are all examples of changes that can result in excess resource capacity.

All of these considerations and more come into play when you compare available capacity with proposed demand. The goal is to establish the capacity profile for your organization as part of the operational planning process. For example, continuing with our capacity charts, the operating plan might conclude that organizational capacity should be revised as shown in figure 10-4.

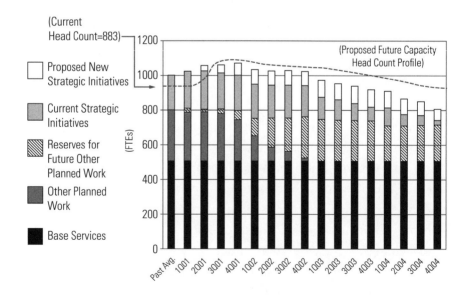

Figure 10-4: Proposed Capacity Profile to Meet Organizational Total Demands

The proposed future head count profile shown in figure 10-4 indicates that current head count will be ramped up beginning in the middle of year 1 in order to increase capacity temporarily to meet the needs of new initiatives. Note how this increase provides a small amount of additional capacity to accommodate a few additional initiatives to be added in future planning cycles. Eventually, the improvements being undertaken by the organization will allow it to reduce capacity slightly over the current head count by the end of the planning horizon, while still reserving about 12 percent of capacity for future initiatives.

MAKING TOP-DOWN RESOURCE CAPACITY ALLOCATIONS

The capacity profile and proposed head count is based on underlying assumptions about how capacity will be allocated across the total demands of the organization, including the number of FTEs needed to support proposed new objectives and strategies. As we illustrated in chapter 8, operational planning establishes the top-down funding and resource capacity allocations at each level of planning. These top-down allocations accomplish a number of control functions besides just establishing the overall capacity "budget."

The relative distribution of capacity reflects the weight that the leadership team places on each mission, objective, and strategy. In essence, allocations become a form of prioritization, indicating how executives and senior analysts emphasize relative importance or needs across competing objectives. Capacity distribution also makes up part of the boundaries provided to respective investment portfolios. Each proposed strategy establishes the expected outcomes, target dates, and the people and money that are allocated to it. This sets the operational parameters that investment portfolio managers need to respect as they develop, analyze, and select the best tactical scenario to fulfill strategic expectations.

Capacity allocations also directly influence funding distribution. As we discussed in chapter 6, there is a close relationship between financial budgeting and the cost of resources; capacity distribution becomes a controlling input into funding. The amount of funding provided relative to the effort required also drives the type of resources that investment managers can consider. For example, allocating four FTEs over a 1-year period and only providing $350K in labor funding will probably drive the investment owner to evaluate the use of low cost, offshore resources. Conversely, allocating $700K in labor funding but only two direct-staff FTEs opens up the potential to consider specialized local contractors.

In addition to enabling new initiatives, top-down capacity distribution also represents a mechanism for changing current operational staffing paradigms and forcing adjustments. For example, the total amount of effort allocated to base services and current other planned work in figure 10-4 diminishes slightly over the planning horizon. Imagine that the majority of this adjustment is actually due to a significant reduction in run-the-business allocations to a single department, perhaps steadily reducing head count by 15 percent to 20 percent over the planning period. What if some of this effort were redirected to other groups? This redistribution of head count would drive internal changes in how the respective parts of the organization operate.

Top-down capacity allocations represent the first proposal in what usually becomes a series of negotiations and adjustments. The initial top-down allocation does not yet have the benefit of additional planning detail that would test the feasibility of the proposed capacity distribution, but it does provide a consciously directed starting point for the organization to work toward as strategic portfolios are refined.

DEVELOPING A RESOURCE CAPACITY SOURCING PLAN

As an understanding of capacity requirements over the planning horizon is developed, the total head count projection is defined, and initial top-down capacity allocations are established, your organization can begin to develop a sourcing plan that details how necessary staffing will be obtained. The resource capacity-sourcing plan should specify what percentage of total capacity constitutes direct staff versus other resources. It may also establish the balance between different staffing partners, locations, skill and role types, the timing of workforce changes, and other related details that are necessary to refine resource costs and to execute the sourcing plan. In the same way that a capacity profile was developed based on the type of demand, a profile of staff sourcing can also be created, essentially creating a resource portfolio. Figure 10-5 offers an example capacity sourcing profile to accommodate the needs of operational planning.

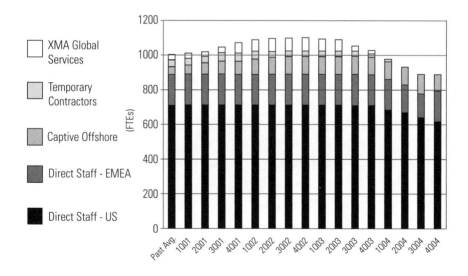

Figure 10-5: Proposed Capacity Sourcing Profile

Looking at figure 10-5, we can imagine how operational planning is driving a reallocation of direct staff between U.S. and EMEA locations, while eventually reducing total direct head count by almost one hundred FTEs. The organization plans to continue using its current service provider, XMA Global Services, to see it through this period of increased demand. However, it is also clear that by year 4, the intent is to phase out this service provider in favor of the organization's less expensive, captive offshore service branch. The organization also plans to shed reliance on temporary contractors by the end of year 3.

Ultimately, the resource capacity-sourcing plan will contain enough detail so that members of HR and procurement and department heads have a clear view of their respective roles in fulfilling these changes. This information is derived from resource capacity-utilization planning.

RESOURCE CAPACITY UTILIZATION PLANNING

If capacity management only required a generic FTE-level analysis of head count, we could accomplish it as a function of top-down financial budgeting, using its associated labor components. However, using funding data for capacity management has inherent limits compared to a more labor-specific approach. Using a blended average cost rate per FTE is a reasonable technique to initially analyze total capacity across general objectives, but order-of-magnitude capacity plans begin to weaken as strategies and tactics add additional insights about specific capacity requirements.

Knowledge workers do not form a homogenous workforce; your staff is made up of many different groups with specialized capabilities. Effective resource capacity planning dictates that we estimate what skills and roles are needed in order to accurately forecast specific resource capacity requirements. To accomplish this, you need to perform enough tactical planning to understand the high level resource requirements of individual programs, services, and projects. This information provides the level of detail needed to plan resource utilization. Role- and skill-based utilization planning provides the information needed to ensure that programs, services, and projects can be adequately enabled with the right type of capacity at the right time. It forms the bridge between the general capacity planning functions accomplished with strategic portfolios and the detailed resource management functions that are part of managing execution portfolios.

The level of work planning detail needed to support utilization planning corresponds with what is required to support tactical planning and due diligence for investment analysis. As we discuss in future chapters, investment portfolios drive the initial pass of planning needed to generally establish the costs, risks, and outcomes of each initiative. Utilization planning does not require every activity to be clearly identified and scheduled; an estimate of the general roles, skills, and amount of effort needed over the duration of the program or project is sufficient to support utilization planning. Utilization planning should also take into account other related considerations as appropriate, such as normal attrition, physical location, and other similar attributes that are important to your organization.

The goal is to analyze the demand placed on each role and skill in any given period, compared to the availability of those roles and skills, to identify hot spots where demand significantly exceeds specific types of capacity. Ultimately, utilization planning becomes part of the bottom-up information that is compared to the top-down capacity targets to validate their feasibility. Chronic capacity utilization issues can result in missing milestone dates, increasing costs, or diluting the expected value of affected initiatives.

While the analysis that follows uses general assumptions, they are useful as working numbers until you can measure and analyze your own specific circumstances. You should be able to provide a reliable breakdown of net capacity by work type based on actual historical results to make accurate future forecasts and estimates.

UNDERSTANDING TOTAL CAPACITY UTILIZATION— WHERE DOES IT GO?

Analyzing true staff capacity can yield surprising results compared to common utilization perceptions and assumptions. As an example, a staff of 500 can be broken down as follows (all values listed are typical approximations):

Typical Staff Head Count by Type

10 Department heads and executives

15 Administrative support and other nontechnical staff

10 Senior managers

30 Resource managers (average team size is 15 members)

435 Individual contributors (including project managers)

For the 435 individual contributors, work availability breaks down as follows (in hours):

904,800	Total possible working hours (435 staff @ 40 hrs/week x 52 weeks)
−87,000	Absence (vacation, holidays, illness, etc.; avg. 25 days/year per head count)
−81,780	Nonwork activities (general staff meetings, training, etc.; approx. 1/2 day/week per head count)
−27,144	3% annual attrition rate (lost effort and time spent training new staff)
−141,800	80% efficiency factor (actually doing work versus breaks, personal phone calls, etc.)
567,100	Total available productive hours remaining

Given the remaining hours available to accomplish deliverables, the following reflects typical effort utilization by general work type:

50%	283,550 hrs: Base services (routine ongoing operations, level-of-effort service delivery
10%	56,700 hrs: Resolution of emergent (unplanned) issues
20%	113,400 hrs: Other planned work (informal projects and unique assignments)
20%	113,400 hrs: Available to plan and execute formal projects

Thus, the typical net effective head count available for formal project work is only about 55 FTEs of the total 500-person workforce, or about 11 percent of the total staff effort available. In practical planning terms, this is enough effort to execute about a dozen medium-sized projects.

KEY POINTS IN THIS CHAPTER

☑ Resource capacity planning is an inherent aspect of overall operational planning and providing top-down guidance to the organization. It is a proactive mechanism for ensuring adequate capacity is available to achieve operational imperatives.

☑ Resource capacity planning establishes a capacity allocation and utilization plan that is based on the existing requirements of the organization combined with additional future demands.

☑ Resource capacity planning provides funding and budgeting inputs into strategic portfolios and ensures that enough human resources are available so those strategic initiatives can be accomplished.

☑ Resource capacity planning leverages the detailed planning that is accomplished with investment portfolios and execution portfolios. It also provides capacity-related inputs into each of these portfolio types.

☑ The resource capacity planning process is iterative in its nature; top-down capacity allocations are eventually reconciled with bottom-up resource planning.

☑ Initially, capacity management is done at the FTE level against broad demand categories and over long time periods.

☑ Eventually, capacity estimates need to be further refined to include the effort, skills, and roles needed for proposed programs, services, and projects so that utilization planning can be performed; this avoids capacity issues emerging later as initiatives are executed.

Section 4

INVESTMENT ANALYSIS

Some readers may simply visualize investment analysis as the senior leadership team gathered to make decisions about which projects to approve. However, if you are to become masterful at taming change, you should approach investment analysis as more than a decision point.

Although operational planning provides high level guidance, the organization needs to commit people and money to specific work activities in order to implement its strategies. Good governance dictates that these commitments be established only after you have reasonable confidence that your investments represent the best approach to achieve intended outcomes. Establishing this level of assurance relies on a series of deliberate and methodical actions that are part of the investment analysis process.

This section contains three chapters. Chapter 11 provides an overview of general investment analysis considerations and the investment analysis process. This process has two major phases; analyzing individual investments, which we cover in chapter 12, and developing investment portfolios, which is the subject of chapter 13.

CHAPTER 11

THE INVESTMENT ANALYSIS PROCESS

THE INVESTMENT ANALYSIS PROCESS collects, assesses, and selects opportunities identified through operational planning that best support the objectives and strategies of the organization. As ideas and opportunities are translated into specific funding requests, tactical planning develops supporting initiatives, programs, projects, or services and associates them with strategic intent. Each proposal is analyzed based on its individual merit to determine its strategic alignment, risk, and cost-benefit.

Those investments that are determined to be worthwhile opportunities are included in an investment portfolio for comparison against competing initiatives. These portfolios use a set of parameters, techniques, and tools to select and recommend the investments that represent the best collective value for the organization.

As part of the process, the planning and estimating that is accomplished in support of investment analysis is reconciled with portfolio constraints already established through operational planning. As shown by the portfolio ecosystem, investment analysis establishes the bridge between operational planning and execution. As a result, the process also drives compromise and consensus by acting as the arbiter between strategic intent and operational realities. Although challenging, the reconciliation process is necessary to ensure that investment portfolios represent a practically achievable approach that can be successfully integrated with ongoing operations.

Each of the functions we suggest in the investment analysis process is necessary if you are to make trustworthy investment decisions that effectively advance organizational objectives. Investment decisions are critically important to the change management process, and every organization tailors its investment analysis approach to fit its specific circumstances and preferences. Yet, most businesses still see opportunities to enhance their investment processes.

Some organizations make investment decisions based on inadequate information or using inconsistent methods. Other organizations do a good job of analyzing individual investments but fail to assess whether the collective results actually fulfill strategic intent or take advantage of synergies between each initiative. Still others may build a seemingly strong investment portfolio from the top down, only to find during execution that major issues threaten to undermine intended results.

These are some of the common concerns expressed by organizational leaders:

- Those who take an informal or simplistic approach often fear they are not doing enough analysis relative to the magnitude and impact of investment decisions.

- Some complain that even after a great deal of number crunching the results still do not provide reliable answers.

- Others feel unsure and tentative if their investment process appears to lack consistency between different opportunities or if the approach shifts from one year to the next.

Such anxiety is a by-product of the fact that there is no single best formula for making optimum investment decisions, as evidenced by the wide variety of contemporary practices, approaches, calculations, and different schools of thought surrounding the subject.

Organizations have a wide range of potential investment types and situations that fall within the realm of investment portfolios, such as:

- Making choices about global markets and positioning
- Determining which product improvements to pursue
- Making trade-off decisions about competing capital investments
- Selecting which process improvements to undertake

The challenge for decision makers is that all of these potential investment opportunities are competing for the same limited capacity. Your organization makes initial investment decisions relative to the uncertainties and operational conditions that are present and known at the time. All of these considerations affect the ability of decision makers to make reasonable assumptions, accurate forecasts, and informed judgments. Nonetheless, leaders have to make difficult and sometimes perplexing trade-off decisions using their best judgment and intuition, regardless of whether financial details fully support them.

Ultimately, the quality of the investment decisions that you make directly relates to whether you are able to successfully tame change. Every approved investment represents organizational commitment to execute some kind of change in your products, services, assets, or in the organization itself. Framing investment decisions from that perspective will help ensure that your organization approaches investment analysis with a clear understanding of what it really represents—the transformation of ideas, opportunities, objectives, and strategies into an approved, funded, and achievable plan of action. The investment portfolio process suggested here shows you how portfolio management offers a methodical and reasonable framework for investment decision making.

OVERVIEW OF THE INVESTMENT ANALYSIS PROCESS

Each organization defines its investment processes based on the practices of its industry sector, the type of investments being made, and its decision-making culture. Regardless of the specific processes employed, there are six distinct functions associated with investment portfolio analysis, as shown in figure 11-1.

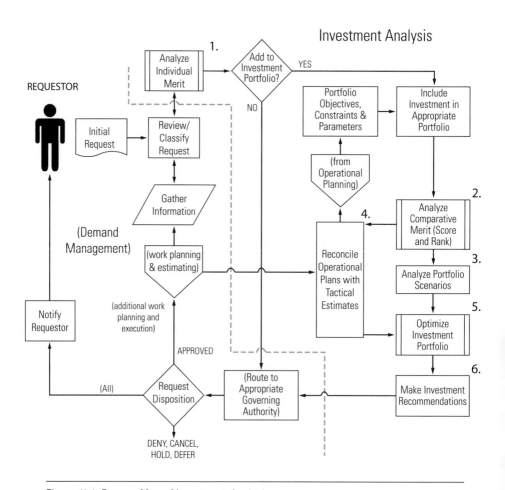

Figure 11-1: Process Map of Investment Analysis

1. **Analyze individual merit:** Each potential investment undergoes analysis based on its individual merit. Regardless of the investment in question, it must stand the test of comparing its presumed value relative to its anticipated costs and risks in conjunction with other considerations such as alignment to strategic direction. To make this assessment, decision makers need adequate information about the investment.

2. **Analyze comparative merit:** Investment opportunities that have merit on their own are placed in a portfolio for comparison against other potential investments.

3. **Analyze portfolio scenarios:** Investment portfolios are tested using different assumptions and variables to account for potential shifts in the investment environment and to establish the possible range of outcomes based on different scenarios.

4. **Reconcile:** The top-down expectations and assumptions used to create the investment portfolio are reconciled with the tactical inputs from bottom-up planning and estimating.

5. **Optimize investment portfolio:** The investment portfolio is refined to select the best possible set of investments to achieve objectives within the capacity constraints of the organization.

6. **Make investment recommendations:** The results of the investment analysis are presented for review and approval by the appropriate decision authority.

This chapter explores general investment considerations such as assessing the investment landscape, investment classification, and information gathering. Chapter 12 will concentrate on analyzing individual investments, with an emphasis on investment valuation. Chapter 13 focuses on developing and managing investment portfolios, including scenario analysis, investment selection, reconciliation, and making investment recommendations.

ASSESSING THE INVESTMENT LANDSCAPE

Every organization has its own unique circumstances and considerations that influence its approach to investment analysis. Macro considerations include the relative stability or volatility of the business; trends in the economy, market, and regulatory requirements; and underlying technology, competition, or suppliers.

Organizational aspects include management culture and risk tolerance, whether investments are targeted at external markets or internal customers (or some combination of the two), and the amount of strategic guidance provided for making investment decisions.

Other factors include the current state and maturity level of investment processes and tools; the analytical skills of the decision makers; the planning horizon; the amount of capacity that is available for investments; the magnitude, type, and nature of the investments themselves; and the availability of information about them.

Modern organizations face a growing dilemma about how to make the best investment decisions in an increasingly uncertain climate. Common investment wisdom tells us not to sacrifice long-term growth and equity for the sake of near-term profitability. But what is "long-term" in this age of growing uncertainty? What is the acceptance level for making large strategic capital investments that may take several years to begin generating value when the risks from unforeseen changes might dilute or eliminate their potential benefit before they can ever be delivered?

The time compression of investment decisions further illustrates the importance of vision and flexibility. Developing a strategic road map as described in section 3 establishes long-term direction. An actively managed investment program provides definitive mid-term guidance and acts as a mechanism to make ongoing adjustments. By adopting an approach that leverages operational planning and investment management as a combined set of tools, leaders are able to develop opportunities that offer a high degree of management flexibility as future circumstances unfold.

Operational planning establishes many of the higher level considerations needed for the investment landscape. For example, market analysis, economic forecasts, competitive influences, general capacity allocations, and similar influences are integral to developing objectives, strategies, and underlying tactical guidance. Having such guidance provided as part of operational planning alleviates the need for individual investment managers to independently research these influences and ensures that they are using a common set of assumptions.

The universal objective of investment analysis is to arrive at a set of portfolios that maximize the value delivered while minimizing cost and risk. However, each organization deals with a unique set of opportunities and constraints, making it a challenge to find the best approach.

Regardless of the approach selected, the keys to successful investment analysis are *consistency, balance,* and *flexibility.*

- **Consistency** ensures that each portfolio of investments is assessed using a common set of guidelines, measures, levels of information, and perspectives. Parity and objectivity of valuation approaches are essential to making fair relative comparisons between competing options.

- **Balance** refers to developing an overall portfolio of investments that is not overly skewed in terms of risk, investment types, time spans, customers, business areas, markets, or other categorical considerations. The financial community has long extolled the virtues of a diversified investment portfolio; such an approach is equally valuable when making business investments.

- **Flexibility** applies the analysis technique most suitable for the initiative being considered. For example, the decision to enter into a merger should only be undertaken after detailed research and analysis has quantitatively validated the opportunity and exposed potential risks. However, applying that same level of diligence to investing in an internal process improvement would result in burdensome overhead and do little to improve the quality of the decision.

The investment analysis process exposes uncertainties that trigger the initiation of several downstream processes, such as risk management, project planning and engineering, or marketing research. Good investment analysis is a critical component in the overall portfolio ecosystem.

INVESTMENT TYPES AND APPROACHES

In most organizations, the investment cycle involves making trade-off decisions that strike a balance between competing imperatives to move the organization forward, maintain operational viability, and to insure the organization from catastrophe. Thus, you can classify potential investments into one of three broad types based on their business driver:

- **Maintenance and improvement** investments are likely to be the largest and the most stable of the three portfolio types from one investment cycle to the next. This includes activities to maintain or incrementally improve the operational performance of the organization and its existing assets or capabilities, for example:
  - Continual improvement (Lean/Six Sigma/TQM, etc.)
  - Operational viability
  - Tactical change management
  - Obsolescence

- **Innovation** investments often vary based on external drivers such as changes in the investment landscape, emerging opportunities, and available capacities as driven by economic factors. Innovation includes investing in new markets, products, services, or other assets, such as:
  - Green field opportunities
  - Growth-oriented initiatives

– Transformational strategies

– Strategic change management

- **Compliance** investments generally represent the smallest portfolio category of the three, although these can periodically create a significant shift in investment balance. Compliance investments can be the most reactionary and least discretionary investment category: risk mitigation and cost avoidance; initiatives designed to satisfy mandatory regulations or policies, to insure and protect the organization and its existing assets or capabilities, or otherwise reduce exposure to potentially costly events. This includes addressing:

  – Regulatory mandates or other legal requirements

  – Security (physical, intellectual, or cyber)

  – Business continuity (production, staffing, supply chain, etc.)

  – Disaster readiness and recovery

In most situations, multiple investment portfolios are built to fulfill a predetermined balance between these investment types, as defined through the top-down allocation of organizational capacities. As a result, portfolios tend to be characterized in one of two ways:

- **Proactive/Progressive:** These portfolios tend to be driven by strategic objectives and are entrepreneurial in nature. They are often controlled via top-down funding and capacity distribution to various initiatives, with enabling programs and projects created to specifically fulfill predefined objectives.

- **Reactive/Demand-based:** Such portfolios are constructed from the bottom-up, usually driven by demand from multiple customers. As a result, initiatives are selected from a population of existing and largely unrelated requests that are usually funded by requesting parties. Demand-based portfolio investment cutoff points are generally dictated by available capacities rather than through meeting a specified value-based target.

The proactive type, driven from the top down by a comprehensive operating plan that balances innovation, maintenance, and compliance, is the preferred strategy. The bottom-up approach essentially defines strategy based on the individual investment decisions that the organization makes.

Realistically, some combination of progressive and reactive opportunities makes up a typical investment portfolio. It is impractical to completely ignore the backlog of internal or external customer requests that are pending disposition in favor of exclusively creating entrepreneurial initiatives to fulfill planned strategies. Operational planning and high level capacity allocation establishes a purposeful balance between competing styles and types of investments.

GATHERING INVESTMENT INFORMATION

Change requests usually undergo reviews by several levels of authority. For example, an investment-grade request generally requires the respective department director and/or a business unit VP to agree to it before submitting an initiative for formal investment consideration.

These internal reviews typically validate that an idea represents a credible opportunity or need, ascertain that its size and nature warrants formal investment analysis, and determine whether it is worthy of expending internal effort to develop the business case. The ultimate sniff test is whether the originator can persuade senior management to get fully behind a proposal as a sponsor. If the head of the originating department seems hesitant or unwilling to actively champion an investment, that should raise an immediate red flag to the PMO and others regarding its necessity or potential of success.

This preliminary chain-of-command approach to evaluating investment proposals, particularly those related to making internal improvements, is a double-edged sword. The obvious benefit is that it effectively weeds out unworthy, inappropriate, or duplicate investments before they have an opportunity to clutter up a portfolio or consume more resources. The downside is that these often-informal assessments are only as good as the leadership team of the originator. Great ideas can flounder because of ineffective communications, lack of thoughtful consideration, or due to internal politics.

To counter this possibility, establishing a mechanism to consistently and systematically gather and analyze ideas and opportunities, such as discussed in chapter 8, aids in developing possible investments as an inherent part of portfolio management.

With this in mind, we will start with the assumption that the opportunity has progressed beyond the point of mere interest and has successfully maneuvered through any departmental assessment gates to mature into a formal investment proposal.

The Business Case

Every investment opportunity should be accompanied by a business case prepared by the initiating party/sponsor. The initial version of the business case includes information directly related to investment decision parameters.

There is a clear distinction between the responsibilities of the business case owner and the delivering organization. Failure to differentiate between these responsibilities is a commonly observed challenge, especially for technology initiatives. Too often IT leadership finds itself in the awkward position of defending the business necessity of a customer-requested service or application. Business need and value should always be driven by the sponsoring business sector, while the provider maintains focus on technological alignment, cost estimates, ongoing support, and other delivery-related aspects.

The business case should focus primarily on the key parameters that will assist in driving the investment decision, along with adequate information to enable initial planning and estimating, including:

- General description of the deliverable(s) or other outcomes
- Business drivers and influences
- Expected benefit (tangible or intangible) with time-phased projections for realization
- Impacts, including those of not proceeding
- Timing (need date/time limits/window of opportunity, etc.)
- Key roles, players, and a defined single point of contact

In addition to information that is initially provided by the requestor, the business case also becomes a vehicle for communicating summary level initial planning and estimating information as it is developed so that both cost and benefit can be clearly established.

The Cost of Considering Potential Investments

Ideally, every potential investment would be thoroughly investigated and analyzed to expose and remove as much risk and uncertainty as possible. Realistically, the cost of routinely employing such a level of diligence could exceed the potential value of the opportunity itself. Such conditions result in "paralysis by analysis."

In addition to the cost of generally developing the capability, each time a potential initiative is analyzed, an incremental cost is incurred in administrative and research effort, time, supporting infrastructure, management attention, and other factors. Such analysis is, in fact, an investment in its own right.

In many respects, the time and effort spent analyzing an investment represents the cost of exercising the option to consider it. If investigation determines that the investment is not worthwhile, then such analysis becomes the cost of failure avoidance. Should a decision be made to proceed with an investment, the cost of data gathering, analysis, planning, and estimating becomes part of the insurance premium paid to help protect its future value.

Thinking of investment analysis as "opportunity costs" tends to temper what kind of opportunity warrants submittal for in-depth analysis. It also establishes a link between the cost of analysis and the potential value of the investment.

The insurance industry offers a relative benchmark for determining how much money and effort is appropriate to invest in analyzing potential opportunities. The cost of comprehensive coverage to insure physical items from loss usually falls in a range of 10 to 15 percent of the annualized value of the item. If we assume that half the cost of "insuring" an investment lies in analysis, then a reasonable cost for analysis of a $1,000,000 investment with a 6-year life expectancy would be around $10,000 (roughly equivalent to 100 hours of analytical effort).

CASE STUDY:
"FREE ESTIMATES, NO OBLIGATION" — MANAGING THE HIDDEN COST OF INVESTMENT ANALYSIS

Members of a technology organization for a mid-sized insurance company found they had a hole in their investment analysis process. They had a policy to scope all project requests at no cost to the initiating business unit, which led to many initial requests that were never funded.

The CIO had mandated that projects could be no more than 6 months in duration. This policy was established in an attempt to curb large projects that never seemed to end. As a result, dissecting the phases of larger projects (including the initial analysis and requirements-gathering phase) into stand-alone "mini-projects" became a common routine. Each of these phase-level mini-projects had its own incremental deliverables, was independently requested, funded, managed, and closed, with no discernable mechanism for maintaining continuity between initiation, design, development, testing, and delivery of the overall business initiative.

In an effort to appear responsive to business units requesting large new initiatives and to encourage the use of technology, initial planning and estimation was performed by IT without charging those associated costs back to the originating organization. As you might imagine, there was never a shortage of project proposals, especially because analyzing an idea was free to the initiator. Over time, the IT group became quite busy exploring an endless stream of potential opportunities. Initial planning would often reveal that proposed initiatives would be far more expensive, risky, complex, or time consuming than originally presumed by the requesting departments, so subsequent requests and funding for downstream design and development projects rarely followed.

Additional investigation revealed that no metrics had been established for tracking how many initial planning projects actually went on to yield actual business value, and there was no measure of how much time was being spent on new opportunity analysis. Senior IT management could only surmise the true impact of scarce technology resources being consumed by initial analysis of ideas that never actually delivered useful results.

In addition to effectively illustrating that requirements gathering, planning, and estimating potential investments has a real cost, this example also serves to demonstrate the importance of maintaining a programmatic line of sight on business value, regardless of how work is structured.

The Importance of Information Parity

In addition to assessing investments on individual merit, information gathered during the initial planning phase is used when comparing one investment opportunity with another. For example, let's say we have a pair of competing initiatives within a portfolio:

- **Initiative A** has been pending disposition for a few months; the review board has previously discussed it, but a decision was deferred until the next planning cycle. Quite a bit of investigation has been done on this opportunity. Its initial optimistic payback has been refined to reflect a more realistic but still profitable valuation. As part of initial planning and estimating, several risks were also identified, analyzed, and documented for their potential impact on the initiative.

- **Initiative B**, a fresh idea that appears to be a great opportunity, was only recently identified and added to the portfolio. Initial planning and estimating is still under way, but it is nowhere near the same level of maturity as the A initiative. As a result, risk analysis is not yet completed and the lucrative ROI projection suggested by the initiator has not been fully vetted.

The "latest and greatest new idea" represented by initiative B might on the surface appear to be a more attractive alternative compared to its more risky A competitor. Initiative A, by virtue of its more complete assessment, may in fact be a more worthy and less risky investment than the B opportunity (or perhaps not). It is difficult to actually make a reasoned judgment between the two until the underlying decision support data reaches similar levels of completeness. This example illustrates the importance of consistency when performing initial planning and estimating for each type and class of investment.

To establish a level playing field for evaluating each opportunity on its own merit and as part of a portfolio, the investment analysis process should strive to:

1. Identify the minimum information and level of detail expected for each type of investment through the use of templates and planning standards

2. Control inclusion of opportunities into portfolios until an adequate amount of information gathering and analysis is completed

3. Recognize the impact that differences in the quantity and quality of information has on making investment judgments

4. Create initial investment portfolios that compare apples to apples, in terms of the types of competing initiatives

With this general understanding of the investment analysis process and related considerations in mind, Chapter 12 turns attention to techniques for analyzing individual investments.

KEY POINTS IN THIS CHAPTER

☑ The investment analysis process collects, assesses, and selects opportunities identified through operational planning to best support the objectives and strategies of the organization.

☑ Every organization has unique circumstances and considerations that influence how it performs investment analysis across different types of opportunities; there is no single best approach.

☑ Effective investment analysis requires adequate information about the investment, an assessment of each opportunity based on its individual merit, and relative comparison of competing initiatives as part of an investment portfolio, based on operational objectives.

☑ Investment analysis forms the bridge between operational planning and work execution; as a result, the process drives reconciliation between the top-down objectives and constraints established for the investment portfolio and the bottom-up planning and estimating required for investment analysis.

☑ Successful investment analysis requires consistency in the overall approach and quality of information, balance between competing categorical considerations, and flexibility to apply proper analysis techniques that are appropriate for each type of investment.

☑ The time, effort, and money invested in analyzing a potential opportunity is a way to insure the value that the opportunity represents.

CHAPTER 12

ANALYZING INDIVIDUAL INVESTMENTS

THE OBJECTIVE OF INDIVIDUAL INVESTMENT analysis is to determine whether a specific initiative presents a viable opportunity. In most cases, it serves as a gate review to establish whether an initiative should be included in a portfolio with other potential investments for further consideration.

There are four main considerations that should be assessed during the initial review of a potential opportunity:

- **Alignment:** Does the investment support operational objectives?
- **Value:** Does its potential net value or benefit meet the hurdle rate or other minimum threshold established for investments?
- **Risk:** What are the chances that the investment can successfully deliver proposed benefits at the costs estimated?
- **Necessity:** Is the investment mandatory for the organization to function or does it represent a discretionary opportunity?

Referencing figure 11-1, the analysis of an individual request is an inherent part of managing demand. Every request for work to be done, no matter how small or routine, receives some degree of scrutiny. When you consider the overall spectrum of demand, the majority of requests are analyzed informally, using little more than the good judgment of the responsible worker or manager as the appropriate governing authority. That individual usually also has the discretion to determine when a particular request will be fulfilled, as compared to other work in the queue. In effect, it undergoes comparative analysis. Even though the reviewer may not consciously realize it, the same four basic questions still apply: "Is this request appropriate?" "Is it of any value?" "Can I do it?" and "Do I have a choice?"

Eventually a reviewer will reach a threshold relating to the size, complexity, cost, or some other established set of values that requires a higher level of authority. Thus, more often than not, there are multiple thresholds, with each level granting decision rights to individual roles or titles. These rights and thresholds understandably differ between organizations, but the one thing that all organizations should have in common is a definition of governance policy. At some point, individual intuition and authority defers to the discipline provided by a more formal and rigorous investment analysis process.

INVESTMENT ANALYSIS PARAMETERS

With this in mind, investment analysis establishes a defined set of parameters and thresholds applied to investment-grade requests, as defined by each organization. Each investment is first analyzed based on these parameters and thresholds to establish whether it represents adequate individual merit. This ensures that only the most necessary investments that are aligned to objectives, represent positive value, and have the greatest potential for success are included for consideration in investment portfolios.

In addition to the primary considerations of alignment, value, risk, and necessity, additional secondary investment parameters, constraints, and decision factors might include:

- Functional constraints (engineering, technological, etc.)
- Functional alignment (to existing production methods, architectures, or standards)
- Timing (tied to a specific window of opportunity, ability to respond by a required finish date, etc.)
- Relationships or synergies with other proposed or approved investments
- Physical and organizational impacts

Note that when analyzing an individual investment, capacity only becomes a consideration when it is analyzed in a portfolio of competing investments or when significant capacity-related risks are known or discovered (e.g., when prerequisite skills required for the investment are lacking or if a single very large, long-term investment would disrupt normal capacity allocations).

Investment Necessity

The relative necessity of an investment reflects business alignment considerations that go beyond quantitative measures related to cost, benefit, or risk factors. For example, a looming regulatory mandate requires an accounting system upgrade. The investment is a complex, costly revision that does not otherwise provide any benefit to the organization. The net value is negative, and the risk is high, but the CEO and CFO will go to jail and business transactions will be halted if it is not done. Clearly, this is a mandatory investment if you want to stay in business. How would the necessity of this investment shift if the driver was to support expansion into overseas markets using different currency rather than regulatory compliance?

As another example, consider the case where the head of a business unit comes up with a proposal to convert manufacturing line waste into energy. The plant will use the resulting power and sell any excess energy back to the utility. It uses proven technology, and projections are that it will provide a net profit after 7 years of operation. However, it presumes that the assembly line will continue to use similar raw materials in the future, is subject to volatile energy pricing, distracts from core business interests, and requires a large amount of capital during a weak economy. While basic financial valuation may support it, there may be little to recommend it as a necessary investment at this time.

Organizations may want to establish a range of options to classify the necessity of a proposed investment, with appropriate descriptions. For example:

- Mandatory (required for continued operations; preapproved)
- Required (necessary to meet a defined business objective)
- Recommended (a preferred approach or significant advantage)
- Desired (optional, opportunistic)
- Not necessary (declined)

Mandatory Investments

The *mandatory* investment classification should be a clear, tightly defined attribute to avoid misuse. As the name implies, a mandatory investment must be such that the near-term consequences of not going forward with it would have severe operational implications for the organization. Examples include actions needed to avoid violating a fundamental operating principle; meet legal requirements that would otherwise expose the organization to debilitating regulatory, criminal, or civil action; hamper the ability to raise capital; or otherwise have consequences that could threaten continued operations. Also included in this category are investments that alleviate a credible threat (existing or imminent) to the health and safety of employees or the public.

Investments that represent a discretionary scenario or viable alternatives should never be categorized as mandatory, no matter how dramatic or compelling they may be. If an investment meets strict criteria for what constitutes a mandatory condition, then no further comparative analysis is required because there is no alternative to proceeding.

However, the consequences of a mandatory investment should be fully explored and identified because they affect the capacity available for other opportunities. If anything, thorough planning and estimating of mandatory investments should be accelerated as soon as they are identified, so that remaining capacity allocations can be accurately adjusted to account for their impact. This includes accepting the mandatory item into its associated investment portfolio as approved. This will maintain visibility and provide a means to account for the capacities it is expected to consume.

INVESTMENT VALUATION

Without question, the most contentious aspect of investment analysis is establishing how potential opportunities will be valued. Valuation includes the revenue or other measures of tangible and intangible benefit over a presumed investment lifetime, less development and ongoing costs. Some valuation methods seek to further condition results to reflect volatility and risk.

Valuation methods range from qualitative seat-of-the-pants judgments to highly detailed calculations and sophisticated computer simulations. These approaches can be broadly classified into three categories:

- **Deterministic:** A mechanical calculation that is employed to derive a single value.
- **Probabilistic:** A range of values and their likelihood that are calculated based on a number of different input variables.
- **Humanistic:** Judgment and reasoning are either added to, or used in lieu of, pure mathematical calculations.

While in no way intended to be a complete listing, the following methods represent examples of each approach to illustrate the range of techniques that organizations employ to establish investment valuation.

Deterministic Valuation

Deterministic valuation methods establish a definitive financial valuation based on specific estimates of revenue or benefit, and in some cases, by attaching financial value to risk. Deterministic techniques are appropriate when input estimates can be reliably established in financial terms and the development and production life cycle of the investment is fairly linear. Deterministic approaches lose effectiveness as the level of volatility, uncertainty, or flexibility associated with the investment increases, or when financial projections of costs or benefit cannot be clearly identified. Some examples of common deterministic techniques are discussed next.

Return on Investment

Return on Investment (ROI) is a measure of investment efficiency, expressed as a percentage by dividing the net value of the investment by its cost. ROI can be calculated very simply without any adjustment in monetary valuation, or it can be derived in present value terms. Because of its simplicity and flexibility, ROI is a popular approach to quickly establish a sense of relative financial value between competing investments.

Discounted Cash Flow

Discounted Cash Flow (DCF) is the most common method used to calculate the present value of an investment or asset based on its estimated future value over the expected life of the product, service, or asset. DCF takes into account the monetary costs by using an appropriate discount rate, depending on its form (i.e., debt or equity, using weighted average cost of capital [WACC] or reinvestment rate). DCF also seeks to risk adjust future value by manipulating the interest rate value used in the calculation (e.g., capital asset pricing model [CAPM]). DCF compounds returns over defined time periods.

Depending on projected cash flow assumptions, the variants of DCF most often applied in investment analysis are:

- Net present value (NPV) as a measure of expected profitability

- Internal rate of return (IRR) as a measure of potential growth

- Multiple DCF calculations embedded within decision trees or real-options analysis

DCF techniques provide more sophistication than ROI, allow for different cash flow rates and assumptions by time period, reasonably reflect the cost of financing, and incorporate some adjustment for investment risk.

Probabilistic Valuation

Probabilistic valuation techniques are useful when an investment represents a large number of contingent options and decision branches, or when input estimates represent a range of possibilities rather than a single value. Probabilistic methods extend deterministic techniques when added sophistication and flexibility is needed to better reflect complex financial investment scenarios.

Decision Trees

Decision tree analysis (DTA) models multiple decision points of an opportunity, along with the compounded valuation parameters at each point along the way. Decision trees (see figure 12-1) are useful whenever an investment offers a number of variations in how it can proceed, as reflected by different iterative stages, associated contingencies, go/no-go decisions (gates), or options.

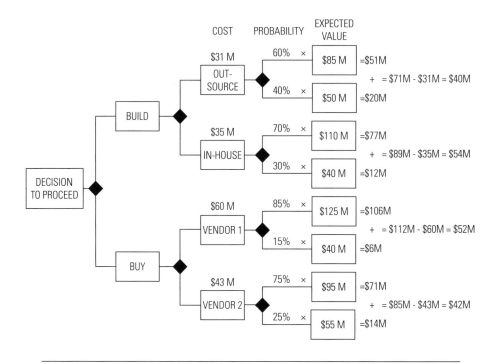

Figure 12-1: Decision Tree Analysis

Monte Carlo Analysis

Monte Carlo analysis is a technique for simulating the range of possible input variables used in DCF to establish the potential NPV distribution for a single investment. A computer program runs thousands of calculations using random values over the predefined range of a given parameter to derive a probabilistic solution.

Real Options Analysis

Real options analysis (ROA) takes the concept of decision trees to another level of sophistication by simulating the range of uncertainty about asset value and market risk at each option node. ROA is most applicable in situations where there is a high degree of management flexibility to respond to moderate to high levels of uncertainty about market outcomes.*

---

* Prasad Kodukula and Chandra Papudesu, *Project Valuation Using Real Options*, (Fort Lauderdale, FL: J. Ross Publishing, 2006).

Humanistic Valuation

Humanistic approaches to investment valuation are appropriate when financial values cannot be clearly articulated or as a supplementary technique to add additional perspective to deterministic and probabilistic calculations.

Delphi Method

This technique uses a facilitated group of qualified experts to predict a future outcome. Unlike mechanical valuation or random sampling techniques, human judgment is used to solve for the most probable result of a given scenario. Each expert provides an anonymous projection about an outcome and his or her underlying reasoning. This information is shared with other members after each round, and the process is repeated in an effort to drive predictions to a point of general consensus.

Investment Review Board

One of the most common methods used in making qualitative investment decisions, especially in cases where the initiative is not directly tied to revenue, is through use of the judgment of senior managers convened as a review board. Investments and supporting data are presented to the board for review and discussion, and resulting perceptions are a primary mechanism to determine relative value.

PUTTING INVESTMENT VALUATION METHODS IN PERSPECTIVE

Many references are readily available that describe the functional details of various valuation methods. Rather than repeat this work, it is more useful to focus on a topic that is referenced less often—the sensitivity and importance of the supporting assumptions that are used.

Most tangible investments of financial significance are subject to some form of quantified economic valuation technique as a major component of making investment decisions. Sadly, organizations often place too much time, energy, and faith in the calculations themselves, without ensuring that the underlying estimates and assumptions have a commensurate level of diligence, rigor, and precision.

Regardless of their level of sophistication, valuation methods represent imperfect forecasting techniques that are only as good as the underlying information on which they rely. All valuation approaches are sensitive to the cumulative uncertainties from factors such as:

- Thoroughness of knowledge about the investment
- Quality and detail of up-front planning
- Accuracy of associated development estimates
- Accuracy of benefit assumptions
- Volume and collective impact of known and unknown risks
- Future economic uncertainty, such as inflation, market valuation, bond ratings, and returns
- Quality and utilization of the data available
- Analytical objectivity and skills applied to the data
- Resulting subjective opinions that are derived from this information to ultimately form the basis of any valuation technique

In addition to these variables, when the valuation process is placed in the broader context of the overall portfolio ecosystem, additional uncertainty accumulates in terms of ability to execute and market performance. While ability to execute is less a factor when investments represent a wealth of experience and high confidence levels, such as repetitive initiatives or traditional construction and manufacturing initiatives, the ability to deliver becomes particularly salient when analyzing competing research or technology investments.

As an example, consider the typical IT portfolio. Gartner Research estimates indicate that approximately 20 percent of IT application development projects fail,* while other studies, such as the Chaos Report

---

* Lars Mieritz, "Exploring the Relationship Between Project Size and Success," Gartner Research, March 4, 2008. (Gartner Research ID Number: G00155650).

published by the Standish Group, regularly place the incidence of IT project failures even higher. This represents a significant impact that is rarely factored into the overall risk posture, but it directly impacts the value created. All organizations would like to believe that "they are different." But being generous, such considerations dictate that an additional 20 percent of standard risk should be inserted into investment valuation calculations *in addition to* opportunity-specific risk factors.

Finally, estimating the benefit or value created has proven so tough that some organizations give it little attention and almost never measure whether it is delivered.

Selecting the Proper Valuation Technique

When valuing an individual investment, selecting the most appropriate technique depends on several considerations, including:

- Magnitude of the investment
- Level of volatility/uncertainty
- Degree of incremental decision flexibility
- Variability of the cash flow streams
- Funding mechanism
- Ability to describe investment value in tangible terms

The size of an investment, either in direct or translated financial terms, is a primary determinant for the level of valuation sophistication and rigor that you employ. Organizations should establish a graded approach to investment analysis based on the estimated value (or cost) of a request that sets incremental minimum standards about how an investment's value is calculated and governed. For example:

- Minimal (less than $10,000) and often short-term investments require a basic ROI assessment or mid-level management judgment to constitute adequate valuation diligence.

- Complex (estimated at $1,000,000 or more) investments indicate the use of a more rigorous valuation approach, such as employing simulation to extend cash flow calculation assumptions or the use of decision trees or ROA.

Such techniques would also consider required minimum levels of investigation, planning, and analysis.

The level of volatility and uncertainty surrounding an investment are two related but different risk considerations that have similar impacts on selecting the proper valuation technique. Volatility refers to a condition where the investment is known to have the potential for a wide variance in outcomes, including different cash flows within different time periods. Uncertainty refers to a situation where a high number of unknown influences have the potential to reduce confidence levels in the outcome. In both cases, investments with high levels of volatility or uncertainty suggest the use of probabilistic valuation methods to incorporate the range of possible values for different variables in the equation being used.

In situations where cash flow is expected to be nonlinear, the use of DCF valuation methods allows estimates for each return period to be independently considered. Market-oriented investments, which are directly linked to a tangible financial return and can be definitively estimated in terms of cost (such as real estate or new product development), represent the most viable candidates for making use of more sophisticated quantitative valuation techniques.

The Impact of Funding on Valuation Method Selection

Whether an investment will be funded privately or through external (market) sources will also impact the valuation technique that is selected and/or how the discount rate is established.

Generally, an internally funded investment represents a more straightforward situation, and thus a more straightforward valuation technique. Typically, its discount rate reflects a low market risk equivalent, such as a federal bond rate. A portfolio made up of strictly private investments may allow you to apply a common discount rate across the board. Note that some valuation techniques are not intended for use with privately funded investments; for example, ROA is intended only for market-funded opportunities.

Additional care is necessary when establishing the discount rate for an initiative that is funded through external sources, often using recognized peer market comparisons to establish the appropriate rate. This can prove to be a tricky prospect, especially in periods of economic instability.

In large, complex investment scenarios, organizations may find themselves lacking the necessary internal expertise and tools to fully evaluate an investment using advanced techniques, particularly if analyzing opportunities of this magnitude are not the norm. In such cases, using specialized consulting support to assist in investment valuation is a prudent move.

Seasoned investment analysts will often uncover valuation implications that are not intuitively obvious from a general business perspective. A shift of only a few points in the discount rate applied or a change in profit assumptions can move an investment from being favorable to being questionable; discoveries such as this can make all the difference in how an investment is approached or in its ultimate disposition.

The Role of Human Judgment in Investment Valuation

Many common investment types are notoriously difficult to value in tangible terms; for example, pure R&D, internal process improvements, staff development programs, advertising initiatives, charitable activities, or community involvement all present unique challenges to quantitative investment analysis.

The more removed an initiative is from directly generating revenue or reducing costs, the more difficult it becomes to establish meaningful valuation in monetary terms. Even an investment aimed directly at revenue generation, such as a new marketing initiative, may be problematic to express in purely financial terms because it is difficult to ascertain whether actual results are directly or exclusively attributable to the specific campaign.

It is for this very reason that benefit management practices are usually applied at a program level or higher, rather than against individual projects. In circumstances where value is intangible or indirect, attempts to make value assumptions only in financial terms can prove to be a dubious exercise. These cases represent situations in which qualitative valuation methods are more appropriate or are used to supplement financial estimates.

Gartner Research* supports the increased application of qualitative analysis of potential IT investments, citing inherent weaknesses in depending solely on the outcomes of typical quantitative financial-based techniques. Using judgment has been shown to provide statistically valid and repeatable correlations in relative value.

There are subtle but important distinctions between judgment and more intuitive or emotional inputs such as perceptions or opinions. To put this in practical terms, applying judgment to determine investment valuation requires assessments to be based on relative, tangible facts. Given good information, managers will usually agree on relative worth within a relatively narrow range, compared to valuation based only on opinion and perceptions. Simply reading a description is likely to elicit an emotional decision based on perception or opinion. Providing assessors with detailed data related to the risks, costs, and expected outcome is more likely to yield a consistent, fact-based judgment of relative value.

Taking Advantage of Investment Flexibility

While investment analysis is often considered to be a one-time decision-making event, relatively few investment decisions are irrevocable or without downstream options. Outright capital purchases offer few choices beyond the decision to proceed, but most developmental investments

---

* Audrey L. Apfel, "A Maverick Approach to the Business Value of IT," Gartner Research, April 29, 2008. (Gartner Research ID Number: G00157347).

tend to represent a variety of decisions and contingencies as the opportunity is pursued.

For example, making changes in requirements and scope, making incremental gating decisions, choosing to put an effort on hold or delay it until better information emerges, or deciding whether to expand or contract production or marketing all represent incremental investment decisions that present themselves downstream of an initial decision to proceed. Such options and decisions that unfold over the course of an investment are not simply downside unknowns; they also offer opportunities to manage risk and defer costs.

There is no greater period of uncertainty around a project, program, or strategy than at its point of initiation. Even though thorough preliminary analysis may help you validate the merits and costs of a proposed opportunity, most of the unknowns about the project remain when making an initial decision to proceed. When it comes to taking control of costs and risk, the decision to go forward should always include a keen consideration of *how far.*

Applying a graduated method to managing investments often takes little more than some critical thought and conscious planning. For example, a somewhat risky project is under evaluation to implement a new and untested business application; the estimate to design, develop, and deploy it is $5 million. Here are some ideas to consider:

- Avoid funding the total cost up front if possible; structure an initiative and contract so that the bulk of the risk is mitigated before most of the money is committed.

- Catalog the major risks as part of the initial analysis; consider the work breakdown structure and overall time line, mapping when each significant risk can be eliminated or reduced.

- Look for ways to move up key activities to eliminate risk earlier in the project; defer as much of the expense as long as possible while working to remove as many unknowns from the equation as soon as possible.

- Build in gate reviews at each milestone to formally trigger a reassessment of progress and risks that consciously drive a decision to continue. At each point, you reach a higher level of confidence in the probability of the outcome and can decide whether to commit additional funding for the next phase.

MAKING INDIVIDUAL INVESTMENT DECISIONS

It is worthwhile at this point to reiterate that any investment opportunity represents making a change. By its very nature, change is disruptive and risky. Given its impacts and the toll that it takes on the organization, a potential change should be considered only when its benefits clearly and substantially exceed the cumulative costs and risks in every respect.

As we have demonstrated in this chapter, subjective judgment and order-of-magnitude estimates find their way into even the most robust assessment of potential investments, further eroding the confidence level of analysis results. There is little point in putting forth a change initiative of questionable value for the sake of change itself. Setting the bar relatively high and keeping a ruthless focus on resulting business value winnows out marginal endeavors before they reach competitive consideration in investment portfolios.

Such a disciplined approach to investment decision making is a common trait that differentiates the top-performing organizations from the rest of the pack, as illustrated by The Hackett Group in its report: "Core Competencies of Financial Top Performers: Managing the Business Value of IT."* This report is part of that organization's ongoing research into the relationship between operational best practices and organizations that perform well above their industry median average in terms of various profitability measures.

---

* Erik Dorr and Philip Carnelley, "Core Competencies of Financial Top Performers: Managing the Business Value of IT," The Hackett Group, April 7, 2009.

As shown in figure 12-2, top performers fund and approve far fewer IT investment proposals; as a result, they are able to place increased focus on a smaller project portfolio and do a better job of executing those high value projects.

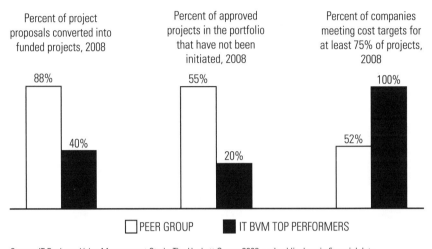

Source: IT Business Value Management Study, The Hackett Group, 2008, and public domain financial data

Figure 12-2: Project Portfolio Measures of IT Business Value Management Top Performers

While this specific study focused on IT investments, it is not a stretch to translate the applicability of these practices to investment management in general.

Most organizations suffer from a glut of discretionary investment requests when compared to real capacities to execute. When only the very best and most compelling opportunities are competing for approval, portfolio managers are in the enviable position of already winning; all that remains is to compound the value of very good individual prospects by selecting the best possible combination of investments for their portfolios.

KEY POINTS IN THIS CHAPTER

☑ Individual investment analysis determines whether an initiative presents a viable opportunity based on its own merits of alignment, value, risk, and necessity.

☑ Analysis of individual requests is an inherent part of managing demand; those requests that exceed a defined threshold are subjected to the rigor and diligence of a formal investment analysis process.

☑ A number of different parameters are used to establish the worthiness of each investment proposal; chief among them are valuation—the comparison of expected benefits and total costs of an opportunity.

☑ Valuation methods fall into three main categories: deterministic, probabilistic, and humanistic.

☑ Deterministic methods such as discounted cash flow and return on investment result in a definitive projected value.

☑ Probabilistic valuation techniques establish a probability of possible values based on a range of inputs to account for uncertainties.

☑ Humanistic valuation relies on human judgment to determine estimated value.

☑ All valuation methods are subject to the quality and depth of information associated with the investment that results from investigation, planning, estimating, and risk analysis.

☑ Selecting the most appropriate valuation technique depends on a number of different factors, including the size of the investment, the level of volatility, the type of funding, and the ability to quantify benefits in financial terms.

☑ Individual investment decisions should favor those opportunities that represent clear value, are well aligned to business objectives, low in risk, and the most necessary.

CHAPTER 13
DEVELOPING INVESTMENT PORTFOLIOS

USING PORTFOLIOS TO ANALYZE and select investments is arguably the purest example of portfolio management. The investments themselves represent clear, tangible choices that offer real value. The portfolio defines business objectives and specific constraints. Several different parameters are weighed and simultaneously considered during the analysis and selection process. People who develop and apply investment portfolios must also navigate the uncertainties of the planning horizon.

Portfolio management offers the unique combination of flexibility, visibility, consistency, and trust that make it ideal for analyzing complex investment scenarios. In this chapter, we discuss the major actions necessary to develop, analyze, and make recommendations through the use of investment portfolios.

THE INVESTMENT PORTFOLIO MANAGEMENT PROCESS

Referring to figure 11-1, the general sequence of actions to develop and manage an investment portfolio is as follows:

- **Define portfolio objectives, constraints, and parameters**: The investment portfolio manager establishes a good understanding of the investment landscape along with portfolio objectives, constraints, and the general investment approach. Given this information, investment parameters are identified, including financial goals for costs, savings or revenue, and risk tolerance.

- **Populate the investment portfolio**: Selecting investment opportunities for the portfolio should include a review of outstanding requests that may potentially fulfill portfolio requirements. New initiatives are created as necessary to fill any gaps in work versus outcomes.

- **Analyze comparative merit**: Each initiative is scored to portfolio parameters, based on initial research, planning, and estimating. Scores are compared with other activities under consideration to rank investments in the portfolio relative to their contribution in fulfilling portfolio objectives.

- **Analyze portfolio scenarios**: With a potential scope of investments identified, they are further validated against different scenarios based on changes in different business conditions, or changes in scope, timing, functional approach, or risk/reward assumptions.

- **Reconcile**: In parallel with portfolio analysis, the top-down objectives and constraints initially defined for the portfolio are compared to bottom-up investment estimates. Any disconnects are assessed and the tactical plans, strategies, or portfolio constraints are adjusted as required. Multiple investment portfolios are also reconciled against overall objectives and operational planning. This cycle continues until a viable approach is determined.

- **Optimize investment portfolio**: Based on investment scores and ranking across different scenarios, the investment manager selects the best-fit portfolio to fulfill the objective, including appropriate backup options. Portfolio selections are prepared for presentation or discussion.

- **Make investment recommendations and get approval**: The recommended portfolio of work is reviewed, modified, approved, and baselined by the designated selection and funding authority for additional work planning and execution.

DEVELOPING THE INVESTMENT PORTFOLIO

Defining Portfolio Objectives

Investment portfolios are based on the general strategy and investment landscape of the organization. While you can think of the complete book of all opportunities under consideration in a given planning cycle as the master investment portfolio, it is typically unwieldy for analytical purposes. As a result, it is usually preferable to group investments into multiple investment portfolios.

The common linkage among the investment portfolios is the portfolio management information structures introduced in chapter 4. Figure 13-1 reflects the typical scope of investment portfolios across the information structures. How you divide the portfolios depends on your unique business needs. Here are some ideas for you to consider.

Whenever possible, develop portfolios of investments that naturally compete for the same resources. Given that most portfolios are capacity constrained compared to potential opportunities as the primary consideration, this arrangement allows you to group and isolate demand and capacity into a series of intersecting sets.

For example, you can group all potential new product development initiatives for each product family into a portfolio that competes for their respective design and development resources. The result is that you will

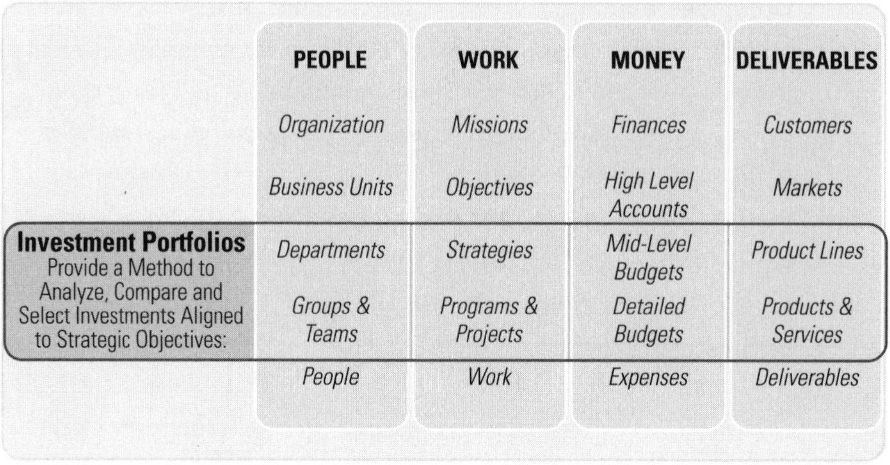

	PEOPLE	WORK	MONEY	DELIVERABLES
	Organization	Missions	Finances	Customers
	Business Units	Objectives	High Level Accounts	Markets
Investment Portfolios Provide a Method to Analyze, Compare and Select Investments Aligned to Strategic Objectives:	Departments	Strategies	Mid-Level Budgets	Product Lines
	Groups & Teams	Programs & Projects	Detailed Budgets	Products & Services
	People	Work	Expenses	Deliverables

Figure 13-1: Scope of Investment Portfolios

minimize the amount of reconciliation needed between different investment portfolios that are fighting for the same capacities.

Often this approach will also correspond to how funding is allocated and how the objectives and strategies of the organization are developed, so investment portfolio objectives naturally align to fulfill a particular strategy.

If this approach isn't possible, or some other consideration besides resource capacity is the most limiting factor, then portfolios can be arranged in whatever manner best suits your needs. Just bear in mind that if multiple investment portfolios are competing for common resource pools, they will likely require added time to reconcile specific resource needs as portfolios are finalized.

Regardless of the approach you take when establishing investment portfolios, each one needs to have a clearly defined business objective. If it is associated to a top-down strategy, then the objective of the portfolio is to fulfill the strategy. The investment portfolio manager should also identify influences and relationships with other portfolios and seek out additional information as necessary. Face-to-face meetings with the strategy owner regarding goals, constraints, and potential investment approaches are encouraged to ensure early alignment. Other guidance may be included as well depending on the nature of the deliverable(s), such as build-versus-buy or in-house versus outsourced.

If an investment portfolio is simply a collection of pending requests, without the benefit of specific top-down guidance, then the objective might be defined as: *Do the work that provides the greatest business value with the capacities that are available.*

While the initial grouping of investment portfolios establishes the primary mechanism for making opportunity comparisons, investments can also be viewed and compared using other definitions. For example, "How do all potential discretionary capital investments for a particular product family or line of business work together to achieve a given objective?"

Provided the portfolio analysis platform you are using offers appropriate flexibility, you can readily see how you can define different portfolios to cross-reference the population of potential investments from several different angles and perspectives. This offers significant advantages over using a desktop spreadsheet, which has practical limits to how many different ways portfolio contents can be grouped for analysis.

Investment Portfolio Parameters and Constraints

The assessment measures used to make comparisons are the core of investment portfolio analysis. When it comes to comparing and ranking opportunities within a portfolio, benefit, cost, risk, and alignment are the *Big Four* of investment considerations. These elements can be further refined for purposes of establishing portfolio comparison parameters, possibly through the use of a four-axis bubble chart like the one shown in figure 13-2.

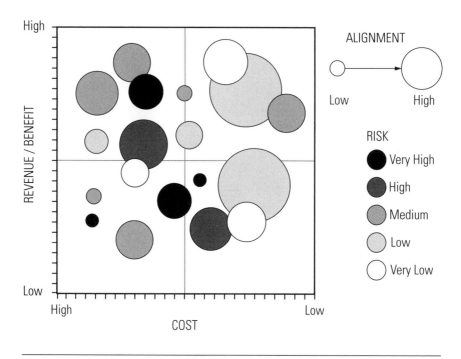

Figure 13-2: Four-axis Bubble Chart for Investment Portfolio Analysis

In terms of financial cost and benefit, portfolio analysis may compare relative value (costs versus revenue or savings), expressed as ROI, NPV, or other terms. You should think carefully about how to group similar investments when defining portfolios because comparing investments that have employed different valuation approaches adds another element of variability into the overall selection process. For example, it is difficult to make a valid comparison between estimated benefits if one investment in the portfolio is valued using a basic ROI approach and another is valued by a method that has risk adjusted the projected benefit.

This also presents potential problems when investments in the portfolio are collectively assessed by adding up their total costs and benefits. When a mix of risk-free and risk-adjusted valuation methods are employed in the same portfolio, it is useful to have two measures of benefit—one column that is risk modified and one column that reflects the raw projected value.

Even if risk is factored into financial analysis, an independent indicator of risk is still an important parameter for portfolio analysis. This offers an insight into the relative risk between different investments and gives you the ability to assess collective risk within the portfolio compared to risk tolerance targets. Being able to gauge the level of uncertainty around collective outcomes can help you identify situations where business objectives and strategies may need to be revisited.

Using an independent measure of risk provides additional analytical flexibility compared to only accounting for risk in valuation calculations. Each parameter can be independently assessed, and complications can be avoided in cases where some investment valuations account for risk and some do not.

Individual investments that simply do not align with organizational objectives should not be considered at a portfolio level. For those opportunities being compared within a portfolio, the question should be, "To what degree do investments in the portfolio align with objectives?" To address this question, individual investments are tagged with an alignment attribute value and description, such as:

- Very high alignment directly fulfills the portfolio objective.
- High alignment directly supports the portfolio objective.
- Medium alignment indirectly supports the portfolio objective.
- Low alignment incrementally supports other investments in the portfolio.

Another option for indicating alignment is through the use of a priority value that has business goals incorporated as part of its prioritization approach.

A portfolio should have target thresholds and constraints set for cost, benefit, alignment, risk, and capacities. As shown in figure 13-3, portfolio development and analysis is undertaken to achieve a defined outcome within specific boundaries: "What results are we trying to achieve?" "How much are we willing to spend?" "How much capacity is available?" and "How much risk am I willing to accept?" With these values set, it then becomes a matter of selecting the best combination of investments to achieve targets within the boundaries identified.

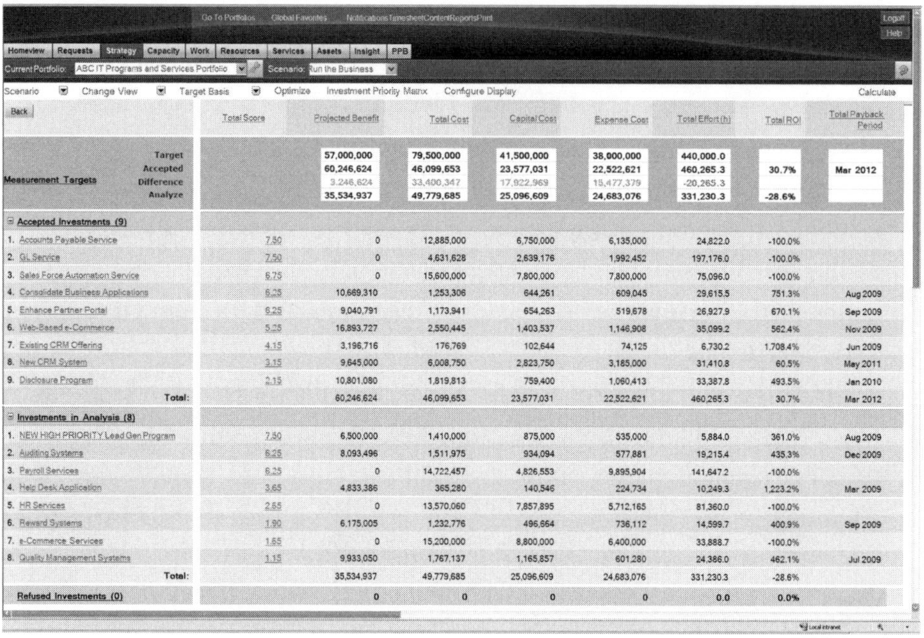

	Total Score	Projected Benefit	Total Cost	Capital Cost	Expense Cost	Total Effort (h)	Total ROI	Total Payback Period
Measurement Targets — Target		57,000,000	79,500,000	41,500,000	38,000,000	440,000.0		
Accepted		60,246,624	46,099,653	23,577,031	22,522,621	460,265.3	30.7%	Mar 2012
Difference		3,246,624	33,400,347	17,922,969	15,477,379	-20,265.3		
Analyze		35,534,937	49,779,685	25,096,609	24,683,076	331,230.3	-28.6%	
Accepted Investments (9)								
1. Accounts Payable Service	7.80	0	12,885,000	6,750,000	6,135,000	24,822.0	-100.0%	
2. GL Service	7.50	0	4,631,628	2,639,176	1,992,452	197,176.0	-100.0%	
3. Sales Force Automation Service	6.75	0	15,600,000	7,800,000	7,800,000	75,096.0	-100.0%	
4. Consolidate Business Applications	6.25	10,669,310	1,253,306	644,261	609,045	29,615.5	751.3%	Aug 2009
5. Enhance Partner Portal	6.25	9,040,791	1,173,941	654,263	519,678	26,927.9	670.1%	Sep 2009
6. Web-Based e-Commerce	5.25	16,893,727	2,550,445	1,403,537	1,146,908	35,099.2	562.4%	Nov 2009
7. Existing CRM Offering	4.15	3,196,716	176,769	102,644	74,125	6,730.2	1,708.4%	Jun 2009
8. New CRM System	3.15	9,645,000	6,008,750	2,823,750	3,185,000	31,410.8	60.5%	May 2011
9. Disclosure Program	2.15	10,801,080	1,819,813	759,400	1,060,413	33,387.8	493.5%	Jan 2010
Total:		60,246,624	46,099,653	23,577,031	22,522,621	460,265.3	30.7%	Mar 2012
Investments in Analysis (8)								
1. NEW HIGH PRIORITY Lead Gen Program	7.80	6,500,000	1,410,000	875,000	535,000	5,884.0	361.0%	Aug 2009
2. Auditing Systems	6.25	8,093,496	1,511,975	934,094	577,881	19,215.4	435.3%	Dec 2009
3. Payroll Services	6.25	0	14,722,457	4,826,553	9,895,904	141,647.2	-100.0%	
4. Help Desk Application	3.65	4,833,386	365,280	140,546	224,734	10,249.3	1,223.2%	Mar 2009
5. HR Services	2.65	0	13,570,060	7,857,895	5,712,165	81,360.0	-100.0%	
6. Reward Systems	1.90	6,175,005	1,232,776	496,664	736,112	14,599.7	400.9%	Sep 2009
7. e-Commerce Services	1.65	0	15,200,000	8,800,000	6,400,000	33,888.7	-100.0%	
8. Quality Management Systems	1.15	9,933,050	1,767,137	1,165,857	601,280	24,386.0	462.1%	Jul 2009
Total:		35,534,937	49,779,685	25,096,609	24,683,076	331,230.3	-28.6%	
Refused Investments (0)		0	0	0	0	0.0	0.0%	

Figure 13-3: An Investment Portfolio in Analysis Compared with Target Values

One of the most common mistakes that organizations make in portfolio analysis is failing to accurately identify and respect capacity constraints. The effects of this cascade through the downstream functions needed to execute investments, often reflected as schedule slippage, missed delivery dates, reduced scope of deliverables, and ultimately, by the actual value received. Capacity constraints are most often established on the basis of top-down human and financial capacities allocated to a given portfolio (although in some cases other physical capacities such as manufacturing lines or infrastructure can also be a limiting consideration).

It may appear at this point that the portfolio analysis process is a somewhat mechanical exercise: simply force rank investments by net value or some other score until all the available capacity is gone. Doing a good job with up-front investigation and individual investment analysis certainly helps smooth the way for analyzing investment portfolios. As we will see when discussing optimization, there are options available for letting computing power take most of the hard work out of portfolio analysis. But there are also other factors that frequently come into consideration at the portfolio level that are not always identified as overt measures and do not lend themselves to automation. This is where the skills and experience of the portfolio manager and investment team become more important.

For example, how can portfolio selections leverage economies of scale or make best possible use of potential synergies between related opportunities? Are there compatibilities (or *in*compatibilities) that need to be taken into account? What about the degree of management flexibility that one investment path offers over another for future adjustments?

The sequencing and timing of investments represent another set of variables that can be leveraged. Even when portfolio managers do a good job staying within gross capacity limitations for any given year or quarter, there can be certain stretches in the execution window where spikes in demand far exceed either human or cash flow capacities. Often, making adjustments in individual investment timing can be used to help overcome acute capacity issues. Some investments are considered time critical to hit a specific market window or for other reasons, but others offer flexibility in how they are scheduled within the portfolio. Making adjustments in investment start dates, consciously increasing durations, or revising how initiatives are staggered can help smooth out periods where planned demands exceed capacities. However, bear in mind that injecting significant changes in investment timing can also affect valuation and risk assumptions.

Finally, it is also important to apply human judgment when assessing how much organizational change the investment portfolio represents, particularly when it comes to internal process improvements or rapid expansion. As we discussed earlier, there are finite limits to just how much organizational change can be successfully absorbed. Although such impacts are often included in overall risk scores, portfolios that include a significant number of cultural impacts should also identify the affected areas of an organization. Including some measure of operational impact as part of portfolio assessment criteria will aid you in this analysis.

Analyzing Portfolio Scenarios

Initial portfolio comparisons use a baseline of assumptions about the investment landscape. Given that investments can span years and that the general volatility of the business climate is only increasing, it is prudent to analyze portfolios over a range of different potential investment environments beyond the most-likely scenario. By making different adjustments to demand, capacity, cost, risk, and benefit parameters, portfolios can be analyzed for sensitivity and outcome differences.

For example, how would key portfolio measures be weighted differently based on weak-versus-strong economic projections? How would these different scenarios impact assumptions regarding available capacities? One large health care provider routinely establishes multiple investment portfolios that reflect different sets of economic assumptions so that as changes occur members of the organization can quickly shift their investment strategy to best reflect actual circumstances.

Beyond general economic influences, scenarios could reflect different assumptions regarding other major changes in the investment landscape. For example, different scenarios may examine shifts in investment strategy based on whether a possible merger goes through or not, or a scenario might be based on changes in the rate of technology advances, shifts in the competitive landscape, or different product and market directions.

If a particular portfolio is intended to plan and execute a defined objective, different portfolio scenarios allow comparison of how alternative strategies might approach achieving the target outcome; for instance, constructing a *build* portfolio versus a *buy* portfolio with each containing the necessary investments or projects needed for the approach in question.

On a macro level, scenarios also enable the comparison of how multiple portfolios might be affected based on differences in strategic capacity allocations. Such a what-if analysis helps reconcile competing needs that emerge when balancing capacity across different demand drivers, such as different lines of business or markets, or internal needs versus customer-facing initiatives.

PORTFOLIO RECONCILIATION

Inevitably, issues arise between the top-down objectives and assumptions that investment portfolios represent and the bottom-up planning and estimating information that is compiled as individual investments are developed and analyzed. When the gears of strategic intent do not fully mesh with the cogs of tactical realities, any differences must be reconciled to arrive at a mutually workable approach.

At a high level, portfolio reconciliation addresses three main considerations:

- Are portfolio objectives practically achievable?
- Do we have enough human resources?
- Do we have sufficient funding?

Whether original portfolio objectives are viable takes into account the intended outcomes and approaches defined by the operational plan. This includes the timing of the outcome, whether it is functionally achievable, and if so, whether outcomes can be realized with an acceptable level of risk.

The next two considerations take into account the obvious issues of the demand represented by portfolios versus the human and financial capacities made available—in total, and how they are divided among different investment portfolios. As we explored in section 2, these two considerations are certainly interrelated but not always interchangeable.

Business case projections for payback should be further refined as part of portfolio analysis and reconciliation. Bottom-up planning of individual investments establishes the functional and/or technical approach and provides additional specific information associated with requirements derived from individual project or service estimates. It also offers a quantified estimate of FTEs by department and functional role relative to the labor constraints placed on the portfolio. As you compile and summarize this information you may find that your portfolios are over or under target capacity for overall effort. Resolving these implications is a critical component of ensuring that the investment process results in achievable outcomes.

Given that several portfolios will likely be in various stages of the analysis process simultaneously, it can difficult for the investment manager to assess whether specific resource needs for an individual portfolio will be available in the proposed time frame; the job of your bottom-up estimate is to quantify the expected requirements.

Taken collectively, these portfolio estimates enable a high level roll up of resource requirements by department and role to help you identify any specific spikes that exceed capacity limits in a given area, even if the overall FTE count is within total capacity. Another consideration for capacity management at the portfolio level is identifying the need for critical skills that are known to be in limited supply.

This information must be evaluated and acted on by investment and strategy managers to determine if bottom-up plans can be executed within resource capacity targets or whether some high level capacity reallocations are needed. You must reconcile demands that exceed capacity, whether they represent a period of general overload or are specific to a certain role or group for a particular quarter.

You may choose from the following reconciliation options:

- Adjust the portfolio contents or timing

- Adjust strategic objectives or timing

- Adjust capacity, either through redistribution or by changing capacity

If capacity is assumed to be a fixed commodity, then the first two options are straightforward enough; you must change either the approach or the expected results. Adjusting human resources has yet other implications.

In addition to using effort estimates provided by the portfolio to manage resource capacity, this information will be used to create a summary of the total cost to deliver each portfolio, based on underlying project budgets. As with resources, you must also reconcile any differences in financial capacity between allocated funding and estimated costs.

Creation of original strategic objectives and constraints often happens simultaneously with the initial planning and estimating of potential investments, so you should not be surprised to find disconnects between them when you compare them initially. Approach mutual refinements as an iterative development cycle, and expect the reconciliation process to take at least four passes as figure 13-4 illustrates.

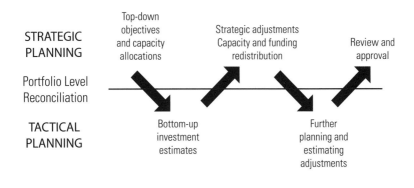

Figure 13-4: The Reconciliation Process Between Top-down and Bottom-up Plans

Portfolio Optimization

As portfolios and various scenarios are analyzed and reconciled, the ultimate objective of investment analysis is to arrive at the best combination of investments that fulfill portfolio goals while meeting target constraints for time, cost, benefit, and risk. Other elements are also considered as part of the process, such as portfolio balance, flexibility, and synergy. In most cases, portfolio optimization is performed manually, testing various combinations of investments to fulfill portfolio objectives until the most satisfactory solution is achieved.

Figure 13-3 shows a typical approach to portfolio optimization. Each investment in the portfolio reflects its associated values for the comparison parameters selected; in this case, projected benefit, total cost, capital cost, expense cost, and total effort. Portfolio-level target values are also set for each of these measurements, as shown across the top of the screen. As various investments are moved "above the line" (investments flagged as accepted), the portfolio-level measurements are automatically updated to reflect the resulting impact of the decision. Note that the investments "below the line" represent the remaining field of available candidates from which to select. Optimization essentially tries different combinations by resetting the status of individual investments to move them above and below the acceptance line.

As this procedure is carried out, different parameters and targets can also be selected to see how the portfolio balances with other measurements. For example, figure 13-5 depicts the investment detail screen for a single investment and the different parameters that are available for comparison in this particular configuration. While initial optimization might focus on cost, effort, and value measures as shown, once those are resolved, the same portfolio selections can then be analyzed against risk and alignment values.

The capability shown in figure 13-5 was specifically built for portfolio analysis, but you can use a desktop spreadsheet program to analyze simple portfolios and make investment decisions. However, as portfolios and scenarios increase in volume and complexity, using an application that is expressly designed to support portfolio decision making becomes more of a necessity, especially when more sophisticated capabilities are required to help solve for optimum solution sets.

In situations where a large number of investments are included in a portfolio, manual optimization can prove to be a very arduous process that yields limited results. In such cases, you can use computer-based tools, such as Efficient Frontier Analysis, to help ease the effort and achieve better outcomes. Efficient Frontier quickly tests thousands of possible complex portfolio combinations to solve for the best possible combination of investments within a portfolio.

Figure 13-5: Portfolio Analysis Application and Investment Attribute Screen

In actual practice, automated selection techniques such as Efficient Frontier can be used to quickly arrive at a general portfolio solution using primary criteria, and then, individual selections can be refined using manual means to further incorporate qualitative considerations and fine-tune recommendations. This combined approach helps you significantly reduce the amount of time and effort needed to achieve a satisfactory result.

INVESTMENT RECOMMENDATION AND APPROVAL

After portfolio managers establish the optimum combination of investments, the final step in the selection process is to seek approval and funding. This step constitutes organizational commitment to not only the portfolio of work itself, but also to the overarching business goals and objectives, strategic plans, resource capacity allocations, and funding distribution model that the portfolios represent. Investment approval signals that it is time to begin the next phase of work planning in sufficient detail to support execution and delivery.

It is important to recognize that initial approval is only the beginning of investment portfolio management. In the same way that an individual monitors his or her personal savings portfolio and makes ongoing adjustments to selected investments, business investments must also be actively managed beyond the initial selection process to respond to shifts in the investment landscape and business objectives, and to address the performance of those investments.

Preparing the Portfolio for Review and Approval

Each organization approaches investment portfolio approval differently, depending on its overall governance model, culture, and other factors. Regardless of the makeup, approach taken, or structure of the approval body, the whole objective of investment analysis is to establish a well-informed position on which decision makers can act. This means that all of the pertinent decision-support information must be presented in a manner that is consistent and easily understood, yet provide a reasonably complete picture of the recommended approach. This includes identifying the other options that were actively considered and any alternative approaches that may also be included in the recommendation.

In most instances, investment portfolios are defined so that they provide a high level tactical plan to execute some parent objective, whether the scope of interest represents a strategy for a product line, a business division, a group of services (such as an IT portfolio), or a business strategy that crosses organizational boundaries. In cases where portfolios directly map back to such elements, any recommendations and supporting documentation from investment analysis simply becomes an input to the respective high level business plan. In the same way that an individual investment must document its business case, a particular strategy should have its own documented basis that is presented for final approval.

In the event that an investment portfolio stands alone, as is the case when the portfolio is built from the bottom-up from a pool of unrelated requests without the benefit of specific strategic guidance, then the portfolio manager must present the recommended selections to the approval committee as a collective investment. Preparing a briefing document that summarizes the overall value, cost, risk profile, time frame, balance, and similar portfolio attributes assists the approval authority in quickly understanding the business implications of the portfolio.

Individual investments and their primary measures can be listed as single line items for further discussion. Specific portfolio attributes that do not stay within cost, timing, or capacity constraints should be flagged and explained, along with any objectives that are not fully realized by the plan. Of course, supporting investment business cases should be readily available if needed to address specific details on an exception basis.

The approval authority and senior leadership team should not be surprised by the final investment recommendation, assuming their involvement (or at least awareness) as strategic plans and tactical inputs were reconciled. If this is not the case, then the portfolio manager should not be surprised to find that the approval process becomes the second round of reconciliation before final consensus is reached.

A sign of organizational maturity is accepting and building on the inescapable interdependencies between setting strategy, investment analysis, and initial bottom-up planning. This allows you to approach the process out in the open, recognizing that operational planning is a team effort. Failure to collaborate as strategies and portfolios are codeveloped inevitably results in an *us-versus-them* mentality emerging between those providing top-down direction and those developing bottom-up plans and estimates—often with the portfolio manager caught in the middle. With this in mind, it becomes apparent that the portfolio manager serves an important arbitration function to ensure that both strategic and tactical requirements are balanced as part of portfolio development, assessment, and optimization.

MANAGING THE INVESTMENT ANALYSIS CYCLE

"A good plan today is better than a perfect plan tomorrow."
—GENERAL GEORGE PATTON

Although the natural inclination of senior management is often to expect (demand!) some guarantee of accuracy associated with the first pass of investment planning and estimating, the number of unknown influences at this stage far exceeds those that are known. Likewise, initial strategy development is an ideation process that strives to expand the planning horizon and provide a common general direction that will be refined over time.

Considering how uncertainties compound at each level of the work-planning structure illustrates the situation. Assuming that *only* 15 percent estimating error is introduced at each level of the planning and development process, the cumulative margin of error can be significant. Add the overall degree of uncertainty and additional influences into this, and it becomes clear that at this stage an order-of-magnitude estimate is both appropriate and sufficient for investment decision making.

It is important to remember that additional opportunities will present themselves for continued strategic adjustments as the planning cycle progresses, and second-pass bottom-up planning will increase accuracy and accountability. Thus, the goal of first-pass planning in support of investment analysis is to assemble an overall approach and evaluation that is plausible.

To ensure a reasonably timely investment analysis cycle and prevent the organizational investment in initial planning from getting out of control, the overall planning and assessment cycle must somehow be contained and forced to completion. This is usually accomplished by consciously limiting the duration of the operational planning and investment analysis period. An "all hands on deck" press to accomplish development, reconciliation and portfolio approval within a calendar quarter is reasonable for most organizations, assuming serviceable processes and tools have been developed and deployed.

Split roughly into thirds, this allows about one month each to focus on strategy development, develop investment portfolios and bottom-up estimates, and to reconcile them. In actual practice, these activities will run in parallel to the extent that reliable input allows.

Taking much longer than a calendar quarter runs the risk of being caught in a cycle of second-guessing shifts in business dynamics before decisions can be made, while accomplishing the process in significantly less time is difficult to do with quality results. As the planning process is repeated, it becomes more efficient. The degree of volatility of the operational plan from one cycle to the next also influences the amount of time and effort required.

This time line, combined with the potential volume of work being considered, reinforces the need for reasonable but limited planning and reconciliation during the portfolio development process. Once again, this is not a one-time event, but rather the start of a dynamic management process that continues through the entire change cycle.

Ongoing Management of the Investment Portfolio

Assuming approval and funding of the investment portfolio, attention then turns to all of the necessary activities to support successful execution and delivery. Referring to the portfolio ecosystem model, it is important to remember that all of the business functions noted are happening simultaneously. Even though portfolio approval means focus shifts to tactical considerations, changes that can affect business objectives and strategies are an ongoing influence that can ultimately drive shifts in the investment approach.

Given various influences that may arise, flexible strategy and agile investment plans are valued for the range of options they provide to counter such shifts. However, this also means that investment analysis must become a more active, programmatic process rather than a single "fire and forget" decision-making event. The senior leadership of the organization must stay engaged in steering overall strategic direction and investment portfolios as an ongoing function. This suggests formal periodic review sessions as an integral part of the governance model.

While routine formal executive review checkpoints are useful, supplementing these with some mechanism to manage investments on an ongoing basis is equally important. Additional information about the investments themselves, which can take the form of new risks and issues, changes in scope, and various actual measures compared to original plan projections, constantly surfaces as work on approved initiatives continues. While individual challenges are often minor in nature and do not necessarily threaten intended outcomes, even seemingly negligible adjustments can collectively erode valuation and similar key parameters over time. Furthermore, a major hurdle challenges almost every initiative at some point. Unless someone is monitoring such developments on a regular basis and analyzing them for investment impact, the business value of projects and programs can become jeopardized before anyone realizes what has happened.

This is where the benefit realization process steps up to provide continuity in management oversight of the investment relative to ongoing shifts in both strategic and opportunity-specific conditions. Unlike a project manager who is primarily concerned with maintaining progress against time, cost, and quality measures, a designated benefit manager is focused on ensuring that the expected business value of investments is delivered on a programmatic level.

KEY POINTS IN THIS CHAPTER

☑ The process of developing and applying investment portfolios begins with defining its objectives, constraints, and parameters.

☑ The primary parameters for comparing investments are cost, benefit, risk, and alignment; additional parameters are added as required by specific circumstances.

☑ As the portfolio is populated with appropriate opportunities, they are scored and ranked based on selection parameters to determine those that best contribute to meeting portfolio objectives at the lowest cost and least risk.

☑ The portfolio of potential selections is further analyzed by running different scenarios that test different assumptions and investment environments.

☑ The planning and estimating information about individual investments is summarized to the portfolio level to assess whether the top-down portfolio assumptions and objectives are practically achievable, and whether enough money and resources have been allocated.

☑ If there are discrepancies between top-down and bottom-up portfolio parameters, then these issues must be reconciled. Any competing needs that emerge between different investment portfolios are also reconciled to arrive at an achievable solution.

☑ The optimum set of investments are selected and presented to the appropriate governing authority for review and approval.

☑ The approved investment portfolio represents a plausible, order-of-magnitude plan that must be actively managed and refined as investments are developed and new information emerges for future consideration.

Section 5

MANAGING EXECUTION

Managing execution refers to the business functions that are associated with creating and processing work requests, tactical work and resource planning, and managing work execution. This section contains two chapters. Chapter 14, "Managing Work Intake," explores the process of managing demand, from classifying and prioritizing work requests to dispatching and backlog management. Chapter 15 covers topics associated with work and resource planning and managing execution.

CHAPTER 14

MANAGING WORK INTAKE

"THERE IS NEVER A SHORTAGE OF GOOD IDEAS." In situations where the portfolio of opportunity far exceeds your capacity to execute it, effectively managing demand is one of the most difficult and important functions that your organization performs. You may not be able to control the volume of all demand asked of your organization, but you can manage how the organization responds to it. Ultimately, the ability to identify, collect, analyze, and control demand is basic to all levels of portfolio management, from strategic opportunities to daily transactional demands.

As illustrated in earlier chapters, operational planning and investment analysis have important parts to play in managing discretionary demand at a high level to keep it in balance with organizational capacities. However, there are tactical demand management functions that are common in supporting strategic analysis and in addressing ongoing operational needs.

Work intake management includes:

- **Work intake:** Receiving work requests in an orderly manner
- **Classification:** Analyzing requests to understand their implications and categorizing them using a defined set of attributes
- **Prioritization:** Establishing the relative importance of the work
- **Initial planning and estimating:** Establishing the amount of time, effort, complexity, risk, and costs associated with performing the work
- **Dispatching:** Establishing request disposition and forwarding approved requests to those responsible for planning and execution
- **Backlog management:** Controlling the volume of approved work pending action

Many people associate portfolio management with managing a group of large projects; however, operational, run-the-business demands can also be managed using execution portfolios. For example, the practice of service portfolio management (SPM) is now a commonly accepted component of IT management. While SPM techniques address project work as *change requests*, SPM also includes methods for managing support requests, problems, and incidents. Likewise, the use of product and asset portfolios is also gaining popularity, and all of these relate to controlling requests for work.

As we discussed in preceding chapters, the ability to control all forms of work is essential to maximizing resource efficiency. Accordingly, we consider work intake in the broadest sense, as any request for work that is placed on an organization, regardless of its source, nature, form, or size. The concept of work types is a key aspect of comprehensive demand management; it allows you to categorize requests so that you can manage and govern each type using the most appropriate stream of process guidance (figure 14-1).

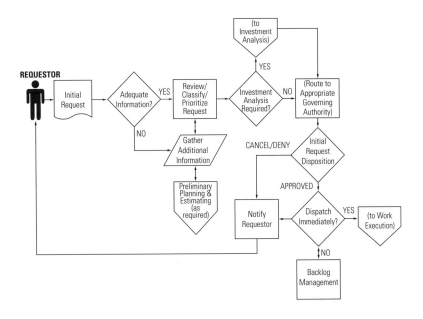

Figure 14-1: The Work Intake Management Process

In addition to classifying work by its type, each request can be categorized using various attributes to further aid in management and reporting. One of those classifications includes establishing its relative priority.

As inbound demand is initially received and analyzed, high level planning and estimating adds additional information essential for investment analysis, requestor feedback, budgeting, timing, and capacity management purposes. Finally, a decision on whether to proceed is reached for each element of demand based on alignment, available capacity, cost, and benefit. If approved, it is either immediately dispatched to assigned owners for near-term execution or managed as part of the inevitable backlog of pending work.

As a general introduction to work intake management, each of these functions is explored in this chapter to establish a reference point for discussing resource management and to support other demand-related portfolio management functions such as operational planning and investment analysis.

WORK INTAKE

Demand management begins with some mechanism(s) for inbound requests to be submitted and processed, which is generally referred to as intake or request management. This can be as simple and informal as e-mail from an internal customer, an action item from a meeting, a phone call, or a conversation in the hallway. At the other end of the spectrum are more structured approaches such as a formal funding request for a new initiative, an order-to-cash system, or the use of a single common web-based request management application that is available across the enterprise. Such systems often incorporate workflow automation capabilities that assist with information gathering, initial processing, and subsequent dispatching actions.

How demand is recognized, codified, and put into a transportable form depends on the general nature of the work itself. However, a good request management system, whether it is a purpose-built system or a basic web form, should have the following characteristics:

- The system should be highly intuitive to users with little or no training; terms, attributes, and menu options should be unambiguous; selection menus should include an option at the top for "I don't know" or "Not applicable."

- If it is handling a broad range of requests, then the system should be able to tailor the kind and amount of information gathered based on the type of work identified. For example, an automated system should serve up specific information fields based on previous selections.

- The system should be able to flag which information fields are required versus optional for the system to accept the request as complete.

- The amount of information required from the requestor should balance reasonable expectations for initiation with the need to support processing; additional information can be added as the request is further investigated.

- The system should avoid drop-down menus that list an excessive number of options.

- The system should include a provision to attach supporting content (drawings, documents, etc.) or hyperlinks to file locations.

- If it is not part of the overall work management system, then the request system architecture should enable easy integration with other systems.

- The system should provide configuration flexibility and extensibility to accommodate future needs.

- Computer-based systems should recognize corporate network logins.

- Access rights should identify levels of authorization for submitting requests.

All of this ultimately relates to how you need to interact with the requestor to categorize, prioritize, and classify work—the subjects we discuss next in this chapter.

CATEGORIZING WORK

There are three broad categories of work present in most organizations: self-contained work, emergent work, and planned work.

Self-Contained Work

Self-contained work refers to predefined request types that are wholly performed by a group of exclusively dedicated resources. Such activities are usually operational in nature and represent high-volume, transactional forms of demand. Examples include: product inquiries directed to an inside sales team, customer calls to service centers, end user assistance provided by help desks, warranty returns to repair centers, or sales and general order fulfillment.

The majority of back-office administrative functions are also self-contained, including accounting, basic HR functions, or logistics. In terms of work intake, self-contained work often uses a dedicated system that is specifically designed for the particular requirements of a given request type.

The characteristics of self-contained work do not present the same level of planning and coordination issues that we highlight in chapter 2, so we will not include it in our scope of interest for portfolio management purposes.

Emergent Work

Emergent work refers to any form of unplanned demand that arises and requires immediate attention. By definition, it is reactive in nature and often a significant source of disruption to other planned activities. For this reason, recognizing and managing this type of work is integral to comprehensive demand management.

Many organizations lack a formal definition or controls for managing emerging crisis activities, leaving it up to the judgment of individuals or managers. Unfortunately, this is rarely an effective approach because of human nature. Everybody loves a good crisis. As an initiator, inflated urgency becomes a method for pushing your needs to the head of the line. If you are the recipient of a hot request, it creates the chance to become a hero, and who doesn't want to be a hero? As a result, these requests too often become manufactured opportunities for crisis resolution rather than being managed in a planned, methodical manner relative to the request's true priority. Is it important? Probably. A true crisis? Maybe.

Without active management, the volume of unplanned work can get out of control, wreaking havoc on productivity, schedules, and resource planning. When explicitly measured, it is common to discover that unforeseen events consume 20 percent or more of the workforce and potentially much higher percentages in highly reactive, chaotic environments.

Although it is impossible to completely eliminate unplanned work, you can manage its disruptive effects. As part of your overall work management or prioritization process, clearly establish criteria for what constitutes critical work that immediately supersedes planned priorities. Establish who has authorization to declare a request or event worthy of an extraordinary, "drop everything" response that displaces in-progress work. This will allow you to approach emergent work in a more controlled manner, often cutting its occurrence by half.

From an intake perspective, immediate response to emergent work may not wait for formal documentation or routine workflows; however, it is important to capture information about unplanned events. Postmortem of a crisis helps the organization understand whether the incident warranted a drop-everything response; if existing processes, practices, and tools supported a prompt and effective resolution; and to further analyze root causes and actions to prevent reoccurrences.

The total number of unplanned events that occur is a very telling business metric. Even though you cannot foresee individual events, documenting them in your work management system allows you to plan for emergent work on a programmatic level. Trend information about emergent work is also important; unless you are specifically in the business of crisis management, a steady increase in such events is rarely a positive indicator! It is also important to know how much effort emergent work is consuming on average so you can factor it into capacity management estimates.

Planned Work

Planned work is our primary interest from a portfolio management perspective. As the term implies, it includes any unique request for action that you can plan for, exclusive of the other forms of demand we have already discussed. Planned work can be as monumental as a billion-dollar program, as diminutive as a request for a new report, and everything in between. Because of its diversity and range, planned work accounts for the majority of demand in a knowledge worker environment.

The potentially unique nature of each request and the type of resources you assign to accomplish it are what makes planned work different from self-contained work. Self-contained work uses wholly dedicated resources to accomplish a specific and repetitive set of activities to the exclusion of other work, whereas planned work usually requires that you define a unique work approach specific to the needs of each request. Assigning staff to a planned work task represents a choice made over other opportunities. Planned work can be an individual assignment or require collaboration with multiple members of the organization. You also usually have some discretion about when the work will be accomplished. In short, planned work presents several unique options that must be analyzed and addressed for each request.

These traits are what make planned work the most challenging type of work to manage; each unique work activity, either as an independent request or as a task that is part of a larger project, must be individually assigned, scheduled, and tracked in concert with many other competing demands, often with little more in common than their need for resources. Because planned work is such a diverse and broad category, it is necessary to classify it in more detail if you are to effectively manage it.

The Importance of Work Types

In the introduction, we explained how portfolio management techniques are applicable to all kinds of planned work. In addition to formal project portfolios, you may also create service portfolios or general work portfolios aligned to product line, geography, or any other major category. Perhaps the most useful way to categorize work is by type. Work type designations do not distinguish priority or the kind of deliverable that is produced. Two primary considerations differentiate one type of work from another: how it is managed and the level of the organization that provides direct control and oversight.

Based on these differences, you should relate each work type to a specific process stream to address how you initialize, evaluate, dispatch, fund, resource, communicate, and manage it to completion. By matching different types of work to appropriate process control streams, you can minimize unnecessary administrative complexity, improve efficiency, and increase throughput. Work is segregated into types based on its expected size, duration, cost and/or value, type of funding, complexity, strategic implications, and level of risk.

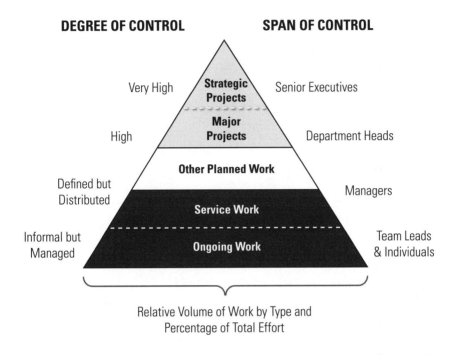

Figure 14-2: Work Types

As shown in figure 14-2, we define five general types of work, understanding that individual circumstances will warrant further refinement to address organizational-specific requirements. The five general types of work are described as follows:

- **Strategic projects** are capitalized investments funded at the enterprise level and under the oversight of an executive governance board. Strategic projects are heavily scrutinized and controlled with rigorous, formal project management standards, processes, and life cycles by virtue of their high costs, large size, complexity, potential for risk, or importance. Strategic projects often span multiple departments or other major organizational units.

- **Major projects** are specific customer or departmental initiatives that are authorized from predefined funding sources. The level of sponsorship and oversight is lower than strategic projects, such as at the line of business or department head level. While the controlling processes are often very similar to their strategic counterparts, there is usually more latitude to treat certain elements as optional, depending on the nature of the project. Although it's not always the case, major projects tend to include internal improvement initiatives, while strategic projects are more often directed toward external customers or large business transformation endeavors. Major projects can be capitalized or expensed, depending on their cost and the nature of their deliverables.

- **Other planned work** is defined as the multitude of smaller planned work requests that result in specific unique deliverables but that do not warrant the level of rigor associated with formal project management techniques. Other planned work typically spans days or weeks rather than months or years. It is noncapital work that is wholly funded and executed within a single department or subordinate group, and functional managers or supervisors have the appropriate latitude and flexibility to determine how the work is planned and managed. Higher-level oversight of other planned work is accomplished as a collective portfolio, with individual work items scrutinized on an exception basis.

- **Service work** is made up of a continuum of minor enhancements; maintenance; and operational support of assets, applications, services, and processes that are directly provided to (and often funded by) internal or external customers. Service work actions may be executed through specialized request and management mechanisms such as support tickets. Because this type of work tends to routinely reoccur, process controls are often in the form of predefined workflows. Formal mutual agreements that are typically documented in service level agreements (SLAs) or other contractual documents may define how support services are to be measured against prescribed performance levels, associated costs and billing, or the level of resources committed for delivery.

- **Ongoing work** is similar to service work in that it too is a continuum of operational activities; however, ongoing work is often funded by overhead accounts and more oriented to internal departmental and indirect functions. Ongoing work also includes basic business support such as maintaining processes and infrastructure that is common to overall operations. As a broad category, ongoing work also accounts for general level-of-effort activities such as meetings, vacations, training, sick time, community services, and similar resource burdens not otherwise addressed by other specific work types. While ongoing work is a recognized type, it is the least formally controlled from a process perspective, allowing ample leeway on a personal or team level about the way work is planned and managed.

Your organization may choose to use different work types or terminology compared to those described here. The important thing to recognize is that every organization has unique types of work that can and should be specifically defined and characterized based on differences in how they are managed and governed. The process you apply to each type of work reflects these differences.

WORK PRIORITIZATION

In our work, we receive frequent questions about work prioritization. Most prioritization issues stem from either utilizing a method that does not fully address the needs of the organization, or from having multiple approaches that create confusion. Establishing a single common prioritization standard within your organization for all types of planned work is core to establishing a proactive work environment, keeping resources and money focused on the work having the greatest business value, and fostering a higher level of internal collaboration.

Developing an integrated prioritization model will compel your organization to clearly define and mutually agree on what is important (or not), as reflected by measurable guidelines with relative quantified values. This ensures that working-level priorities are consistently based on business criteria rather than by ad hoc measures such as the order of request receipt, emotion, coercion, personal interest, or hunches.

On a tactical level, a common priority model enables a consistent perspective on relative work priorities *between* functional areas and the activities they perform. Established guidelines are a highly visible standard that can be applied to all work, so that managers can understand its relative importance. To make sense of competing demands for limited resources across a wide variety of work types, managers must be able to call on consistent priority guidance that encompasses the complete spectrum of work placed on them. This allows them to make better decisions about how to best deploy staff, whether for activities within large complex projects or more discreet, less formally managed tasks.

In lieu of a common and consistent method to evaluate and score inbound requests, individual workers, team leads, and managers are left to assess priority based on their own perspectives and what information they have available. Different conclusions almost always result, which hampers the teamwork that is so critical in a matrix organization. When managers are armed with a uniform understanding of how pending work stacks up in terms of priority, they are able to collaborate more effectively to meet common objectives.

Why Forced Ranking Is Ineffective as a Prioritization Approach

Force ranking formal projects into an ordered list is a common method employed for project prioritization. While this is an appropriate approach when making investment portfolio decisions, maintaining a forced ranking of hundreds, if not thousands, of work requests is impractical. Forced ranking involves making a relative value judgment between different work items—an impossible task when dealing with a steady stream of new requests for different types of work across a wide range of business needs. Forced ranking in such a dynamic situation would result in constantly changing the priority of each request as new work is added ahead of it, adding confusion and administrative burden.

The Integrated Prioritization Approach

Applying priority to projects alone is of limited value unless they are the only type of work being done. Prioritizing only part of the workload does little to help the managers who must ultimately make day-to-day work and resource assignment decisions across all types of work. The integrated prioritization model is designed to accommodate all types of planned work, from strategic projects to ad hoc support requests. The objective is to establish the relative value for all planned demand to determine how to best apply limited capacities. The more that your staff has to multi-task across different assignments, the more valuable this process becomes.

Integrated prioritization establishes an objective score for each incoming request that is based on its overall merit as compiled from several potential categories. This score is then used to place each request into one of a handful of priority groupings (e.g., very high, high, medium, etc.). Because individual priorities are not subject to change based on the assessment of other work requests, there is much less maintenance compared with a forced-ranking system. The resulting population of work is managed collectively, with the objective being to work down the most important work first in a planned and methodical manner.

Assuming that project tasks are always more important than other types of work and should therefore take precedence is a common prioritization mistake. The relative business importance (thus priority) of work has little to do with its type. Projects are often discretionary endeavors with little impact on near-term business operations, while countless work activities are undertaken on a daily basis that have immediate implications for operational viability, even though they are often well under the radar of senior management.

Establishing the Integrated Prioritization Model

The basis for an integrated prioritization model begins with determining the high level missions of the organization. Just as we described them with the MOST model in chapter 8, these top-level categories provide an overarching structure so that requests can be analyzed for relative fit. This should result in the alignment of any work under evaluation to one or more mission categories. The best way to explain mission categories is through some examples:

- We will be good stewards of shareholder investments by making prudent decisions that yield profitable results.

- We will delight our customers with an outstanding shopping experience and exemplary service.

- We will maintain a safe, respectful, and positive work environment.

Note that in every case, these mission examples make basic value statements but avoid specific terms of time or benefit. This gives them year-after-year durability and consistency that can weather the inevitable changes in specific business objectives.

After mission categories have been identified, six to ten attributes that represent a range of relative importance are developed for each one. These are intended as examples of relative value that the planned work will be scored against. The goal is to create a reasonable framework for guidance, rather than attempt to account for every possible situation. Each statement is assigned a point value, for example:

Mission: We will maximize shareholder value.

Points	Attribute
10	Performing this work is expected to directly impact net profit margin in excess of 1 percent.
8	Performing this work is expected to directly impact net profit margin between 1/2 and 1 percent.

7	Performing this work will directly reduce operational costs by 1 percent or more.
6	This work directly supports an approved strategic initiative.
4	This work will significantly reduce the incremental cost or effort required to perform a routine function and has an ROI of greater than $500,000/year.
2	This work has a positive ROI less than $500,000/year.
0	This work has no hard dollar value.

As you compare work against these attributes, select a point value that best reflects the request. Any given request will accumulate points from each applicable mission category to arrive at a total score.

Once the model is fully developed, it is validated using a statistically representative, random sample of requests that are scored using a panel of knowledgeable representatives, and scoring adjustments are made as needed. An optimum prioritization model will result in the scores of the existing backlog of routine work forming a bell curve, as shown in figure 14-3.

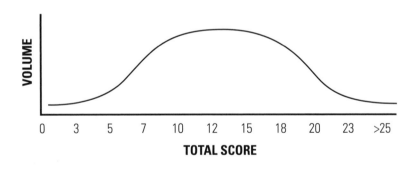

Figure 14-3: Optimal Distribution for Initial Work Prioritization

What matters the most is that the majority of the work should initially cluster around the mid-range, while the remaining items that are clearly higher or lower in priority should consistently populate either extreme of the range.

We need to reiterate that it is not the intent of this model to a yield a precise forced ranking. Minor differences of a few points in one direction or the other are inconsequential when the integrated prioritization process is placed into service because the methodology is applied to a large and diverse population of work that is constantly turning over.

Instead, raw scores are used to place the request into one of a handful of descriptive priority categories. This ensures that end users can easily comprehend the assigned priority in practical, unambiguous terms, for example:

Score Range	Priority
> 17	High
12–16	Medium-high
7–11	Medium
4–6	Medium-low
0–5	Low

For those people who actually determine work priorities, it is important that they understand the business drivers for employing the process, its purpose, and a general idea of how priority will be used downstream. When dispersing responsibility for assigning priority over a large population of users, it is critical that scoring attribute descriptions be unambiguous. If guideline intent isn't inherently clear or is open to broad interpretation, it will impact the consistency and effectiveness of the process.

All of these considerations, and the mechanics of how the prioritization model itself is deployed, should be documented as a procedure or guideline. How the process is engineered as part of the request workflow can be as simple and low tech as filling out a hard copy cover sheet that is attached to a paper request. Alternatively, you can keep track of prioritization in a spreadsheet or utilize sophisticated automated workflows. Such systems walk users through the selection of scoring attributes and update the priority field in the request.

Use of the Integrated Prioritization Process

A common priority system applied to all types of planned work should:

- Guide the order of work that is released for planning and execution
- Determine the pecking order for work to receive resources
- Establish a priority that is commonly recognized and respected across individuals, teams, and groups to improve coordination and collaboration
- Minimize disruptions from reactive, unplanned activities

Like the air traffic control system at a busy airport, the prioritization process allows you to systematically line up and execute work in a highly efficient, methodical manner to increase operational efficiency and maximize work throughput.

As a practical example, let's assume your organization has 1,000 approved requests in the system representing pending work. If only 75 of these requests have a high priority ranking, then you probably have sufficient resources available to plan the immediate and simultaneous execution all of 75 requests with few conflicts, given they are such a small percentage of the total workload. Whether an individual request with a high priority has a score of 17 or 20 has little relevance when it comes to work release and execution.

Extending this example further, you should also be able to plan for near-term execution of most of 150 work items ranked medium-high priority as well. There may be occasional delays resulting from key resources being allocated to higher priority work in progress. The process of planning and scheduling work for execution based on relative priority continues until all available near-term resource capacity is fully utilized. As work is completed and more capacity becomes available, additional work from the backlog is released.

As this work is performed, additional new requests will continue to come into the system with their own priorities. New work requests with a relatively high priority value should not displace lower value work that is *already in progress!* That has a highly disruptive effect that undermines the value of the process. Instead, new high priority work should be ordered appropriately relative to the priority of other pending work for planning and dispatching purposes as resources allow. Remember, this is still routine work; only bona fide emerging crisis activities trump currently planned in-progress work.

Referencing figure 14-4, the result is that over time you work down the backlog by methodically choosing the most important, highest value work to accomplish first, thus reducing the net business impact of the work pending execution.

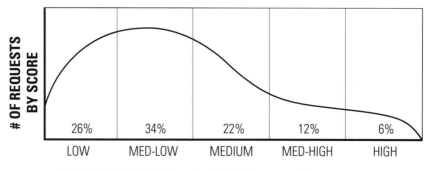

PERCENT OF WORK IN BACKLOG BY PRIORITY RANKING

Figure 14-4: Shifting the Priority Distribution of the Backlog over Time

Once work is actually in progress, this process ensures teams or work groups are using a common set of priorities whenever they must collaborate. Lack of consensus about what is important between functional groups is one of the biggest barriers to maximizing efficiency in a matrix organization. When asked for support, managers must respect the assigned priority of a work activity to determine how resources are deployed, even though they may not have direct responsibility for task completion. This ensures that the highest value work has first consideration for staffing and skills, regardless of who "owns" that work.

The process as described is a proven method for fostering proactive work control. However, priority is only one consideration when determining how and when work is accomplished. Other factors include time sensitivity, opportunities to combine similar efforts to reduce total effort, or release and configuration management.

Sometimes it makes sense to perform relatively low priority work in conjunction with a high priority task just because it simplifies the work or greatly reduces effort required. Given that the whole objective is to increase organizational efficiency, opportunities such as this should be seized when they present themselves. With these and other considerations in mind, use of this prioritization process yields a level of reasonableness, consistency, and organizational effectiveness that make it a highly valued improvement that helps make sense of complex environments and balances the needs of multiple types of work from multiple customers.

When working properly, the prioritization process will increase collaboration, reduce reactive responses to new items, and lower the level of multi-tasking across too many different activities at once, all of which can dramatically improve efficiency and productivity. This should in turn lower the overall backlog of pending work.

The prioritization model we describe here is a summary-level description. Readers who would like additional details are encouraged to download a free whitepaper: *How-To Guide: Developing an Integrated Work Prioritization Process* from www.tamingchange.com.

CLASSIFYING WORK

To complete the intake processing function, other work attributes beyond work type and priority are needed. By defining consistent terminology, definitions, business rules, and methods for making these classifications, data integrity is maintained for reporting and analysis purposes. Because some of this information may not be known at the time of its initiation, each organization should determine the minimum required information necessary to be considered a complete request for each type of work.

In addition to typical basic request information such as originator information, long and short text descriptions, status, ID numbers, various date fields, and so on, other common work classification categories that round out the "five Ws"—who, what, when, where, and why—include:

- Work type
- Priority
- Related product or service
- Work class
- Funding source
- Funding type
- Strategic alignment
- Requesting department
- Work owner
- Location
- Sponsor
- Performance rating

Work type and priority have already been explained at length, while other categories such as product or service, funding, or sponsor are self-explanatory. However, a few of the categories listed here bear additional comment.

Work class is typically used to establish the kind of work being performed and its necessity; for example, menu options under this category might include selections such as:

- Preventive maintenance
- Corrective maintenance
- Enhancement
- Regulatory requirement
- New development
- Internal improvement
- Other discretionary

When a work class selection is used in conjunction with one of the work type options previously discussed, a general portrayal of a given work item is created even before its description is read. For example, "a major project that satisfies a regulatory requirement" allows you to begin immediately visualizing the work in terms of size, duration, cost, and need. Contrast this with the mental picture created by the type and class of "service work that is preventive maintenance." Note that any type of work could potentially be categorized as any of the class options listed.

Strategic alignment is used to link a particular request to some level of the work planning hierarchy as discussed in section 3, or it can be used to reflect alignment in more general terms: very good alignment or not aligned.

Performance rating denotes the overall risk to successful completion in terms of cost, rate of progress, or severity of issues encountered; for example, using good, fair, and poor options aligned to green/yellow/red options enables easy creation of a stoplight report.

The number of work classification categories established and options listed within each one can become quite sophisticated, sometimes to the point of being unmanageable. Having helped hundreds of organizations establish work and resource categorization approaches, it is our experience that organizations initially tend to create too many categories and options only to later find in actual practice that the data cannot be accurately maintained, or that users do not understand the intent and subtle differences between the many choices.

It is more important initially to create a data set that can be reliably maintained with valid information than it is to account for every potential consideration. We recommend starting as simple as possible to capture high value information that will be specifically used for core reporting and then let necessity drive further refinement. Remember that text fields, notes, business cases, requirement documents, and a host of other references are available to contain additional supporting information for work of significance. Avoid setting yourself up for problems by creating opportunities for possible conflicts between the same kinds of information stored in different information sources; when discrepancies are discovered the level of trust about information accuracy will suffer as a result.

The basic examples we have suggested provide a lot of flexibility when it comes to developing work portfolios and reporting capabilities, often meeting 80 percent of common management information needs. For example, using these classifications, you could quickly create an execution portfolio that includes all capital projects for corporate operations that support a specific strategy, sorted by priority, status, and relative performance.

INITIAL PLANNING AND ESTIMATING

An important aspect of intake management includes a general assessment of the amount of work involved with any given request, in terms of cost, effort, and expected duration. This information is necessary to categorize work by type and to support capacity management. As an integral part of the intake process, these preliminary estimates also offer quantifiable information that is useful for backlog management.

General Estimating

It is important to point out that the intent of initial estimates developed during intake is to provide a preliminary, order-of-magnitude assessment that will be subject to refinement by more detailed planning as each request is dispatched for work. As we noted in the investment analysis section, preliminary planning should be commensurate with the magnitude of the request itself.

One of the long-term benefits associated with classifying work by type is that a historical record of actual results accumulates over time, which is very useful for making initial estimates. For example, past records for a routinely accomplished, specific work type might indicate that on average it consumes 100 hours of effort and $10,000 over a period of 4 weeks. You can automatically apply average estimate information as each request of that type is received and categorized to populate fields as part of an automated request management system, or within a schedule template that is associated with the request in a dedicated work and resource management application. You may choose to make adjustments as you individually review each request, or the initial estimate reflected in the template may be all that is necessary to dispatch work to the responsible manager.

Initial Planning for Investments

As the magnitude of the request goes up, so does the importance of initial estimating. As we discussed in section 4, initial planning and estimating takes on greater importance for demand that warrants formal investment analysis. Making sound investment decisions depends on having adequate supporting information. This information is usually contained in a formal business case that is prepared to facilitate investment analysis and in other supporting documents such as project charters, plans, and requirements documents.

All of this data ultimately relates back to increasing the information available about the basic investment decision parameters of alignment, benefit, cost, and risk. Depending on the nature of the investment, the details of such topics may populate individual line items in a six-page project charter or could fill volumes of research material.

DISPATCHING AND BACKLOG MANAGEMENT

Work intake culminates with the distribution of approved work requests to the groups or teams responsible for planning and execution, commonly referred to as *dispatching*. To the extent that work intake is in equilibrium with work throughput, then dispatching is a pass-through function: identifying the proper responsible manager and transferring an approved request to that person for action. However, it is relatively rare that the rate of work demand is in balance with capacity.

One area that is often inadequately addressed by organizations and business guidance alike is how to manage the inevitable backlog of work pending action. All demand has a customer, and all customers share one universal trait—they do not like waiting, especially if the duration of the wait is beyond the expected norm, or worse yet, unknown. Unfortunately, waiting is inherent to situations where demand exceeds capacity, which is often the case in knowledge worker environments. While some shy away from the using the term *backlog*, no matter how you choose to describe it, the subject of pending work is an important element of managing demand.

No one understands this better than groups responsible for operational, self-contained forms of work. For these teams, the volume of requests sitting in a queue awaiting response is critical. Metrics, measures, and tools carefully track call durations at help desks, order processing throughput, average customer wait times and other cyclic indicators, all in the interest of managing customer expectations and the backlog.

Yet for some reason, this same sense of importance seems to diminish when it comes to managing the backlog of routine planned work in other areas of the organization. In our new world of unbridled opportunity, it is not uncommon for an organization to have a years' worth of approved planned work pending action at any given time. Some of it will come and go in a relatively short time span, while other low priority requests may languish for several months, perhaps never to be worked.

Like any other area of the business, the key to successful backlog management lies in practical processes, information, and communications.

As demand data is gathered over time, each work type can be analyzed to determine the average number received, amount of effort required, duration from receipt to delivery, and so on. This information offers insights into how the backlog should be managed. Additionally, using the prioritization method we described generates some very telling and easily obtained work control metrics. Simply adding up the point value assigned for everything pending in the queue and trending it on a monthly basis easily establishes the total value of the backlog over time. An obvious extension of this is calculating the average value of work in the backlog. Comparative measures include value by requesting department, value of monthly demand versus work completed, and so on. Prioritization metrics can also be used for overall production measures: the total throughput of work through the organization and the volume and priority of work received versus delivered.

You should periodically review work that remains in the queue over a defined period (e.g., a quarter) to determine if priority has changed due to shifting circumstances. This is primarily a consideration for mid-level priorities that may keep missing the cut-off for authorization and dispatching because of being repeatedly displaced by higher priority work.

CENTRALIZED VERSUS DISTRIBUTED WORK INTAKE PROCESSES

The act of accepting, analyzing, and transferring responsibility for a request is relatively straightforward. However, there are variations in how the work intake process itself is designed and who is responsible for performing its functions. For example, will all approved requests be immediately dispatched to the respective manager on approval, or should you manage them in a central repository where managers pull work as needed? For that matter, is there a central receiving authority, or should work intake be managed in a more distributed manner? Does a single request always relate to a single work entity, or can it be broken up into multiple independent work items that are dispatched to multiple owners? Clearly, the answer to each of these questions and more will depend on the specific circumstances of your organization.

Many organizations identify the project, program, or portfolio management office (PMO) as the central intake point for formal projects. Increasingly, the PMO is becoming the focal point for collecting and dispatching requests for other types of planned work, although it is still most common for non-project requests to be sent directly to individuals responsible for fulfillment (the role and scope of the PMO regarding work management is discussed in more detail in chapter 16).

From a customer service perspective, there is a strong case for minimizing the number of parties between the requestor and those responsible for fulfilling the need. However, there are practical considerations as well. For example, in very large organizations can you reasonably expect the requestor to know who the responsible party is for every possible need? Can that person provide adequate information for an automated system to route it to the right point for review?

Perhaps the best compromise is to establish a single system that is centrally administered but accommodates a distributed group of users who actually analyze and distribute work. Often this approach is aligned to the concept of a corporate or enterprise PMO, with intake and dispatching responsibilities assigned to local department PMOs. Each local PMO can then work with department managers to further refine local rights and responsibilities appropriate to their needs. This offers a reasonable compromise between enterprise consistency and local control.

KEY POINTS IN THIS CHAPTER

☑ Work intake management includes request receipt, analysis, classification, prioritization, estimating, disposition, dispatching, and backlog management.

☑ Emergent work refers to requests of a critical nature that require immediate management attention.

☑ Emergent work must be managed in order to minimize work that is addressed in a reactive manner and to mitigate disruption of planned work

☑ Work intake accommodates all forms of demand, from formal projects to routine operational requests; planned work is classified into five general types:

- Strategic projects
- Major projects
- Other planned work
- Service work
- Ongoing work

☑ Each type of work is distinguished by the different process controls that are applied and the level of the organization that provides governance.

☑ All planned work should be prioritized using a single integrated method to establish its relative business value, regardless of its source or type.

☑ Work is further classified using primary descriptive attributes to enable reporting and development of specific execution portfolios.

☑ A preliminary estimate should be developed for each new request in terms of cost, effort, and expected duration to aid in assessment and disposition.

CHAPTER 15

MANAGING WORK AND RESOURCES

BRILLIANT STRATEGY AND SHREWD INVESTMENT decisions are of little value until they result in the delivery of products, services, and assets. Effectively driving project and operational work through the efficient use of your resources is the key to successfully getting products to market and serving your customers. This chapter offers proven techniques for successfully managing work execution and resource management for any environment that uses knowledge workers and technology.

When coordinating dozens, hundreds, or even thousands of specialized resources working simultaneously to complete myriad tasks, it is essential that all staff members have a common understanding of the applicable techniques, business processes, planning methods, priorities, and progress measures. Execution portfolios provide your organization with the common working environment and sources of information needed to coordinate and manage daily activities (figure 15-1).

	PEOPLE	WORK	MONEY	DELIVERABLES
	Organization	Missions	Finances	Customers
	Business Units	Objectives	High Level Accounts	Markets
	Departments	Strategies	Mid-Level Budgets	Product Lines
Execution Portfolios *Provide a Method to Collectively Manage Work and Resources:*	Groups & Teams	Programs & Projects	Detailed Budgets	Products & Services
	People	Work	Expenses	Deliverables

Figure 15-1: Execution Portfolio Scope Relative to Management Information Types

THE ROLE OF PROJECT PORTFOLIO MANAGEMENT

From its beginnings in the late 1980s, project portfolio management (PPM, alternatively referred to as program/portfolio management or project and portfolio management) has become one of the most respected and mature applications of the discipline. In our PMO survey, 85 percent of respondents indicated they were practicing program/project portfolio management in some form.

PPM as we know it today was born from the emergence of the modern Technology Services Organization (TSO) as defined in chapter 2. TSO characteristics created the need for better methods to address the complexities of multiple project environments, rather than managing each project as a wholly independent entity. Today, the application of some PPM products extends well beyond its roots in the information technology sector. PPM is becoming increasingly popular in the areas of new product development, product and service life cycle management, marketing, engineering, R&D, and the public sector. PPM is applicable in practically any environment where development and delivery of products and services via projects intersect with the use of knowledge workers and technology.

Over this same period, the Project Management Institute (PMI) has enjoyed a steady growth in membership and is now one of the largest professional associations in the world, boasting more than a quarter of a million members in more than 170 countries. PMI has done much to codify standard practices for project management functions such as planning, risk and quality management, issue and scope management, and other subjects within the discipline. Recognizing the PPM trend, PMI has also steadily extended its interests to develop standards and certifications for program and (project) portfolio management to address multi-project environments.

However, despite wide adoption of the PPM practice, a rich body of knowledge, abundant subject matter expertise, and a broad range of supporting software applications, many organizations still struggle to fully realize the potential value of PPM. Part of this stems from not recognizing and addressing the interconnected nature of the portfolio ecosystem and the unique requirements of the modern knowledge worker environment.

While focusing on a collection of formal projects is certainly a valid use of the portfolio management discipline, employing such an approach as the *exclusive* mechanism for managing resources and work frequently fails to deliver on the promise of PPM. As we described in chapter 6, the reason for this is that the availability of resources for project work is often directly and substantially affected by other concurrent run-the-business responsibilities. In such a scenario, it is important that you approach project management as a subset of the overall portfolio of work.

How the various elements of project planning and execution intersect with other areas of work and resource management presents the central challenge to managing the modern business environment. Rather than adding to the abundance of information already available about the general execution of project portfolio management, we will instead direct our attention to some key techniques for using execution portfolios to comprehensively plan and manage work and resources.

We have found that supplementing common PPM methods with these practices ensures successful execution of the complete portfolio of work and increases the overall effectiveness of the organization and its resources. Some of the key elements associated with this include:

1. **Being flexible**: Martial arts teach us that it is often better to leverage the opposing force's momentum than to bluntly resist it. Similarly, the realities of today's fast-moving business environment must be embraced rather than opposed; no amount of denial will overcome the internal and external influences that force change on a TSO environment.

2. **Taking a resource-centric approach**: Manage the workload of those people with critical skills by factoring in all of the demand, instead of just the needs of a few major projects. Planning work to avoid reactive juggling of staff and to limit inefficient starts and stops is the key to moving from chaos to success. The result is greater control over assigned work and higher morale for workers who are able to maintain greater focus, be more efficient, and meet realistic expectations.

3. **Operating within the limits of the planning horizon**: The considerations of the planning horizon, first introduced in chapter 6, are equally important when it comes to planning the details of work and resources.

4. **Recognizing that work and resource management are inseparable functions**: During planning and execution, recognize the interrelationships between managing work and managing resources. Each is wholly dependent on the other to develop viable plans and successfully accomplish work. The level of detail that you can apply to resource planning and assignment is predicated on the level of detail you have about the work to be accomplished and vice versa.

ESTABLISHING WORK PORTFOLIOS

Typically, thoughts of project management conjure up visions of a fully developed plan for a complex investment to create a large physical result, like a building, ship, or bridge. The schedule wraps around the walls of the project office, containing thousands or even tens of thousands of activities, planned down to the precise day the activities should occur. The project manager and his staff spend countless hours planning and updating the schedule, calculating multiple critical paths, rearranging constraints and task relationships, and carefully tracking earned value data. Based on that information, he chairs a meeting each day to choreograph the activities of a large dedicated staff through a team of superintendents and supervisors.

In such a situation, all work activities relate to achieving a common outcome and thus have logical relationships. Resource management is much more straightforward because the workforce is fully dedicated to the project. The entire team is free to focus on a single priority and objective—getting the project done; on time, on budget, and in a way that conforms to defined requirements.

While this kind of project management environment is still alive and well, it is not the scenario we address. Instead, we look at an even more complex set of circumstances where work portfolios are far more interesting and useful. Most projects undertaken in a TSO environment are shorter, smaller, less predictable, and face a very different set of challenges compared to what we previously described. Perhaps most important, many such projects are being performed simultaneously, along with other types of work, with little more in common than the fact that all of them are fighting for the resources you have, or need. Agile-based approaches are becoming increasingly popular because they add greater flexibility and better alignment with modern considerations. The project manager who continues to apply techniques intended for managing a single large project within a dynamic TSO environment is likely to have a career marked by frustration, lost productivity, and disappointing results.

For our purposes, a work portfolio consists of a population of independent activities grouped together for collective analysis and management. In the previous chapter, we identified a number of work attributes that enable work portfolio development. Depending on the purpose of the work portfolio, you can use these attributes to group, sort, and compare portfolio subjects in different ways. Work portfolios also draw from the different levels of the work information structure that we introduced in chapter 4 to select the subjects to be included.

For example, consider the needs of the typical line manager who is responsible for a particular group and its workload. To manage her active workload, she might construct a portfolio of subjects that consists of:

- All work assigned to the group with an approved status
- With a scheduled start date of the current month
- Sorted by priority

And parameters that include:

- Work type
- Work class
- Performance rating
- Assigned resources
- Associated product or service
- Total estimated effort
- Actual effort expended
- Estimated effort remaining
- Schedule start and completion dates

As the manager checks in with her staff to discuss progress and issues, she has the information available to provide guidance about possible conflicts, ask the right questions about utilization, and identify what work plans need adjustment to prepare for the next few weeks. This portfolio also allows her to quickly determine whether the total amount of work scheduled for the month exceeds the available effort of the team. What if this is indeed the case? The manager needs a resource portfolio view to support making reassignment decisions.

PLANNING WORK AND RESOURCES

Work and resource planning leverage many of the techniques that we explored earlier in this book. Practices such as balancing demand and capacity, defining work by type, prioritization, and managing the planning horizon all come into play. We will add some variations and a few new techniques to our repertoire to help manage the tactical aspects of demand and capacity planning.

Previous topics illustrate how the work and resource details intersect in different portfolio views. Planning work and managing resource assignments go hand in hand. How far in advance you are planning work, the stability of the planning process, the level of task detail that you develop, and who is performing the planning all dictate how you should plan and assign resources.

Planning Work

There are as many different approaches to planning work as there are kinds of work. One of the most common questions associated with work planning practices asks, "What is the right level of detail?" Once any prescribed minimum process requirements are met, additional planning detail is often a matter of personal preference on the part of the work owner.

Too often, a high degree of detail in the work breakdown structure (WBS) is mistaken as a sign of planning sophistication, when in fact it may be counterproductive. Excessive detail makes the WBS ineffective as a communication tool, creates genuine problems when making changes and updating progress, and adds a significant reporting burden.

The degree of work planning detail should be commensurate with the risk and complexity of the work and the skills of the contributors. A work plan should never repeat defined process steps or the common toolbox skills of assigned resources. When a higher level of detail is necessary, consider using a checklist or supporting work practice guidance instead of including it as schedule line items.

"Never plan to more detail than you are willing to manage" is a very simple but effective planning rule. When you define the lowest-level tasks between 8 and 80 hours in duration each, you can establish a balance between reasonable resource and duration estimates, a minimal planning burden, and a reasonable level of detail for progress reporting.

With this general guidance in mind, other factors will influence the planning detail for any single activity, including the nature and complexity of the work. For example, it is perfectly appropriate to have a task that is only 4 hours long when it represents an integrated testing event that must be coordinated across several resources or when it achieves a major milestone. When constructing a large work plan, the use of peer reviews often provides valuable objective insight and feedback to ensure that planning is at an appropriate level.

Regardless of the planning method and level of detail employed, a good work plan should be able to withstand the following test questions:

- Does the plan meet defined process and procedural requirements?
- Does each element of the work plan represent development of a specific tangible sub-deliverable that can be objectively measured for start, progress, and finish?
- Is the terminology and naming convention clear and unambiguous?
- Do child activities directly and exclusively relate to the parent?
- Does the plan adequately segregate tasks for cost accounting, subcontracting, or similar purposes?
- Are important milestones, stage gates, or other process control points incorporated?
- Does the work plan effectively communicate and control?

- Does the plan balance control with flexibility in how it uses relationships and constraints?

- As the completed work plan is rolled up and summarized from one level to the next, does each level make logical sense?

- Does the work plan respect the planning horizon by using a level of detail that is consistent with the degree of uncertainty?

If you can answer yes to all of these questions, then you likely have an appropriate and effective work plan. You can probably think of additional questions to add to these to create your own work planning checklist.

Resource Forecasting and Assignment Options

Over the past several years, we have made it a point to ask groups of first-level managers in different types of organizations and industry sectors how far in advance they can reliably allocate workers to tasks.

The majority of those who responded told us that it is difficult to define specific resource assignments more than 3 to 6 weeks into the future without facing the need to re-plan. Even in stable, highly project-oriented departments, individual task assignments made 8 to 10 weeks in advance are in jeopardy of actually being carried out as originally planned.

The net result is that the farther out individual assignments are planned, the greater the probability that they will have to be re-planned. This significantly increases the amount of planning overhead and potential for confusion. To avoid this, you can employ the different resource assignment types we describe here, commensurate with the level of detail and confidence in work plans. The general options for resource forecasting, estimating, and assignment are as follows:

- **Requirement**: A generalized resource need that is identified at any level of a work plan, described by identifying resource attributes such as skill; role; level of organization structure (i.e., from a particular department, team, or group); and/or other resource attributes such as physical location, resource type, and so on.

Requirements are highly versatile; you can define a single broad requirement as a general resource estimate for an entire project or specify multiple requirements with more specific information on a single phase or activity. The requirement often represents multiple unnamed resources and always includes an estimate of the total effort and the general time frame that the resource is required.

- *Example*: The Aries Global Product Expansion Initiative has a requirement for 100 hours of effort for a marketing specialist from the EMEA Product Solutions Group during the first quarter. The resource needs to be familiar with the Aries product line and EU customer demographics and must be able to speak both French and English.

- **Reserve**: A proposal or request for a specific named individual at any level of a work plan (also referred to as a soft booking). A reserve can reflect a possible assignment that has not yet been committed to or confirmed, or it could represent a request from a work authority (such as a project manager) to a resource assignment authority (such as a line or resource manager). A reserve may employ a status flag (proposed, accepted, rejected, etc.). Like a requirement, a reserve includes: the activities to be assigned, the planned time period, and an estimate in hours of effort that will be required. Reserves can also be used to establish capacity estimates for effort that is expected to be needed for nonspecific or unplanned activities.

  - *Example*: A pending reserve has been created for Janette Alba for 100 hours to manage the Aries central Europe advertising campaign in Q1 under the Aries II expansion project.

- **Allocation**: A specific task assignment and effort estimate for a named individual created at the lowest level of planning detail. An allocation represents an expectation for a specific deliverable to be produced within the constraints of a specified date range and defined amount of effort.

- *Example*: As part of the Aries II expansion project advertising campaign, Alec Anselmo has been allocated to design and place a print advertisement in *Avec Le Temps* to run in its April 3rd Paris edition; the estimated effort is 20 hours over the 2-week period between March 12th and 26th.

- **Authorization**: Establishes authority for a defined group or individual to expend effort on a prescribed portion of a work plan over a specified period of time. No level of effort is identified; therefore, authorizations do not affect the resource effort profiles (histograms). Authorizations are frequently employed in conjunction with time-reporting categories to enable you to book effort on a level-of-effort or ad hoc basis.

  - *Example*: While he does not have a specific planned assignment, Bill Jones, the Aries product manager, is authorized to charge effort to the Aries II advertising campaign in Q1 in the event he is called on to provide casual assistance.

In chapter 6 we introduced the concept of the planning horizon. While that chapter dealt primarily with planning work and resources at a strategic level, the concept is equally applicable to tactical planning. To forecast resource needs efficiently in a TSO environment, we recommend that you apply an iterative planning approach, as shown in figure 15-2.

Use of resource assignment options in an iterative manner as illustrated in figure 15-2 leverages the planning horizon by adding more work and resource planning details as the potential for uncertainty and re-planning decreases. Long-term projects are most likely to fully utilize all of the stages noted. For example, establishing high level requirements to a phase-level project template is often done in support of investment analysis decisions.

All of these resource assignment and planning options may be employed simultaneously depending on the length of a project. For example, at project initiation, the requirements definition phase establishes all the tasks and allocations needed to fully understand the scope of work, proposes the approach to be taken, and estimates design and

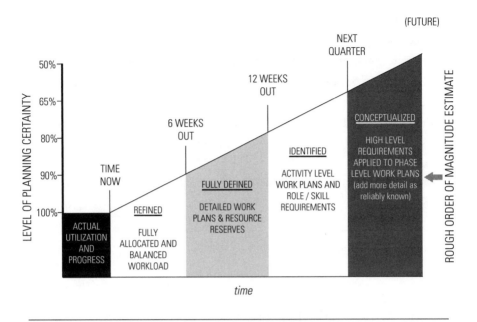

Figure 15-2: Iterative Work and Resource Planning Cycles over Time

development activities and their resource needs. As this phase continues, resulting information is added to subsequent design and development phases as it is identified. If a funding gate is positioned to follow requirements gathering, the activities and tasks that were added to the subsequent phases may use reserves to demonstrate a workable resource plan and better estimate costs to get capital funding approval. Meanwhile, the testing and validation phase (which may be several months out) could employ resource requirements with only basic skill, role, and effort estimates until design is complete and more details are known.

Other types of work may not use all of these iterations. For example, a work request that represents a simple, quick-hit activity may come into the demand cycle and be immediately dispatched to an assigned owner for action in a matter of days or a few weeks. In such a case, the assigned manager may immediately know who he wants to assign to the work and directly allocate resource effort to a plan that consists of only a few underlying tasks.

The continuum of day-to-day operational activities represented by service work and ongoing work types are accounted for by establishing reserves to general level-of-effort work categories. For example, a reserve can be used to denote that a percentage of a specific resource's time will be utilized for general product management functions. This is important to ensure that utilization profiles reflect true workload in a manner that is flexible enough to absorb the weekly fluctuations that naturally occur in these efforts.

These resource assignment approaches represent a classic example of "using the right tool for the job." It is always preferable to have a complete toolbox of options rather than relying exclusively on a single resource assignment approach.

MANAGING WORK EXECUTION

Measuring Utilization and Progress in a TSO

As we identified in chapter 6, measuring actual utilization is the starting point for go-forward planning assumptions. Given the different types of work and resource demands of the organization, understanding how time and effort is actually being consumed is important. Besides the obvious benefit from knowing how individuals are spending their time, a firm understanding of actual consumption allows utilization to be assessed at various levels of the organizational breakdown structure (OBS). The most effective way to achieve this is to collect actual utilization data, and time reporting is the most widely used method to get this information.

Most organizations have some form of time reporting capabilities in place, but often these systems are intended for general accounting and charge back purposes rather than measuring utilization. In such circumstances, detail is often limited to time reported at the project level and on a monthly reporting frequency. While this may be adequate for accounting purposes, it does not offer enough detail or timeliness to facilitate effective work and resource management.

Time reporting as designed in PPM systems fulfills multiple functions in addition to meeting accounting needs. Because the primary mechanism for getting work done within a knowledge worker environment is by expending human effort, time reporting becomes the equivalent of an inventory control system, tracking how "raw material" is consumed for production. Because effort tracking is in the context of what work is being done, it can also be used as a highly effective means of reporting work progress. For knowledge work, effort expended versus effort required is the most accurate measure of progress reporting.

For example, if you are developing a requirement document that is initially estimated to take 20 hours of effort, then reporting 5 hours effort applied toward that deliverable constitutes 25 percent completion. It does not matter that a twenty-page document is expected and ten pages were written in the first 5 hours—the final ten pages might be the technical "meat" of the deliverable that takes far more effort to complete. Using a 50 percent completion rate because of page count progress would be very misleading.

Another benefit of time reporting is that it provides a feedback mechanism so you can manage based on your reality as changes emerge. As we discussed in chapter 2, one of the common issues associated with knowledge work is that accurate up-front estimates can be difficult to achieve. This is partly due to the often unknown or iterative nature of the work itself. To continue the requirements document example, it would not be a surprise to find that once the first 5 hours are expended on the requirements document, the initial 20-hour effort estimate may require adjustment to reflect new insights into what it will really take to accomplish the deliverable. In addition to reporting actual time spent, having a provision for updating remaining effort estimates as a part of time reporting and subsequently integrating that information into work schedules and progress measures is a desirable feature of a PPM system.

Some managers may question the wisdom of giving individual contributors the ability to adjust initial work estimates as progress is made. The fundamental issue is not really whether work and resource plans will have variations, but rather how managers and stakeholders will be informed of such changes so they can respond. These factors are why time reporting is such a highly prominent component of integrated work and resource management.

The Manager's Role

Perhaps the heart of the issue in many organizations is rethinking (and redefining expectations for) the primary role of the manager. Too often in today's business environments we find that the role of the manager has been transformed into something akin to a "lead engineer," rather than a true management role. While a manager certainly has a duty to ensure the technical viability of the work and workers he or she is responsible for, if the majority of the manager's effort is spent *doing* work rather than *managing* it, a leadership vacuum for other responsibilities often results.

The manager's primary responsibility should be to ensure that the work and people he is responsible for are effectively fulfilling the needs of the business. It takes both time and discipline for a manager to make work assignments, set expectations, remove roadblocks, coach the team, adjust work plans, coordinate with peers, and generally maximize the effectiveness of the resources he or she has been entrusted with.

While such a discussion is too often dismissed without much interest, consider this: a typical manager in the United States who is responsible for a dozen professional knowledge workers has the equivalent spending power of over a million dollars annually, often with relatively few checks and balances as to how that money is spent. Compare that to the level of controls that your organization places on an expenditure of that magnitude from an accounting perspective.

One of the goals of the practices described in this chapter is to help establish a better sense of accountability to achievable expectations throughout the organization. We have continually stressed the importance of establishing workable strategies about how demand will be comprehensively balanced in line with resource capacities. On a tactical level, managers are responsible for giving individual workers a realistic workload and a clear understanding of their priorities as a prerequisite to establishing a culture of personal accountability.

KEY POINTS IN THIS CHAPTER

☑ Project portfolio management (PPM) emerged with the advent of the TSO to address the complexities of a multi-project environment.

☑ For PPM to be fully effective, it needs to incorporate the total workload of the organization and use techniques appropriate to the unique challenges of the TSO.

☑ The keys elements associated with conducting integrated work and resource management in a TSO environment include

- Flexibility to respond to business dynamics

- Taking a resource-centric approach to how work is managed

- Operating within the limits of the planning horizon

- Recognizing that work and resource management are inseparable functions

☑ Work portfolios allow you to group, compare, and manage disparate work activities to obtain a complete perspective of your workload.

☑ Resource portfolios give you similar capabilities to manage your workforce; resources are classified and arranged into an organizational breakdown structure (OBS) to facilitate creating portfolio views.

☑ The level of detail, stability of work plans, how far in advance the work is planned, and who performs the planning all impacts how resources are planned and assigned.

☑ We recommend that work tasks be planned to a level of detail that is between 8 and 80 hours of duration.

☑ Resource forecasting and assignment options include defining

- Requirements

- Reserves

- Allocations

- Authorizations

☑ The option selected depends on the type of planning being performed, the planning horizon, and the rights of the individual planning the work.

☑ These elements enable you to take an iterative approach to planning work and assigning resources.

☑ Time reporting provides a mechanism to measure resource utilization and work progress, and to update resource estimates based on emerging information and experience with the task.

☑ The managers' role is to maximize the work and staff for which they are responsible to meet the objectives of the organization.

☑ To accomplish this, as part of the work and resource management process, execution portfolios can be applied to establish reasonable expectations and accountability.

IMPLEMENTING PORTFOLIO MANAGEMENT

This final section contains four chapters dedicated to implementing portfolio management and a concluding summary chapter. Chapter 16 explores how the role of the traditional program or project management office is increasingly evolving into a portfolio management office. We will explain how to create a unified network of portfolio management processes in chapter 17. Chapter 18 takes a look at the role technology plays in enabling the practices we have discussed, and chapter 19 offers proven approaches for implementing a portfolio management initiative in your organization.

CHAPTER 16

THE PORTFOLIO MANAGEMENT OFFICE

THUS FAR, WE HAVE FOCUSED on how you can apply portfolios to unify your entire organization, manage change, sharpen your strategy, and create measurable value. This chapter begins the section by explaining why the PMO is an important component in taming change.

Traditionally, the P in the acronym PMO has stood for the "project" or "program" management office, with its focus primarily dedicated to the tactical execution of formal projects or groups of projects. In that respect, the PMO has always been an important part of managing change, given that projects are change mechanisms by definition.

Today, this acronym is just as likely to stand for "portfolio" management office. We coined the term "PMO 2.0" in 2005 to differentiate between those PMOs that have evolved into a next-generation portfolio services organization and the more traditional project-centric PMO. As we will explore in this chapter, the modern 2.0 version of the PMO is emerging as a full-service business management and integration center for managing change.

Throughout this book, we have stressed approaching portfolio management with a broad perspective, discussing how to apply this technique to manage markets, strategies, resources, products, and more. As explained in the opening chapters, the portfolio environment functions as an interdependent ecosystem that employs different perspectives and applications. Whether it is linking strategic direction with work execution or managing the relationships between customer demand and your products and services, a significant amount of coordination is necessary to sustain these different relationships.

In a growing number of organizations, the portfolio management office has become that centralized point of coordination. The PMO also serves to establish the array of different tools and techniques needed to foster enough consistency across the enterprise so that it can function as a single cohesive ecosystem such as we described in chapter 1.

This chapter first draws on recent industry data to explore current PMO trends and then analyzes the underlying reasons why the project or program management office is evolving to become a portfolio management office.

Next, we present the case for the corporate PMO to become established as an essential shared services provider which is similar to how IT, corporate accounting, and HR are viewed. Before that can become a reality, organizations need to address some common roadblocks to PMO success and longevity. We close the chapter with the key elements that you'll need for PMO success.

PMO TRENDS

As introduced in chapter 3, we conducted an extensive survey* of PMOs that focused on technology services organizations. The objective of the study was to quantify PMO performance, identify the scope of services

---

* "2008 PMO 2.0 Survey," January 15, 2009, available through www.tamingchange.com.

that PMOs provide, and ascertain the presence and impact of the issues facing organizations and their PMOs. Over 450 respondents participated, representing a broad cross-section of organizational sizes, types, industries, and maturity levels, from massive multinational institutions to government agencies and local businesses. The results yielded several key findings that added to our overall understanding of modern PMOs and the organizations they serve. We present the findings that are most relevant to the role of the PMO in portfolio management in this chapter.

The "Project" Management Office Is Now a Minority

The PMO that focuses solely on formal projects is no longer the de facto standard. As shown in figure 16-1, over 60 percent of the PMOs surveyed indicated that they were extending their scope of interest in work and resource management to either include all forms of planned work in the organization but not operations (33 percent), or that they were fully engaged in comprehensive work and resource management—including routine operational activities (28 percent).

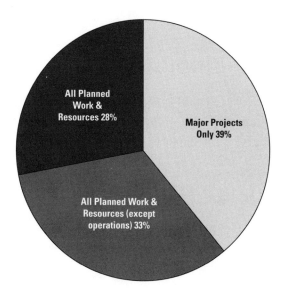

Figure 16-1: General PMO Work and Resource Management Scope

The PMO Is Reaching Upward and Outward

According to our findings, the majority of PMOs reported directly to the c-level (55 percent) or to a vice president (10 percent) and 26 percent of PMOs operated at an enterprise level, serving across the board as an integration point for different departments, lines of business, or similar divisions. Almost half of all respondents were operating in a multi-PMO environment. Around a third of the PMOs were associated with information technology organizations.

The PMO as a Business Management Center

In terms of the services provided by the PMOs, 85 percent of respondents indicated that they were involved in program and portfolio management, the highest percentage of any of the 38 functions listed. The next most prevalent functions included process improvement (82 percent), high level reporting (78 percent), and strategic planning (68 percent). On average, the typical PMO reported involvement with fifteen of the thirty-eight activities listed in figure 16-2.

ANALYZING THE EVOLUTION OF THE PMO

Before we can discuss how and why the PMO is changing, we must first examine what it is and what it does. Any PMO—large or small, old or new—is generally responsible for:

- Collecting and distributing information
- Managing demand and capacity
- Providing analysis and reporting
- Enabling coordination and communications

- Identifying and addressing opportunities or roadblocks
- Developing, distributing, and maintaining processes and tools
- Providing and promoting specialized skills and expertise

Note that these functions are not exclusive to the PMO; in fact, departments routinely perform these activities as a normal part of general administration and management. What distinguishes the PMO is that it provides these services *across* functional silos and different levels of the organization. The true value proposition of a PMO lies in its ability to effectively traverse departmental and hierarchical boundaries as a mechanism to establish consistency and interoperability. A secondary benefit is the consolidation of specialized business functions to improve quality and take advantage of economies of scale.

The Expanding Role of the PMO

To be clear, when we refer to the evolution of the PMO, the basic *functions* it performs are not necessarily changing. However, the *business processes* that the PMO supports with these functions are changing. As a result, the constituents of those functions and the value they receive from the PMO are shifting as well.

To illustrate this point, consider the traditional PMO that limits its scope to supporting project management; it gathers project proposals and related information, reports on project progress and performance, provides project tracking tools and expertise, addresses project scope and risk issues, and so on. When applying these capabilities to the discipline of project management and related processes, the PMO constituents primarily consist of project managers, project staff, and functional sponsors. The resulting benefit delivered is largely tactical in value.

Referencing the activities in figure 16-2, consider how the PMO constituency changes when it also supports strategic and investment

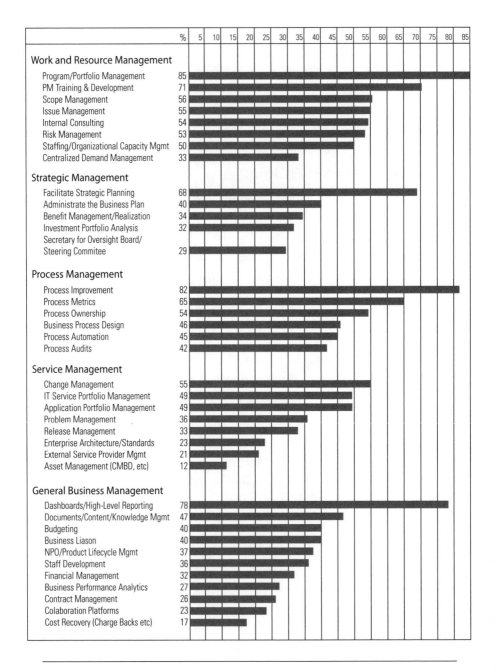

Figure 16-2: Survey Results: Percentage of PMOs Engaged in the Functions Listed

portfolios. Now the PMO is gathering information about proposed strategies, analyzing how potential investments align with those strategies, providing tools and expertise in support of making portfolio trade-off decisions, and reporting on progress toward achieving business objectives. As a result, the constituency served by the PMO shifts to include the leadership team. Equally important, the potential for the PMO to add value to the organization goes up by an order of magnitude.

In both cases, the PMO performs essentially the same basic functions and acts as a bridge to coordinate activities across different groups and layers of the organization. However, the target portfolio management processes in its scope of interest have changed. The data suggests this trend has a significant amount of momentum behind it. While there are several reasons for this transformation, much of the impetus stems from the very issues discussed in the previous section. The complexities that accompany matrix organizational structures, the added difficulty associated with tracking knowledge-based work, and the operational dynamics that we face from constant change have driven the need to "put a head on the monster."

The PMO as a Portfolio Management Office

As a technique for collectively managing change, portfolio management uses six basic elements:

- A subject change event
- Viable supporting information
- Analytical skills and capabilities
- Decision parameters
- Resulting decisions and actions
- Analysis and decision-support tools

These are universal techniques, whether managing a strategic, investment, or execution portfolio, regardless of whether the subjects are products, markets, work, or resources. When you compare these elements with the basic functions that any PMO already provides, extending the PMO to be a centralized group that is dedicated to facilitating portfolio management is a completely intuitive and natural step in its evolution; this is what we mean by "PMO 2.0."

Some people misconstrue the concept of a portfolio management office as a high level, prescriptive decision-making authority. The very notion can be alarming to senior executives, product managers, and department heads, who might see such a group as encroaching on their own responsibilities and power. Although a PMO may indeed create, analyze, and make portfolio recommendations in some cases, it is more often intended as a shared central service rather than a center of decision making.

The PMO *can* efficiently provide the underlying information, tools, and process support necessary to enable others. The portfolio management office can also be a practical location to concentrate business analytics and reporting skills, coordinate actions across multiple portfolio managers during planning cycles, and provide arbitration and facilitation when making trade-off decisions between competing portfolios. The PMO also provides the necessary administration to keep track of portfolio decisions and the status of portfolio activities.

To the extent that the PMO is actively involved in up-front decision support and "back office" functions, it is also well situated to smoothly translate those decisions into actionable work and to facilitate effective execution.

The PMO as a Shared Service Provider

While it is still somewhat uncommon for a PMO to be as firmly embedded in an organization as IT, HR, or accounting, we believe the corporate

PMO is on a trajectory to gain such acceptance in the coming years. This will occur for the same reasons that these other groups were ultimately embraced; the PMO is yet another example of consolidating essential shared services and specialized competencies to increase effectiveness and reduce costs.

Few would suggest that it would be a wise move to disband your existing corporate technology, HR, or finance groups in favor of dispersing their staff and functions to individual departments. Besides the inevitable inconsistencies and chaos that such a move would create, you would also need to replicate the processes, tools, and skills within each department. This would greatly distract line organizations from their primary objectives, and the functions themselves would suffer from a predictable loss of focus, effectiveness, and economies of scale.

Contrast this with organizations that have not yet employed a PMO. The need to establish business management processes and tools, manage strategies, make investment decisions, deal with work demand, assign priorities, control capacities, identify and address issues, and track progress are inescapable and ubiquitous. Yet, without a centralized mechanism to establish common approaches and competencies, each department performs these functions independently, with responsibilities either divided or duplicated across that department's management team.

Some organizations have not yet embraced the PMO concept because it has failed in the past or they still consider it a luxury that adds needless administrative overhead to the bottom line. For organizations that have made a long-term commitment to creating a strong, full-service PMO and nurturing it to maturity, actual results suggest otherwise: an investment of less than 2 percent of the total workforce can achieve gains of 20 percent or more in long-term productivity. However, to realize these gains, the cycle of PMO creation, destruction, and resurrection must first be broken.

IMPROVING PMO CONTINUITY AND SUCCESS

In our own contemporary PMO research, as well as that conducted by leading analyst firms, Hobbs and Aubry,* Pennypacker,† and others, we consistently find that the average age of a PMO tends to fall somewhere in the 2- to 3-year range. The PMO is a transient entity in many organizations because of perceptions about its role, natural business and economic cycles, and other factors.

The majority of survey respondents view their PMOs as reasonably successful despite their relatively short average life span; as figure 16-3 shows, 58 percent of PMOs were ranked "Good" or better. However, a significant minority (42 percent) struggle to meet their mission, usually resulting from a combination of poor execution; low levels of organizational maturity; and inadequate staffing, sponsorship, and support.

Studies also consistently indicate that overall PMO effectiveness increases with time in service; however, there is often a lack of patience or understanding about how long it takes a fledgling PMO to mature into a fully effective contributor and its true role in the organization.

Unfortunately, even PMOs that achieve moderate levels of success are not immune to being routinely purged from their organizations. The reason that PMOs are abandoned is often rooted in why they were initiated. Some PMOs have become, in effect, "a temporary solution to a permanent problem."

The decision to embark on a PMO initiative is often event triggered. Perhaps it is due to the arrival of a new executive that is a PMO supporter. More likely, organizations initiate a PMO in response to a period of high growth and prosperity, or because a new requirement drives the need to improve processes or information. In each case, these situations represent a perceived acute need to manage an increasing amount of change.

---

* Dr. Brian Hobbs, BASc, MBA, Ph.D, PMP, and Dr. Monique Aubry, Ph.D, of the University of Quebec at Montreal; ref. as referenced in the *PM Network* journal, PMI, Vol. 40 Issue 1, March, 2009. Building Value Through Sustainable Project Management Offices, Mimi Hurt, MI2 Consulting, Calgary, Alberta, Canada; Janice L. Thomas, Athabasca University, Athabasca, Alberta, Canada

† James Pennypacker, *The State of the PMO 2007–2008*, The Center for Business Practices, 2007.

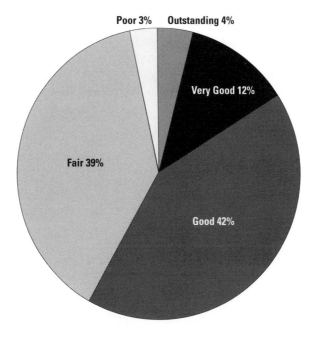

Figure 16-3: Survey Results: Percentage of PMOs by Effectiveness

In cases where the PMO is not an established shared business service, one of two scenarios typically play out within the first few years of PMO operation: (1) the initial business drivers for the PMO have subsided or have been substantially satisfied or (2) it has failed to fully achieve expected improvements.

Either outcome results in the PMO becoming a target of questions about its continued necessity in the subsequent months and quarters. Organizations abandon their PMOs when these questions coincide with one or more of the following conditions:

- Normal business rhythms reduce the volume of discretionary projects.
- Economic pressures drive workforce reductions.

- Initial executive sponsorship is lost due to changes in leadership.
- Early PMO successes are perceived as a threat, and a backlash emerges.
- The organization loses focus on the original objectives of the PMO initiative.
- The PMO fails to show substantive value.

Thus, too often young PMOs suffer a high mortality rate when organizations perceive change itself as a temporary situation. In those cases, it may become the phoenix of the organization chart; regularly abandoned after only a few years of operation, it rises again from the ashes when a new cycle of intense change emerges. The biggest obstacle to the long-term success and acceptance of the PMO is overcome once an organization accepts that managing change is a persistent and inevitable part of managing the business and recognizes that the PMO's role is to facilitate change.

PMO Success Factors

Besides recognizing its role in the organization, many other factors go into creating a successful PMO. Several books on PMO development and operation are dedicated to the subject, such as *Business Driven PMO Setup* by Mark Price Perry (Fort Lauderdale, FL: J. Ross Publishing, 2009). However, we have identified some general considerations that will go a long way toward establishing the foundation for an effective PMO.

PMO Vision

As the idea of a PMO initiative goes from inception to approval, it needs to be recognized for what it is—the insertion of a specialized support group into the organization. You should approach a PMO as a long-term commitment to create a valuable shared asset. As such, it should be treated no differently than any other programmatic investment as it is refined, analyzed, approved, developed, and deployed. The decision to embark on a PMO program requires a measure of clarity on the part of the primary stakeholders for its basis, purpose, responsibilities, and expected outcomes. These conclusions need to be clearly stated in the business case and charter of the PMO.

Initiation of a PMO in an environment that has had no prior experience with one can be a potentially contentious undertaking. Leaders are naturally wary of any inference that improvements are needed, especially when they are going to be "helped" by an entity outside of their control that may impose new requirements, demands, and oversight mechanisms. Because of this, to unilaterally initiate a PMO through the brute force of a single executive is to likely invite its prompt destruction as soon as that individual is no longer in a position to protect it. That is not to infer that a strong PMO benefactor isn't useful—just that it isn't enough on its own.

Because the PMO is a group that will serve multiple parts and levels of the organization, it is important that primary recipients of the service understand the business case and have a voice in determining what the PMO will and will not do. While it is unlikely that you will get 100 percent consensus, it will give stakeholders the opportunity to offer their opinions. These insights are invaluable in understanding concerns and areas of sensitivity that will need to be addressed during PMO initiation and operation.

PMO Service Span

Before we discuss success elements in more detail, this is a good place to first make some clarifying points regarding the service span of a portfolio management office and about the application of portfolio management in general. Most of the discussion in this book has necessarily centered on applying portfolio management at a high level, such as across the entire enterprise, or a largely autonomous organizational unit that has unique markets, strategies, resources, and products. We have done this to both illustrate the wide applicability of the technique and to approach the subject of portfolio management in the broadest sense.

However, the vast majority of the practices and concepts we have offered are applicable at the departmental level as well. For example, an engineering department within a manufacturing environment has defined markets, strategies, resources, and products, even though you may not express them in those exact terms.

There is an element of relativity to consider when discussing portfolios and the PMO. For example, compare the application of portfolio management techniques in these two situations:

- Across an entire company that has $300 million in annual revenue and a staff of 400

- In an Information Systems department of a global financial services institute that has an annual budget of several billion dollars and 8,000 employees

In the latter case, it is not unusual to find an "Enterprise IS PMO" in place with several satellite PMOs around the world providing local support, whereas the former might be best served by a single PMO.

When discussing the scope of the PMO, you first need to define its intended span of control and influence. Once you reach agreement about those areas, additional discussions can be held about defining its scope.

PMO Scope

Two broad categories need to be addressed when discussing the scope of a PMO. The first is its general scope of work and resource management interests within the defined service span, and the second is the scope of supporting services and functions that the PMO provides.

We discussed the different types of work and the challenges presented by the TSO environment in earlier chapters. Because of these factors, it is preferable that the PMO's scope of influence create an intersecting set of both the body of work and the resource capacities used to perform that work as illustrated in figure 16-4.

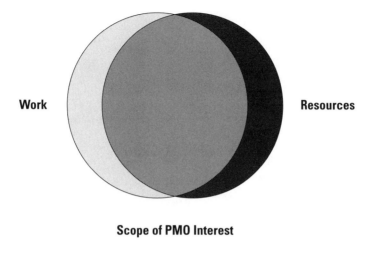

Work

Resources

Scope of PMO Interest

Figure 16-4: Defining the Work and Resources in the Scope of the PMO

The reason for this goes back to one of the early basic concepts for managing demand and capacity—it is difficult, if not impossible to effectively manage one without the ability to manage the other. The example in figure 16-4 is representative of a PMO that has both the workload and workforce of a single department within its scope. The scope does not totally overlap because there will always be some work that relies on the support of external resources and some resource capacity that works outside the department. The important point is that the PMO has a substantial majority of both demand and capacity within its scope and thus can influence how they are co-managed.

Failure to recognize this relationship is part of what limits the success of a PMO in a matrix environment that focuses only on project work. In such a scenario, the PMO does not have the total workload assigned to resources within its span of influence. As a result, the PMO has little control over ensuring resource availability to perform project tasks as scheduled. Figure 16-5 illustrates such a scenario.

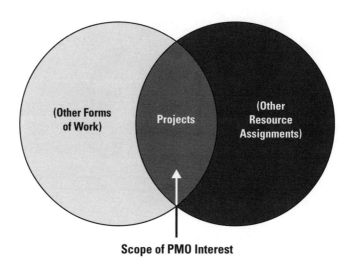

Scope of PMO Interest

Figure 16-5: Limited Intersections of a PMO Focused Only on Projects

The second component of PMO scope focuses on the functions and services it provides within its defined span of work and resource influence. The scope of PMO services are defined on two operational planes— the range of its involvement along the continuum of change and how much strategic versus tactical support the PMO will provide.

The first consideration of scope includes establishing the points where the PMO begins and ends its involvement along the portfolio ecosystem. Will the PMO be involved in reporting on current state operations, or will it begin its support with providing request management services? Will its involvement end with project completion, or will it play an ongoing role in managing the life cycle of its deliverable or in measuring benefits?

The second consideration is how strategic or tactical the PMO is to be: Will its scope of responsibilities include functioning as the secretary for operational planning? What is its role in investment analysis? What should its level of involvement be in financial management and budgeting functions? In tactical terms, more IT PMOs are getting involved in operational activities like change management, service level management, managing service catalogs, application portfolio management (APM), and outsourcing and vendor management.

When it comes to defining both PMO span of service and scope, the most important consideration is how its responsibilities intersect with other management roles. Failure to adequately define and communicate the role of the PMO relative to other leadership positions within the organization leads to stressed relationships, turf wars, dropped responsibilities, and unclear expectations. The PMO is but one element in the overall management repertoire, so it is critical that you clearly identify PMO responsibilities relative to those of line managers, resource managers, project managers, department heads, investment owners, and so on. Use of tools such as a RACI matrix, in conjunction with the process framework we provide in the next chapter, will help you identify which functions the PMO should be involved with. Ensure that there are no gaps or conflicts in responsibilities for core portfolio processes.

Organizational Placement

The PMO must influence without authority, yet have leverage without being seen as a threat or overbearing. To achieve this delicate balance, the PMO manager should hold a peer-level position relative to the PMO's span of service and the other parts of the organization it supports. For example, a PMO that serves the interests of the entire IT department should report directly to the CIO. If the PMO is expected to operate across the enterprise, the PMO should report to the COO, CFO, chief strategy officer, or other senior executive. If the PMO manager is positioned at the same level as the managers he must work with and influence, then the inherent parity of their positions and the fact that they report to a common superior make it more likely that others will actively engage in collaborative efforts.

Conversely, a PMO placed in a subservient position faces a literally uphill battle when trying to influence other areas of the organization. Unless an unusually savvy and politically adept manager leads the PMO, chances are it will routinely have to rely on outside authority figures to broker incentives so that other senior positions actively cooperate. A PMO that is perceived as weak or insignificant will find that adoption of its policies and guidance to be more likely considered an optional suggestion rather than an operational imperative. Obviously, it takes much more than a title for the PMO to garner respect. However, the lack of one makes the process that much more difficult, particularly if it is perceived to signal a lack of executive support and commitment.

Executive Sponsorship

Highly visible and consistent sponsorship of the PMO is one of the most important elements of PMO success. Survey respondents showed a high correlation between the level of active sponsorship they were receiving and the overall effectiveness of the PMO. As discussed in organizational placement, sponsorship is yet another method of providing the PMO with the authority to influence others. However, too often support for the PMO hinges on the continued presence and benevolence of a single executive.

To ensure that sponsorship is a shared responsibility among executive stakeholders and that the PMO stays in alignment with expectations, we recommend establishing a PMO steering committee as part of its charter. Holding meetings on a quarterly or semiannual basis to review progress toward objectives and to discuss related issues helps maintain an open line of communication and continued support.

PMO Staffing

Our survey indicated that on average, PMOs that had achieved an effective level of service usually have a minimum of four or more staff members. Given that modern PMOs are providing a wider range of services, more people are likely to be necessary just to address the diversity of skills required. Based on the scope of services that the PMO is chartered to provide and the size of the constituency it must serve, PMO staff members must achieve adequate critical mass or risk spreading themselves too thin to be effective. Partially staffing a newly formed PMO with seasoned individuals who are already known and respected in the organization will help garner confidence and acceptance.

While each PMO situation will dictate the appropriate staff quantity, the roles they most often play fall into some general categories and descriptions. Particularly in smaller organizations, individuals who make up the PMO staff should have a broad range of competencies because each person in the PMO will likely fulfill multiple roles. The following personas suggest the various roles needed to achieve PMO effectiveness:

- **Leader**: The leader must clearly understand the objectives and challenges of not only the PMO, but also the organization it supports. The leader needs to be respected as a team builder, mentor, and internal consultant and to be able to think strategically and communicate at an executive level. The leader should be politically astute and know the importance of building strong allies across the organization. He or she needs the wisdom to offer sensible alternatives to sticky issues and get everyone back on track. The leader must also be an evangelist to inspire the organization to follow the lead of the PMO.

- **Instructor**: Often, one of the main functions of the PMO is to educate, which is a deceptively difficult task when dealing with a wide constituency of adult learners. The PMO often needs to build its own curriculums on specialized topics, so the instructor needs to be competent and confident on a variety of subjects and administratively adept. As an instructor, he or she must be able to command the respect and attention of the staff being supported, whether in a formal classroom setting, on a remote web presentation, or during one-on-one mentoring sessions.

- **Mechanic**: Enthusiasm and information has to be backed up with workable solutions; the mechanic of the PMO must be able to disassemble and rebuild processes, configure supporting applications, and generally make sure that PMO solutions work. The mechanic should be able to troubleshoot automated workflows, write documentation, or develop templates equally well.

- **Reporting specialist**: Regardless of the system of origin, disparate information types must be obtained and presented in a number of different ways for different audiences. Data should be summarized so that it is readily digestible by busy executives or meaty enough to satisfy the needs of working managers. Beyond excellent technical skills to mine information sources, the PMO reporting specialist should also inherently understand the business so as to anticipate what information end users need and how that information will be used.

- **Analyst**: The analyst should be adept at mining actionable information from various data sources, spotting trends, and recognizing emerging issues. To accomplish this, the analyst must have a certain level of intuition about what information is viable and a keen sense of how different types of information are related.

- **Financial specialist**: Everyone wants to know, "What does it really cost?" or "What did we really get?" Every PMO needs someone who can deftly turn labor, time, benefits, and other elements into dollars and sense, as well as act as a liaison with the accounting department. A PMO financial specialist should be as comfortable with a business plan as an accounting ledger, know his or her way around a project schedule, and be adept in various investment valuation techniques.

- **Marketer**: For the PMO to effectively influence without authority it must successfully promote its concepts, information, and processes to an often wary and fickle audience. The marketer constructs internal campaigns to gain buy-in and compliance for process improvements and other alignment initiatives. Do not underrate this skill—sessions where practitioners relate how they market their programs to their organizations with inventive and catchy approaches often draw the biggest crowds at user groups and industry forums.

MAINTAINING PMO CONTINUITY

As we write this, the world is slowly emerging from a global recession; many PMOs fell victim to significant cost-cutting measures during the downturn. Current economics aside, most organizations routinely go through business cycles, including periods when cost control becomes paramount.

Rather than facing the start up of a new PMO while on the path to recovery, there is a strong argument for maintaining continuity of PMO assets and functions in such circumstances, even if it is greatly scaled back. Besides avoiding the loss of your substantial investment in time and intellectual capital, there are certain critical services that the PMO can provide to help reduce costs wisely, keep systems functional though a lean period, and put the organization in a better position to quickly ramp up innovation during revitalization. Being the first mover coming out of an economic downturn has historically proven to be one of the greatest advantages a business can have.

The processes and infrastructure that a PMO puts in place will need to be ready to support new investments if organizations are to get maximum benefit from a period of growth. If an existing PMO is shut down and all of its staff members are released, it is unlikely that a new manager tasked to restart the PMO later will embrace abandoned systems, tools, and processes. Without PMO continuity, the organization loses its knowledge base and its ability to keep management assets maintained in a functional state. In the end, the cost of missed opportunity and restarting the PMO will far outweigh the additional savings gained by temporarily cutting a few more staff members. Consider retaining a minimum PMO staff during a period of retraction to maintain basic support functions, keep systems operable, provide continuity of intellectual assets, and greatly reduce PMO recovery time and expenses.

In the final analysis, the functions performed by a PMO must be done, the effort must be expended, and the results achieved; it is simply a matter who does the work and at what cost relative to the quality of the outcomes. By concentrating common business management and integration functions into a dedicated center of excellence to improve efficiency and effectiveness, organizations are finding that a well-managed PMO is becoming an increasingly essential element of the overall governance structure.

KEY POINTS IN THIS CHAPTER

☑ As the challenges of managing modern dynamic environments continue to increase, the PMO has emerged as a mechanism to foster alignment across a broad footprint in today's organizations.

☑ For organizations that choose to apply portfolio management, the support of a PMO may make the difference between successfully reaping its value or struggling to make the practice viable.

☑ The PMO is a valuable resource in helping to identify problems and opportunities; provide information; manage portfolio processes and decision parameters; provide analytical assistance, capabilities, and tools; and ultimately, to help make resulting decisions actionable.

☑ The PMO can help provide continuity for portfolios, ranging from strategic intent to making investment decisions and executing work.

☑ The PMO is a logical point to assess the true benefit of products, assets, and services delivered.

☑ The PMO can ensure that related business processes form a single cohesive network.

☑ The scope of work and resource management interests of the PMO should span the total demand of the organization it supports and include the workforce needed to accomplish the body of work.

☑ To be successful, the PMO must have consistent and visible executive sponsorship so that it has the leverage needed to influence the organization and the support for its mission.

☑ It is critical that the PMO be clearly chartered with objectives and functional responsibilities that facilitate decision making and corrective actions; this keeps the PMO from becoming just a passive reporting function that contributes little value.

☑ Extra care should be taken to ensure that the PMO is supported as it matures to avoid the trap of constantly setting up, abandoning, and then restarting PMO initiatives.

☑ PMO staffing needs to address the scope of services it provides, the skills needed to provide those services, and adequate members to deliver those services to its constituency.

☑ Consider maintaining a minimum PMO staff during periods of economic adversity to ensure change management processes and systems are ready to take advantage of inevitable upswings

CHAPTER 17
CREATING A PORTFOLIO PROCESS MAP

THROUGHOUT THIS BOOK, we have necessarily touched on a host of different business functions as we described how to apply portfolios. Sometimes the discussion has been at a conceptual level about a general topic. Other times, we have delved deeper into subjects, including the use of specific process flowcharts. Through all of this, we have consistently used the portfolio ecosystem in figure 1-1 on page 9 as a visual reference to show how different portfolios and business functions work together to manage change.

However, to meet the working-level requirements for implementing portfolio management, we need a more robust map. It should still give us a unified view of core change management processes, but we need enough detail to map specific functions and their interactions in a format that is better suited to using established process development tools and techniques.

This chapter builds on several of the basic portfolio management concepts we have already introduced to construct an integrated portfolio process map. We provide a generic example map and explain its underlying framework so that you can create a process map to reflect the specifics of your organization.

This process map is an invaluable tool for depicting operational interdependencies across the organization and for deploying portfolio management. To that end, we leverage the portfolio process map in the remaining chapters in this section for several different implementation-related purposes.

MODELING THE PROCESS OF CHANGE

Maps have been important instruments of progress since man first etched mountains and rivers on cave walls. Throughout history, a good map has been essential to anyone whose business depended on knowing location, direction, and distance.

You are probably familiar with several modern mapping technologies; in a remarkably short period, these devices have become so ingrained in our daily lives that we now take them for granted. For decades, satellite images have allowed us to make better maps, study geology, and forecast the weather. Now, Global Positioning Systems (GPS) allow us to navigate in real time from our automobile dashboard, PDA, or cell phone. Regardless of the platform or its use, maps allow us to better understand our environment, locate where we are, and track changes in our position.

A process map gives you these same capabilities to visualize and manage your business environment. In the same way that cartographers and navigators use a commonly accepted set of coordinates, standards, and descriptions for geographical maps, we apply some of the concepts introduced in the opening chapters to create a universal framework that generally describes the world of change management.

Mapmakers overlay roads, subways, and points of interest on a geographic topography; we will use the portfolio management framework as a foundation to visualize the network of processes and information flows, along with the supporting tools and infrastructure that make up our business environment.

Creating your own process map affords your organization a comprehensive vantage point to measure and control how the business ecosystem operates as a single dynamic entity. It also enables you to anticipate unintentional consequences that you may otherwise miss if you narrowly focus your process improvement efforts.

BUILDING A FRAMEWORK FOR THE PROCESS MAP

Process architects often use an open-ended flowchart to depict a single process. An off-page initiating event "from somewhere" triggers some defined left-to-right sequence of actions to culminate in a given result. To border our efforts, we do not give much thought to "what initiated the initiator," nor do we often dwell on what happens next to "the result." Both the preceding and subsequent events at either end of the target process are handily out of scope.

But, as the portfolio ecosystem concept points out and the process map will illustrate, no single process adds bottom-line value or operates as an independent function; like the parts of an engine, each must work together (with a minimum of friction!) to deliver optimum results. Thus, the objective of the process map is to provide a blueprint of how major portfolio management functions interact so that they can be designed and managed to efficiently operate as a single cohesive network.

However, first we must lay out the basic topography for our map. We refer to this first layer as our framework, and we will use that to lay out our core portfolio management processes.

Defining Basic Framework Relationships

We introduced the fundamental relationships between demand, capacity, cost, and benefit in chapter 6. We will use the relationships between these elements and how they relate to the cycle of change to begin forming the general topography for our process map, as shown figure 17-1.

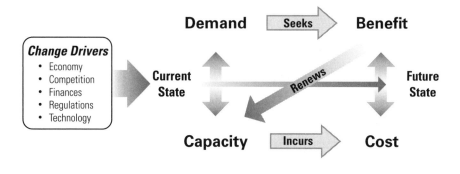

Figure 17-1: Using Portfolio Balancing Act Relationships to Develop the Process Framework

The process of fulfilling demand by consuming capacity to produce benefit is a reasonable description of "work." (Cost is an unfortunate and inevitable consequence.) The idea that we need to perform work to move the organization forward becomes the anchor point for relating processes to this framework. The process functions that directly depict work as it moves through the cycle of change will occupy the center of the framework.

With work processes located along the centerline of our process map, we will logically place any processes associated with managing demand and benefit in the upper half and those that manage capacity and costs in the lower portion.

Referring back to our portfolio ecosystem, we segregated the cycle of change into some major phases including operational planning, investment analysis, work and resource management, and value delivery. We apply these basic phases to sequence how change traverses the framework, which helps us locate specific process functions relative to the phases they support. Figure 17-2 gives us the basic coordinates of our process framework.

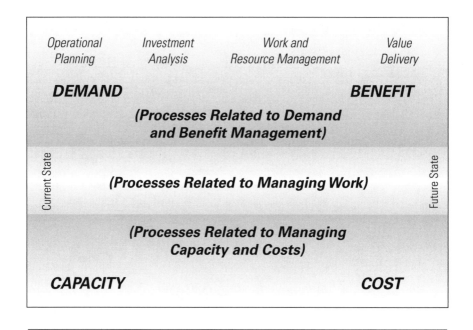

Figure 17-2: Basic Coordinates of the Process Framework

Locating Processes Within the Framework

Before we can begin to locate individual processes on our framework, we first need to identify the core processes we want to include. For our example process map, we will concentrate on the processes that we have discussed that relate to managing change and using portfolios. These are processes that we have covered that directly relate to managing work:

- Intake (request) management
- Planning and estimating
- Project management

- General work management
- Product and service delivery

These are the processes that we have discussed that are involved with demand management:

- Operational planning
- Investment analysis
- Benefit management
- Program management

These are the processes that we are most interested in and that are associated with managing capacity:

- Resource management
- Financial management
- Asset and infrastructure management

Finally, measuring operational performance is the leading function for analyzing the current state of the organization, and it is integral to all other processes.

When developing your own process map, we encourage you to modify our basic list and include the processes and terminology that works best for your organization. Regardless of the processes you select, you should be able to find a home for them on the general topography we have described. For example, if you need to include inventory management, manufacturing, or logistics as key processes, just remember that they all relate to managing a type of capacity. If customer relationship management is a critical process, note that it is a mechanism for managing demand.

Given the topography of the framework and the scope of processes to be included, we can begin to establish their relative location based on their relationship with each other and the phases of the change cycle where they are active. Note that locating processes on the framework is just an interim exercise to help facilitate general placement of their underlying functions. We are including it here to describe the general approach that we take when constructing a portfolio process map.

Figure 17-3 is an example of how these processes roughly fall within the coordinates of the framework. In this rendition, you can begin to get an idea of how you will be able to use the framework in discussions about how your organization operates.

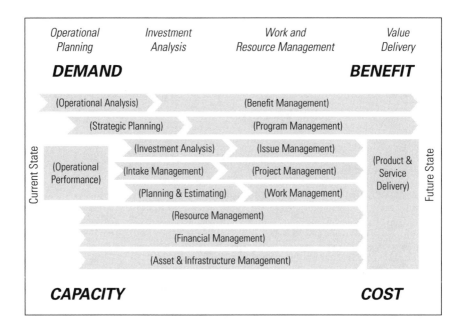

Figure 17-3: Locating Portfolio Processes on the Framework

MAPPING PROCESS FUNCTIONS TO THE FRAMEWORK

Identifying Process Functions

In chapter 3, we defined a process as a pre-established, event-triggered sequence of actions that produces a specified result. You can generally describe any process by the handful of major functions that it performs. As a simple example, the benefit management process (sometimes referred to as benefit realization) includes the following basic functions:

- Define target benefits.
- Manage benefit design.
- Manage benefit development.
- Measure benefits delivered.

In most cases, accomplishing any given function requires you to perform several discrete steps, but the function itself represents a primary activity that contributes to achieving the process objective.

More complex processes might include a dozen or more functions, and some of those may run in parallel or be repeated multiple times; for example, as a process, "Project Management" includes functions such as defining requirements, design, development, work planning, managing issues, scope management, risk management, scheduling, progress reporting, and quality management, among others. It is important to recognize the following about process functions:

- Performance of each function is triggered by the output of some upstream function.
- Each function adds incremental value.
- The result becomes an input to one or more subsequent functions, no matter which process those downstream functions reside in.

Some functions within one process will have relationships with those of another. For example, Project Management functions must interact with those in other processes such as investment analysis, resource management, procurement, financial management, and so on.

After we identify the major functions for each process we want to include in our map, the next step is to collectively locate them on the framework.

Completing the Portfolio Process Map

Locating all the functions on the framework to create a process map is a bit like working a jigsaw puzzle. Each function is placed relative to its logical sequencing, the phase it occurs in, and how it interacts with nearby functions. Depending on the processes you have identified, this may mean that you will have to make some practical concessions with respect to your interim process layout, such as we illustrated in figure 17-3. It is more important that the final layout depicts the functions and their major interrelationships in a manner that reasonably reflects how your organization works (or in the case of designing improvements, how it should work). Figure 17-4 is a simple example process map based on the processes we identified earlier and their functions, which provides a visual review of the subjects we have discussed.

In actual practice, you may want to include more functional detail in your process map than the example we provide. However, the functional view of the process map is most useful when you can keep it on a single page. Additional detail can be added later as subsequent layers of the map. Consider the functional level of your process map as the *visual table of contents* for how your organization works and the guidance it uses.

You can easily see how any one of the functions we show on our version would include another level of process detail. Process steps depict the sequence of specific actions needed to execute a given process function. These steps are often reflected in the familiar flowcharts, swim lane diagrams, or documented procedural guidance we commonly see whenever discussing processes. This level of detail is ultimately necessary for those who must execute or manage processes on a daily basis. You should establish the level of guidance provided by process steps with input from managers, designers, and users as to how much detail is necessary and appropriate.

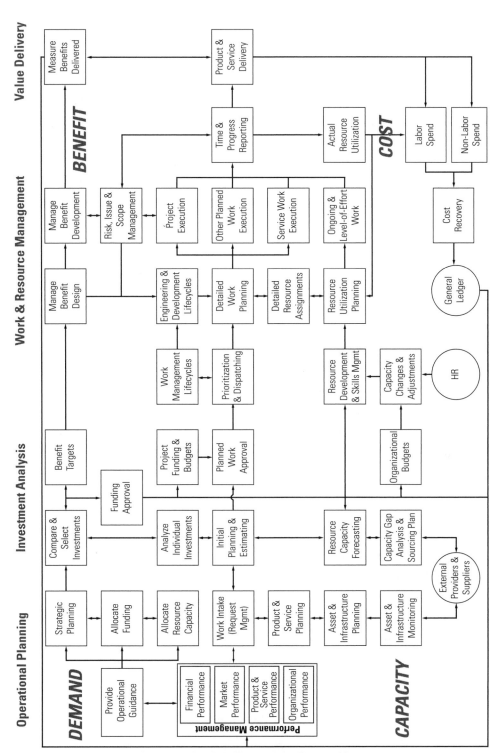

Figure 17-4: Example Integrated Portfolio Management Process Map

Insights Gained from Developing a Process Map

Once you are able to get a unified view of your processes and functions as a single comprehensive network, new insights begin to emerge about how your organization operates.

First, you'll recognize that most, if not all of the process functions shown are being performed simultaneously as a normal part of business. We tend to think of a process as a series of sequential left-to-right events that occur and then stop; in reality, many are ongoing functions that create a highly dynamic, machine-like environment with many moving parts that are always running.

For example, even as a project is underway to execute a given strategy, someone is likely re-assessing strategy, which may affect the continued need for the project deliverable. Resource assignments are constantly adjusted based on work progress, emerging new activities, movement of staff within the organization, or changes in priority. Product and service performance is under continual scrutiny compared to shifting customer demand and market forces, and those results potentially affect investment portfolios and capacity planning. Each function represents a flurry of continuous activity: taking in information, adding incremental value, and passing it forward. This explains why even minor, seemingly contained changes to the demand-capacity/cost-benefit equilibrium can have far-reaching and unintended implications.

Second, you can determine how you might define and measure organizational performance. Making comparisons along the horizontal or vertical axis of the process framework allows you to derive many common business metrics. You can also collect information about the location of any single element as it traverses through processes. As functions act on an entity, you can intercept and employ information about status for performance management purposes.

The process function view in figure 17-4 strikes a balance between providing a comprehensive, single-page perspective of the model while offering sufficient detail to support many different management functions. It offers a clear view of the interface points between different functional groups and gives managers a better understanding of how their inputs and outputs affect overall operations.

The underlying process steps delineate how business functions are executed, which allows an organization to completely catalog, communicate, control, and revise the working-level details required to operate the entire ecosystem. For organizations that want to go to this level of sophistication, the process map makes an excellent basis for designing and configuring an automated business process management (BPM) system, as we discuss later.

APPLICATION OF THE PROCESS MAP

Having a universally recognized and understood single point of reference of how the organization operates offers significant advantages when managing daily operations, looking for efficiency opportunities, or analyzing the impacts of change. The portfolio process map provides a single common blueprint of related management functions to model and mange key aspects of your business environment—your people, the work they do, and information and supporting technology. It is a mechanism to:

- unify perspectives,
- improve performance, and
- manage enabling technology.

We briefly describe the major benefits of the process map as a prelude to how we can apply it later to implement portfolio management and supporting technology.

Achieving Organizational Alignment

As organizations continue to develop into ever-more complex global and virtual environments, it is becoming increasingly difficult to keep everyone focused on a common set of objectives. Organizational compartmentalization and specialization can further narrow perspectives of the business, which erodes alignment and collaboration.

The magnitude of the issue should not be underestimated—these are among the areas that have the greatest impact on organizational effectiveness and efficiency. Referencing another major finding of the PMO survey as illustrated in figure 3-1 on page 29, "departmental silos" were ranked as the single greatest operational challenge, with 66 percent of respondents listing them as a "Critical Problem" or "Significant Issue."

What is perhaps less evident is that organizational separation is unwittingly propagated by building "process silos." While highly tuned approaches that cater to specialized areas of the business are useful to make a particular functional area more efficient, they can have unintentional consequences if you do not manage their adoption within the broader organizational context. Communication barriers arise when a specialized approach unilaterally attaches a different meaning to commonly used business language or introduces unique terminology that other areas of the organization do not share or understand.

This situation is exacerbated when multiple standards or methodologies are used to manage different areas of the process map. Standards and methodologies are independently developed and controlled by different governing bodies such as professional associations, government agencies, international standards groups, or vendor consortiums. As a result, it is easy to see how overlaps and gaps might be created as they are applied to different functions on the process map. Even homegrown processes and methodologies are not immune to this issue.

As the process map aptly demonstrates, different groups must interact with each other to accomplish common business functions. When multiple approaches lay claim to the same process function, conflicts for ownership and management of the function or the process inevitably arise. Gaps are also created when interacting functions are not fully incorporated into, or recognized by, adjacent methodologies.

A comprehensive process map that describes how functions interact is an effective tool for managing the adoption and interaction of specialized standards, methodologies, or bodies of knowledge. Using the process map to draw lines of demarcation between certain functions that fall under the control of one approach versus another avoids the issue of conflicting terms and approaches. You can also apply such boundaries to clarify responsibility for who defines and manages process functions. Of equal importance is the identification of orphan functions that do not fall within the scope of any of the approaches as defined, or that do not have a designated owner.

Silos also emerge as a result of different perspectives in the hierarchy of leadership. To achieve integrated operations across multiple departments or lines of business, executives must define and actively articulate a common vision, while still managing their respective areas of responsibility. Department heads have a similar responsibility to ensure that their groups recognize and embrace the interdependencies between each other to function effectively.

The process map illustrates that regardless of where each group in the organization "lives" within the ecosystem, functional relationships cross department boundaries and management levels in all directions. Instilling this view among the staff helps foster improved relationships and cooperation.

Improving Business Performance

The interconnected network of processes and business functions within your organizational ecosystem are the highways on which work and information travels. Accordingly, there is a direct link between the rate of work throughput (efficiency) you can achieve and the effectiveness of your process network. Traffic jams or poorly designed intersections can snarl up the flow of work or information along these process roadways.

You can apply the process map in a number of ways to ensure that the organization is operating at peak efficiency. As an inventory of core business functions, it provides a method for systematically assessing the effectiveness of those functions. Because the functions are displayed relative to their associated process streams, the performance of the processes themselves can be analyzed and measured. We further explore how to use the process map as an assessment tool in chapter 19 "Implementing Portfolio Management."

Automating the process map using business process management (BPM) technology raises performance assessment and management to the next level. Like a control center that dynamically monitors and adjusts traffic controls in a metropolitan area, an organization can interface the process map with enabling applications to provide a real-time command system that manages operational performance.

An automated dynamic model of your process map can assist in *what-if* analysis to assess the effect of proposed changes. By automating the framework, you can introduce potential changes into a baseline model to test for unforeseen impacts and consequences. For example, transferring capacity from one type of demand to another because of a growing backlog may cause another problem to emerge elsewhere. Because of the interconnected nature of process functions, removing a performance barrier at any one point often simply moves the traffic jam a little further downstream, resulting in little or no net business benefit. Such information allows stakeholders to understand cause and effect before any functional changes are actually undertaken.

Managing Enabling Technology

An increasingly serious issue in many organizations is the unfettered expansion of business applications that are used to facilitate the business. This happens as a result of mergers and acquisitions, when different groups independently acquire different but functionally similar solutions, or simply because a mechanism to identify and decommission obsolete platforms has not yet been put in place.

The incremental costs associated with a bloated portfolio of business applications can become staggering. In addition to the money wasted on the initial purchase of duplicate systems and the inherent inefficiencies they create, the ongoing costs associated with maintenance and licensing, support, upgrades, and training, along with the incremental costs of associated supporting hardware, infrastructure, and facilities can consume a significant portion of the overall technology budget, leaving little room for truly innovative advances. In chapter 18, "Leveraging Technology," we explain how to use the process map to analyze your current application footprint, develop strategies to consolidate applications, and manage interfaces between different systems.

THE ROLE OF THE PMO IN CREATING THE PROCESS MAP

As discussed in chapter 3, processes play a critical role in general business and in portfolio management. Associated functions (including process design and improvement, process automation, process ownership, process metrics and audits) are among the most common PMO activities cited by our PMO survey respondents.

From an integrated portfolio management perspective, individual processes need to seamlessly connect core transformation activities as a single network of change management guidance through the ecosystem. Such an initiative requires alignment across different departments and levels of the organization. Adequate staff with the necessary skills and experience is also necessary to consistently manage and maintain processes as an ongoing program. The PMO is a logical point of ownership and motive force for establishing a cohesive portfolio process map.

The PMO itself has a major stake in the effectiveness of business processes. As a group that must span multiple parts and layers of the organization, processes are the primary method for the PMO to gather information and exert influence, given that it has no direct authority over the organizations it seeks to align. All of these factors make the PMO a natural custodian of the network of processes within an organization.

KEY POINTS IN THIS CHAPTER

☑ For portfolio practitioners to be effective at initiating and controlling changes in their organizations, they must have a functional understanding of their environment.

☑ A model of portfolio management processes give us a visual map that describes the organization and how various functions and groups within it interact as a collective entity.

☑ The benefits of applying the portfolio process map include:

- Better organizational alignment when reacting to change

- Improved business performance by focusing on performance measures

- Enabling technology to leverage the change events

☑ The process map can be used to align disparate elements of the organization, whether they are groups, methodologies, standards, or perspectives.

☑ The process map also gives us a platform to define key performance measures, assess effectiveness, identify bottlenecks, and monitor the flow of work and information through the organization.

☑ The portfolio process map offers new insights into how the organization functions to manage change.

☑ A process-based model of our environment gives us an operational baseline to identify, communicate, and control changes within it.

☑ An important part of building change management competency is recognizing that portfolio management processes are both change enablers and targets of change themselves.

CHAPTER 18

LEVERAGING TECHNOLOGY

THE ROLE OF TECHNOLOGY
IN PORTFOLIO MANAGEMENT

WITHOUT QUESTION, MODERN INFORMATION TECHNOLOGY plays an important role in our ability to practically apply portfolios in the ways we have suggested. Comprehensive portfolio management is a relatively new discipline, in part because the enabling information management capabilities have only become available within the past several years. Some may find this to be a surprising statement, but the basis for it will be more evident as you read through this chapter.

If any readers still doubt that the pace of change is as significant as we have suggested, consider that it was not that long ago that computer support for the portfolio ecosystem consisted of little more than a few mainframe programs to manage financial and logistical transactions. Everything else was slow and labor intensive, relying on huge numbers of staff armed with drafting boards, electric erasers, typewriters, and carbon paper. The use of computerized scheduling systems was limited to only the largest of projects because of the size, cost, and complexity of the applications.

Today, your organization probably has one or more specialized software applications to support many of the functions on our example portfolio process map. This is a bit of a "good news, bad news" situation; the good news is that the information used for portfolio purposes is more likely now than ever to be available in digital format. The bad news is that this information is equally likely to be located in any number of different software systems, databases, and files, from myriad spreadsheets and documents in desktop applications to centralized (and tightly controlled) corporate financial systems. When we review how an organization is implementing portfolio management capability, we rarely find that there are no supporting applications—we usually find that there are too many.

As organizations first embark on a portfolio management initiative, there is often some debate and confusion about the technology capabilities that are required. Simply having systems that give you capabilities for portfolio-related functions is not enough. For example, software packages designed primarily to support the needs of project managers may not be able to provide project portfolio management capabilities. Although the application may contain some information that can be used in a project portfolio, it still needs to be presented as part of a defined collection of projects that includes all information that is pertinent to decision making.

Information related to work, resources, money, and deliverables constitutes the data of primary interest to portfolio management. The discipline requires that you be able to collect, store, associate, retrieve, display, and analyze that information in a way that empowers you to make good business decisions and then to act on them. Thus, the primary technology challenge to implementing portfolio management for most organizations is how to gather and present a variety of information about a number of different business elements, often from a variety of different platforms.

In this chapter, we first show you how to apply the portfolio process map from the last chapter to assess and improve your current technology. There are two aspects to this discussion—enabling your processes and enabling portfolios. Second, we discuss practices for implementing a portfolio management system, with particular emphasis on dispelling some common myths and misconceptions about portfolio management tools and vendors.

DEFINING PORTFOLIO TECHNOLOGY RELATIONSHIPS

The portfolio process map we introduced in the preceding chapter is a great tool for describing and managing relationships between business functions and supporting technology. These relationships are important because the applications that you use to support different business functions throughout the change continuum ultimately define what technological improvements you may need to consider when implementing portfolio management.

To begin, imagine using a projector to place the portfolio process map on a whiteboard so that a team of business analysts can mark how different software tools currently support each function; figure 18-1 illustrates what such a session might yield.

Although your exercise might produce different results, it is not uncommon to discover that the same degree of gaps and overlaps exists between different applications as those we discussed previously about methodologies and standards. You might find instances where multiple applications support a single function depending on which group performs that function. In several cases, the team may not know what systems are being used, particularly if the process itself is not formally defined. Depending on your organization, perhaps some of the tactical functions are left up to the discretion of individual managers. In those

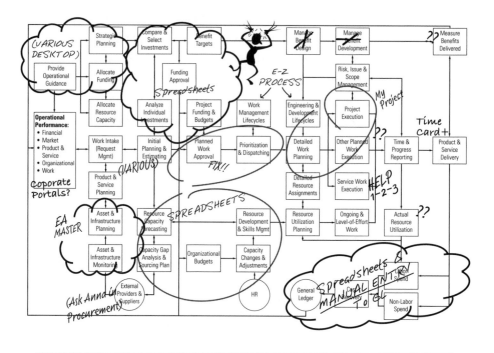

Figure 18-1: Results of Software Application Mapping Exercise

cases, supporting technology ranges from using personal documents or spreadsheets to using the task management capabilities in your e-mail system. Of course, we cannot forget the low-tech and popular approach of keeping a running to-do list on your whiteboard, cordoned off in the corner with a "do not erase" warning scribbled below it.

The gaps and overlaps you discover represent potholes along your portfolio information highway. The important thing to recognize from the technology mapping exercise is that supporting software provides two related but different capabilities: a way to share data among various business functions and a way to create, view, and manipulate portfolios of information.

An automotive analogy may help explain—the portfolio process framework as a whole represents your organizational vehicle. The different functions within it and the underlying technology that supports them form the engine of business that powers your organization forward. However, in addition to ample power, you also need a way to steer the business in the direction you need it to go, and that is the role of portfolios.

Your first job is to get the engine of business to run smoothly and to generate plenty of horsepower. To do this you need the free flow of data between the different functions and supporting software platforms. To the extent that you are able to tightly integrate all the functions, applications, and information within the portfolio process map, you will have the different moving parts of the business engine working well together.

However, you still need a mechanism to direct its power and manage the organizational throttle. Thus, the second technological consideration is that you need to be able to tap into the information within business functions in a manner that enables portfolio views. To get business value from these portfolios, you also need to be able to add or modify information to carry out the decisions you make, which allows you to control and steer the organizational vehicle.

Again, these are related but different technological considerations. You can pull portfolio information from an array of disparate databases and systems to create portfolios, but if the business functions do not operate smoothly, you may not have enough power to move your decisions forward. Conversely, a powerful, highly tuned power plant is most effective when you manage it to efficiently drive the organization where it needs to go.

Integrating Technology Applications

Referencing figure 18-2, wherever you have adjacent applications that support related functions on the portfolio process map, there is a transfer of information. The more separate applications you use to enable the continuum of change, the greater the number of transfer points. At each data junction, transfers are enabled either by a technology interface or human intervention. Both add incremental costs and levels of complexity to business operations, however human intervention also introduces the added potential for slowdowns, bottlenecks, and errors.

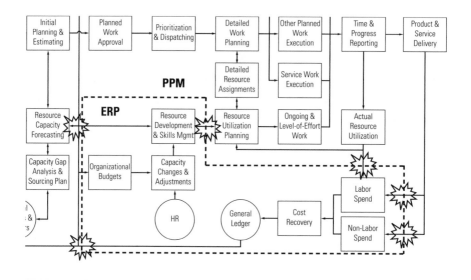

Figure 18-2: Example Interface Points Between Adjacent Supporting Applications

Organizations that have several different systems in place to support their process map face making trade-off decisions when interfacing supporting technology, such as:

- Creating direct data interfaces between existing applications
- Consolidating information using a data warehouse approach
- Consolidating applications to reduce the number of interfaces needed

Each option has costs, risks, and benefits that differ depending on circumstances. However, reducing the number of applications that you use across the portfolio process map is always a desirable condition for a number of reasons, including:

- Better data integration and access with fewer external interfaces
- Fewer user interfaces improve use and adoption

- Greater potential for more streamlined and consistent processes
- Less risk of process gaps and overlaps
- Reduced technical complexity, risk, and maintenance
- Lower total cost of ownership due to economies of scale, fewer vendors, fewer licenses, and so on

Using the portfolio process map as an integral part of an application portfolio rationalization initiative can help you assess your "as-found" state by aligning software with supported business services, identify consolidation opportunities, and allow you to envision and communicate the "to-be" streamlined future state.

Establishing Portfolio Management Capabilities

Once you have the types of portfolio information needed readily accessible from across the process map, the next technological consideration is presenting it in a manner that allows you to perform portfolio management actions. As we have addressed throughout the book, portfolios give you the means to define, view, and manipulate information. Although these three functions should be essentially seamless and transparent to the end user, they each represent different technical capabilities that you need to consider when developing or acquiring portfolio management technology.

Defining Portfolio Information

Defining portfolio information is associated with gathering the right information to suit the decisions you need to make. Thus, a portfolio management platform should structure data to define the subjects of the portfolio and the kinds of measures or attributes that you want to use to compare those subjects.

(Depending on your technical background, an important point regarding this process may not be obvious: Users are not actually moving information into a portfolio, just reading it from a defined location. This allows multiple users to simultaneously access the same information and use it in different ways.)

Individual portfolio users have different requirements for what their particular portfolio might contain at any given time. For example, most users will have portfolio definitions that they consistently use to manage their ongoing responsibilities. The contents and values included in the portfolio will change, but the definition of the information required is constant. At other times, users will have a unique need that requires a specific portfolio definition created on an ad hoc basis.

These considerations mean that users need both the ability to define the portfolio information they need and a mechanism to name, store, modify, and delete these definitions. Additionally, they need to be able to refresh and/or save the results of a particular query for baseline, reporting, and "as of" reference purposes.

Establishing the access rights of each user is an additional consideration associated with defining portfolio information. This is where having defined information structures for your people, money, work, and deliverables as described in chapter 5 comes into play. A full-featured portfolio management platform should give you the ability to define these structures, gather and store all four types of information within them, and provide the means to administer and control user rights to various levels of information in each structure as read-only or read-write access.

Viewing Portfolio Information

Viewing portfolio information involves presenting it in different ways so that you can adequately analyze the results. One primary consideration is having the ability to easily compare the information associated with each subject. This would include being able to sort portfolio subjects by different parameters and using different analytical methods to view it. For example, you might be thinking of looking at portfolio data in a spreadsheet format, however, there are also graphical views that are very useful, such as the four-axis bubble chart shown in figure 13-2 on page 204.

In addition to comparing individual portfolio subjects, you will also want to be able to compare the total values of a given portfolio against defined portfolio targets. This is particularly useful when allocating capacities or managing investment portfolios. For example, given all of the subjects in my portfolio, what is the total amount of cost and effort that they represent? How does this compare to the target values I have established? What is the difference?

To support this, you should have the ability to change the status of different subjects in the portfolio to vary the total values of approved subjects versus those that you have rejected or that are still pending disposition. An example of this is shown in figure 13-3 on page 206.

While displaying the contents of the portfolio *as defined* is important, the more advanced commercial portfolio management technology also provides drill-down capabilities, which is very useful in allowing you to actively manage the portfolio. For example, while analyzing a strategic portfolio, you note that a certain strategy is exceeding its expected cost; the next logical action is to find out why. Being able to click on the strategy in question and view its associated projects allows you to quickly understand which projects are causing the overrun. Continuing to drill down into those projects and their performance measures provides you with additional insight into what is happening so you can take corrective action.

The examples thus far are related to the end user of the portfolio interface being able to view information directly. However, portfolio management is most effective when you are able to collaborate. This means that you should be able to share your portfolio views with others, either online or through various reporting mechanisms. As of this writing, some leading portfolio technology vendors give you the capability to embed portfolio information into common office platforms—*with drill-down capability.*

This functionality has significant implications for your ability to share portfolio information seamlessly across the organization, without ever logging in to your portfolio management system. You can now provide your company executives with the ability to call up and drill down into real-time graphical market performance information by product line and region without ever leaving their e-mail system. This technology now allows you to embed revenue pie charts into a slide deck and drill into the underlying data as an integral part of the presentation. With each passing year, modern technology is increasing the transportability of information, and product providers are finding new ways to leverage it to the advantage of their customers.

Manipulating Portfolio Information

Being able to effectively define and view portfolio information improves your decision-making capability. The ability to manipulate portfolio information means you can put your decisions in motion. Being able to change the source information from within your view requires real-time bidirectional data transfers. For example, if you have a portfolio of investments that you are analyzing, and you reach a decision about which investments you want to proceed with, your portfolio management platform should allow you to change the status of those investments and update the host data records accordingly. Conversely, if you do not like the way a particular strategy is developing, you should be able to put that strategy on hold until you can gather additional information.

This capability extends down to execution portfolios as well, enabling managers to reschedule work, reassign resources, accept scope changes, or resolve issues. While some of these features may actually occur with the applications you have drilled down to from within the portfolio, the end result should appear to be a highly efficient, fluid series of events to the end user—collect, analyze, decide, and *act*.

IMPLEMENTING PORTFOLIO TECHNOLOGY APPLICATIONS

The next chapter discusses implementing portfolio management in general terms, so we limit our discussion here to considerations for implementing supporting technology. As we have seen through the use of the portfolio process map in this chapter, the line between technology and processes is increasingly blurring. If you ask to view a particular process, chances go up each year that the response will include opening up a particular application. Processes describe what we do, and technology enables us to do it.

The sole purpose of any business application is to improve and enable your processes. It does not matter if it is for portfolio management, financial management, or any other group of business functions. To the extent that you have a good process foundation, software applications can help you automate and streamline the functions needed to execute them. If the target processes of an application are poorly defined, then the use of technology merely allows you to confuse the organization more efficiently.

A developmental dilemma arises when you employ software to support a process. The capabilities and functions of the application itself have an impact on exactly how you design the process. A great deal of published general process guidance is available, but almost all of it is suspiciously lacking the detailed steps about how to actually do something. Part of the reason is because those details will differ depending on the

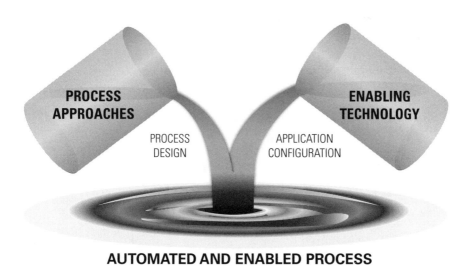

AUTOMATED AND ENABLED PROCESS

Figure 18-3: Co-developing Processes and Enabling Technology

type of enabling technology that you use. By definition, product-agnostic process guidance is inherently limited to how much detail it can offer, regardless of its source.

With that in mind, we recommend that you implement supporting technology and develop processes as an iterative, parallel endeavor (figure 18-3). Using the portfolio process map and guidance we have provided will help you narrow down your areas of interest and needed capabilities. Applications tend to align to certain approaches and functional areas. Your enterprise (IT) architecture preferences will also have a bearing on the products you consider. If you have particular policies, methodologies, or standards you want to support, that will assist you in continuing to narrow down the applications of interest. Specific objectives and key functionality requirements for your initiative will eventually lead you to a manageable list of applications and vendors that you can evaluate in more detail.

Co-developing processes and technology should begin in earnest during the evaluation phase; if a single vendor cannot support a particular process approach that you propose, ask them why. If none of the vendors can support it, ask yourself why. The reason is usually one of three likely options:

- You are proposing an approach that is not a generally accepted method for accomplishing the business function.
- You are talking with the wrong vendors.
- You are asking for something that is not technically feasible.

Given that software providers are in the business of supporting target process areas across a wide range of customers, they strive to design their capabilities based on how the majority of constituents successfully execute those processes. Inherent product flexibility has also increased dramatically through configuration choices. As a result, outright customization of software code for a particular customer is almost extinct. If you find that you consistently fall outside of the envelope of capabilities supported by leading vendors in that functional area, it should raise an immediate flag to your team. You may indeed discover that you have truly new or unique business requirements, but it is equally likely that there could be a better approach to achieving the desired results.

As you continue through the evaluation process, use it as an educational opportunity. You have at your disposal some of the best and most experienced authorities on what you are trying to achieve, and they will be eager to share their thoughts to win your business. Ask questions about your initiative and your approach. Seek out suggestions about how you might improve your potential for success. Most leading vendors have helped hundreds, if not thousands of customers go through the process you are just beginning; as a result, they know as well as anyone what works and what doesn't. Of course, you should not expect a single vendor representative to hold the combined experience of the entire corporation in his or her head, but the sales team members should be very knowledgeable about their product and customers and be willing to put you in contact with their subject experts.

Nontechnical vendor considerations are often as important as the software. When you narrow your portfolio technology down to the final few technology options, take the time to thoroughly understand the respective strengths, capabilities, and limitations—of the applications and the vendors. Any product design (not just software) reflects the philosophies and beliefs of the company that creates it. Make sure you understand and are comfortable with what those driving principles are as part of your selection process.

Look at the support they can provide to help your initiative. Given that application capabilities and process design are codependent, your software provider often functions as your process adviser as well. Make sure that your provider's expertise extends to include published guidance, plenty of training options, and robust consulting. Beware of situations where vendors rely only on third-party integrators to implement their solution. The software vendor should be fully committed to the long-term success of your portfolio initiative and providing a complete solution.

PORTFOLIO MANAGEMENT TECHNOLOGY FAQs

We find ourselves answering many questions (and refuting erroneous assumptions) about options and alternatives associated with portfolio management applications. What follows are answers to some of the more common subjects that we address.

"Should we purchase a site-installed portfolio application or lease it by going the SaaS route?"

Software as a Service (SaaS) is now a popular alternative to purchasing a business application and deploying it in your own environment. Typically, SaaS providers administer and host the software on their hardware from a remote location and lease the service to you under a periodic contract.

The initial investment in a SaaS application is less than purchasing and self-hosting an equivalent application. However, the total cost of ownership typically begins to reverse after 3 to 4 years of use, so be sure you evaluate comparable deployment options by calculating costs through several years of operation. You should also take into account the policies of your organization regarding preferences toward spending capital funds versus operational money.

The question of whether a SaaS application is *better* than a site-installed package is totally dependent on your business needs. One thing to consider is that vendors who offer either deployment model give you the option to start with a SaaS approach and later convert to an on-site installation. This gives you a low cost of entry to prove the capabilities, while opening up more choices as your needs change in the future.

Make sure you also consider your data integration needs between platforms; interface development approaches will probably differ depending on the deployment model.

Ultimately, we recommend that you separate the acquisition model from your analysis of capabilities; compare applications on a functional basis, and compare deployment options on a platform basis.

"Do we really need the complexity of an enterprise-class portfolio application?"

Consider that the needs you have today will likely be very different from your requirements 2 to 3 years from now as your portfolio skills and maturity levels increase. Enterprise software providers like to demonstrate the rich capabilities of their products, which can seem daunting to those who have relatively basic immediate needs. Make sure that the vendors you invite to demonstrate products understand your current specific interests and maturity levels and your long-term goals in advance.

The simplicity or sophistication of a portfolio application is primarily dictated by two factors: the user interface and how the product is configured. Many vendors offer the concept of "roles" to configure the user interface. Your processes ultimately drive the configuration of an application; elegant, streamlined processes tend to yield a straightforward user experience. Both processes and configuration are within the control of the implementing organization, which has a significant impact on how end users apply the product.

"Don't I need to buy all my software from the same vendor to get different applications to reliably work together?"

Not necessarily. Best-of-breed vendors can actually offer improved integration flexibility over big-box software providers, given that they need to design their systems to work with a wider array of platforms and architectures. Conversely, many software vendors acquire their capabilities by purchasing other companies; just because different applications have the same corporate logo, do not assume that they are all seamlessly integrated. Ask questions about whether the software was developed internally or acquired, and verify that the different applications you are considering will work well together.

"I used a particular software application in my last company and I had a (good or bad) experience; do I need to review the product again?"

Your last company has a culture, process orientation, and state of maturity that is probably not the same as your current employer. The software industry continues to move at a blistering pace. New platforms for collaboration, productivity, and performance measurement change the way you can use technology to address portfolio management functions. As you consider the business processes that you are automating, it is advisable to take a fresh look at the current offerings and technology options.

"It seems like portfolio management software is primarily designed for IT, will it work for my needs in other areas of the business?"

Each vendor has different target markets. Over the years some have focused on the business functions in IT, product portfolio management, or enterprise portfolio management. Others have focused on project management and offer limited portfolio functionality. The question to ask is "What business processes do I want to automate today and within the next 3 to 5 years?" Build your high level process maps and weight your selection criteria more heavily to your short-term needs without ignoring the long term. You know more about your immediate needs than your future needs. While some vendors continue to focus almost exclusively on one functional area, other enterprise portfolio management providers have expanded their interests to include idea management, corporate performance management, and other arenas.

KEY POINTS IN THIS CHAPTER

☑ Portfolio management technology serves two related but distinct functions:

- It enables the functions associated with the portfolio management process map.
- It allows you to define, collect, view, and manipulate portfolios of information.

☑ Whenever different applications supply the information that you need to make decisions about change events, an information integration point is created.

☑ Organizations that have several different systems supporting their process map need to make trade-off decisions among:

- Creating direct data interfaces between existing applications
- Consolidating information using a data warehouse approach
- Consolidating applications to reduce the number of interfaces needed

☑ It is always desirable to minimize the number of different applications that you use to support your portfolio ecosystem.

☑ Portfolio management applications include capabilities to define, view, store, and manipulate portfolio information, based on the needs of each user.

☑ Technology advancements offer a number of new methods for sharing portfolio information across your organization, including embedding graphics into your suite of typical office applications.

☑ Use an iterative development approach between process design and application configuration when implementing portfolio management technology.

☑ When evaluating applications, use it as an educational opportunity by asking the right questions of application providers.

☑ Nontechnical considerations are as important as application capabilities when evaluating portfolio management solution providers.

CHAPTER 19

IMPLEMENTING PORTFOLIO MANAGEMENT

PORTFOLIO MANAGEMENT INVOLVES an organization-wide set of business processes, and you should approach implementation as a long-term process improvement initiative. Implementing portfolio management is about changing how the organization works together. As a result, it is subject to the same dynamics as any other change event. Although cliché, it is indeed a marathon rather than a sprint. However, in this chapter, we offer an implementation approach that delivers near-term benefits with a positive return on your investment and a long-term process improvement program.

We recommend that you set a goal to methodically establish a level of parity in your competencies throughout the entire portfolio ecosystem. We have emphasized the importance of the interrelationships between the various business functions within the portfolio ecosystem. The game of golf illustrates the value of "playing the entire game." Becoming an expert with your putter is of little value if you are unable to keep your long shots on the fairway. Golfers intuitively understand that the key to improving their game begins with first concentrating on the fundamentals across all aspects of the game, and then building on that foundation to continue to refine their skills.

Similarly, your organization will perform at its best when it is able to execute portfolio management capabilities at a common level of maturity. For example, attaining a very high level of project planning and execution competency is of little value if you are weak in defining your strategies and making wise investment decisions. The result of such an imbalance could be that you execute the wrong changes more effectively, while wasting organizational capacities with great efficiency!

We recommend that you use the process map introduced in chapter 17 to identify your areas of relative strength versus those that need work. Improve the weak areas until those capabilities equal your strengths. Then you can go about the process of making small but steady improvements across all of your business functions, continually increasing your overall change management expertise until you are satisfied with your performance. The process of implementing portfolio management is not a single rotation through the cycle of change, but rather an iterative series of changes that build on past improvements to continually evolve and refine your portfolio management capabilities.

So, just how *do* you approach this undertaking? Actually, the answer lies in the very structure and content of this book. Consider this your first opportunity to apply the concepts and practices we have offered to facilitate a proactive change in your organization. What follows is an overview about how to initiate, plan, and execute your portfolio management initiative using the guidance we have offered.

ASSESSING YOUR CURRENT CAPABILITIES AND PERFORMANCE

Every journey begins with your starting point, and every initiative begins with assessing your current state. You should approach this analysis from several different perspectives to accurately determine what needs to be changed and why. This includes:

- A general operational assessment
- An organizational assessment
- A functional assessment of your change-related processes
- An assessment of your supporting technology (as discussed in the previous chapter)

Whether you treat the assessment process as informal as writing in the margins of this book or as structured as hiring an outside consultant and using industry benchmarks, the important thing is to first clearly identify the starting point of your journey. *Do not skip this step!!*

Before you can conduct these assessments, the first order of business is to define your scope of interest and influence. Given your role in the organization, are you in a position to sponsor this effort yourself, or is this something that you need to propose to others? As a C-level executive or leader of the Enterprise PMO, are you interested in taking an enterprise-wide approach to managing portfolios? If you are a department head or are in charge of a business unit, is your scope of interest limited to your own part of the organization? These answers shape your approach to the assessment process and the initiative.

Once you define your general scope of interest, you can begin to assess where you are in terms of performance. Consider the following questions as examples of those to include as part of a general operational performance assessment of your change-management capabilities:

- Does your organization have defined operational objectives?
- Are specific strategies in place to achieve those outcomes?
- Are objectives and strategies documented in an established business plan or road map?
- Are key stakeholders knowledgeable and supportive of them?
- Does your organization understand all of the demands being placed on it?

- Do you know how your people, money, or other core capacities are being utilized?
- Are you able to control demand within the limits of your capacities?
- Can you effectively innovate as well as operate?
- Do you know where your products and services are in their respective life cycles?
- Are they adequately meeting customer and market needs?
- Do you know what each one is costing you to deliver them?
- Can you effectively execute work on a tactical level?
- Are you in compliance with various requirements?
- Are your infrastructure and other assets sufficient for today? Tomorrow?

In addition to assessing your general operational performance, take an objective look at your organization itself as well; remember, your people are your raw material and most precious commodity. Assess organizational health by asking the following questions:

- Is your organization generally proactive or reactive?
- How is morale? Turnover? Integrity?
- Is your staff enthusiastically engaged in a common vision?
- How does your organization generally handle change? Crisis?
- Are reasonable expectations clearly defined and communicated?
- Is your organization accountable to those expectations?
- Does your organization easily collaborate across organizational boundaries, or are silo walls tall and thick?

Although general assessment questions help paint a picture of your current situation, process-specific questions help identify underlying causes and opportunities on a more functional level. To accomplish this, we once again turn to the portfolio process map to provide an assessment framework. Figure 19-1 shows how you can use a version of the map to assess the maturity and effectiveness of your core portfolio-related processes and functions.

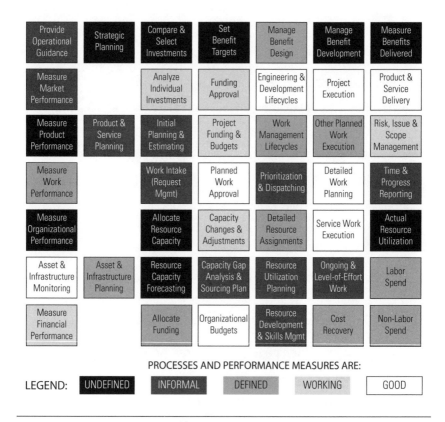

Provide Operational Guidance	Strategic Planning	Compare & Select Investments	Set Benefit Targets	Manage Benefit Design	Manage Benefit Development	Measure Benefits Delivered
Measure Market Performance		Analyze Individual Investments	Funding Approval	Engineering & Development Lifecycles	Project Execution	Product & Service Delivery
Measure Product Performance	Product & Service Planning	Initial Planning & Estimating	Project Funding & Budgets	Work Management Lifecycles	Other Planned Work Execution	Risk, Issue & Scope Management
Measure Work Performance		Work Intake (Request Mgmt)	Planned Work Approval	Prioritization & Dispatching	Detailed Work Planning	Time & Progress Reporting
Measure Organizational Performance		Allocate Resource Capacity	Capacity Changes & Adjustments	Detailed Resource Assignments	Service Work Execution	Actual Resource Utilization
Asset & Infrastructure Monitoring	Asset & Infrastructure Planning	Resource Capacity Forecasting	Capacity Gap Analysis & Sourcing Plan	Resource Utilization Planning	Ongoing & Level-of-Effort Work	Labor Spend
Measure Financial Performance		Allocate Funding	Organizational Budgets	Resource Development & Skills Mgmt	Cost Recovery	Non-Labor Spend

PROCESSES AND PERFORMANCE MEASURES ARE:

LEGEND: | UNDEFINED | INFORMAL | DEFINED | WORKING | GOOD |

Figure 19-1: Using the Portfolio Process Map to Assess Change Management Capabilities

Once you have constructed a process map that works for your organization, you can use it to ask the following types of questions about each function you have identified:

- Is the function part of a formally defined process?
- Is the function/process efficient and effective?
- Is the process being followed?
- Does it have performance measures and limits?
- Is there adequate supporting guidance?

- Does it have a clear point of ownership?
- Is it adequately enabled with appropriate technology?
- Are the supporting applications well integrated?
- Are we getting the information we need from them?

Alternatively, you may choose to model your assessment to follow industry models such as the CMMi model from the Software Engineering Institute, or the Project Management Institutes' OPM3 approach. Regardless of the method employed, the objective is to assess whether change-management process functions are formally defined and if so, whether they are understood, followed, and effective. As each important question is answered, a clear picture will begin to emerge of where you are today.

SETTING YOUR GOALS

Deciding to undertake a portfolio management initiative is a top-down prerogative that must have executive support. Ultimately, you need to approach implementing portfolio management as a strategic imperative for your organization. Otherwise, you are left trying to make incremental, tactical improvements as conditions and opportunities allow.

Once you have identified the sponsor of the process improvement initiative, get a clear understanding of the issues you and your sponsor wish to address. Change is almost always associated with some pain or fear of future pain. What is the concern you or the sponsor is expressing for the organization? Maybe projects are always late. Maybe your people are always overloaded with the wrong type of work. Perhaps strategic decisions are not being communicated and worked with the right levels of staffing or funding.

Once you know the issues that the sponsor considers important, make that your first priority for the implementation. It might be as simple as building a high level reporting process to inform the sponsor of the current work in the organization. We can tell many stories about how organizations have mobilized executive sponsors by giving them what they need first. We have seen implementations deliver real value to the sponsor just a few weeks after starting a longer term implementation initiative.

Use your assessment results to set objectives, prioritize gaps, and identify opportunities. If your assessment yielded the results in figure 19-1, then perhaps you would establish specific objectives for formalizing operational planning and supporting performance measures. Another objective might relate to how you would establish capacity planning and resource management capabilities. Yet another might focus on how you should analyze and prioritize work.

As plans and opportunities begin to emerge, think about how your objectives and strategies relate to each other. Begin to prioritize and sequence improvements relative to how much change you can reasonably expect to implement, the relative value of those improvements, and how they affect different parts of the organization. You can run multiple improvement projects in parallel in different parts of the organization.

Your goal should be to determine which areas represent the greatest need, in balance with the best opportunities to be successful. Work with your sponsor to organize short-term and long-term goals. Again referring to the assessment results in figure 19-1, deciding to formalize your operational planning in the absence of a currently defined process is an objective that has the potential to yield substantial results. Given that anything will likely be an improvement over your current approach, it is low risk. It directly affects a comparatively small number of staff, is relatively fast and easy to implement, and the technological footprint is manageable. It also actively involves and benefits the senior leadership of the organization.

The beauty of leading with such an approach is that as a natural result it also helps drive further improvements. Once a well-defined operational planning process is established, members of the leadership team will be anxious to make sure it is equally well executed so they can see the benefit of their strategies!

Continue to define your objectives to build a long-term improvement program that takes into account how much financial and organizational capacity you are willing to invest in this initiative for each period.

As objectives for the initiative are identified, you can begin to formulate strategies, brainstorm ideas, and define improvement opportunities in specific, actionable terms.

PRIORITIZING YOUR PROCESS IMPROVEMENT OPPORTUNITIES

By assessing your current capacities and setting goals for your improvement program, you will identify process improvement opportunities. Each opportunity represents a potential investment option to consider, aligned to your overall objectives. As we discussed in section 4 "Investment Analysis," consider each item based on its own merits, including its benefit, costs, and risks. Each opportunity should also identify the capacities that will be needed, specific stakeholders, and success measures.

When developing your investment opportunities, we encourage you to define them so that each one represents a discrete improvement with a specific, measurable business result. It is equally important to avoid long, overly complex projects that try to do too much at a time. Focus on specific processes or functions within a process, and limit their duration to 3 to 6 months each.

As you analyze your opportunities and make selections, try to arrange them so that you are able to execute multiple projects simultaneously in different areas of the organization, up to your allotted capacity limits. Referring to our example assessment results in figure 19-1, as you are implementing a formalized operational planning process with the senior leadership team, you could also be implementing time reporting improvements for your current level of work planning. Once again, it is a relatively simple, low risk, high value project, but this time it involves staff at a tactical level. As a result, it is functionally and technologically independent of the operational planning initiative, yet the results of time reporting will provide insights into current state utilization. This information is important for improving capacity management and better enabling operational planning.

IMPLEMENTING IMPROVEMENTS

Leveraging the PMO

A portfolio management office (PMO) is a valuable way to manage your portfolio management initiative. The PMO is in a position to give the initiative momentum and oversight. As with any cultural change for an organization, there are layers of involvement in implementing portfolio management as shown in figure 19-2.

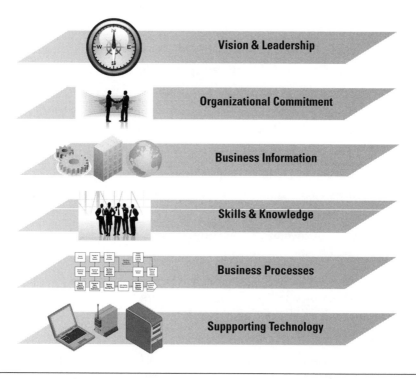

Figure 19-2: Implementing Portfolio Management Involves Changes on Many Levels

It begins with the vision and leadership to drive the initiative forward and continues with communicating the case for action and setting expectations to build organizational commitment. Portfolio management improves your ability to create and leverage accurate business information and supports performance measures, which affects how information is gathered and managed. For the initiative to be successful, individuals may need new skills and capabilities to help the organization operate differently. The organization collectively applies those skills and knowledge to execute new or improved processes, supported by new or improved technological assets and applications.

As a general business process improvement, portfolio management includes more coordination than a typical project management initiative. By using the PMO as the motivating force to keep everything moving forward, you establish a centralized and dedicated team charged with keeping the different parts of the initiative on track. Equally important, the PMO has a vested interest in ensuring that the end result constitutes an effective, cohesive business management framework. "No better boat will ever be found than one built by a man who intends to sail the seas with it."

One of the authors witnessed the following a decade ago; it puts real meaning behind the concepts of vision and leadership:

A large IT group for a well-known industrial manufacturer was making a second attempt at implementing portfolio management in its department. Vendor selection was complete and the project team was assembled. An impressive array of preparatory materials had been distributed to those involved, including the project plan, charter, and business case.

Within the first few pages of the business case was a discussion about the previous attempt at this initiative a few years earlier that had not been successful. It candidly stated that the outcome was not due to the previous application or poor support; it was because the organization was not ready and the leadership team was not committed to the initiative's success. It went on to list what the organization had learned from the previous attempt and why those mistakes would not be repeated.

The CIO chaired a formal kick-off meeting at an off-site location, which included all of his direct reports and the project team—a total of twenty-four people. He laid out the case for action relative to aggressive corporate goals, talked about the previous attempt, introduced the team, and reviewed his expectations for what they were to achieve.

As he looked around the room at each person, he said, "We have all prepared for this project for several months. If you have any lingering concerns over this initiative, any outstanding questions, anything you want to get off your chest, now is the time to speak up and be heard. Because when we walk out of here this afternoon, we WILL walk out of here in lockstep, with the attitude that failure is not an option."

What followed was among the most successful and well-run implementations we have been involved with, in part because there was never a hint of doubt that objectives would be met. In addition to the leadership and commitment the CIO showed with his words, the initiative was well planned; the schedule was realistic; and the effort was adequately funded and staffed with professional, dedicated, and skilled people. The entire department was well aware of what was being done; in fact, the staff members were impatient for deployment—all managers knew they had a lot of work to do once they were trained and given access to the new system. Several hundred staff members demonstrated a uniform understanding of what was happening, why it was happening, and their role in transforming how the organization operated.

Defining Your Results

One of the best things you can do to keep implementation focused on outcomes is to clearly define the outputs you expect from each improvement. In this case, we are not talking about general objectives, but rather mocking up specific outputs in terms of reports, dashboards, application screens, and other tangible results. To the extent that your project team and technology consultants know exactly what information is expected and how it will be used, they can ensure that the right inputs are designed into the improvements.

This is particularly important when it comes to developing reporting capabilities. Define your list of key reports, who will use them, and how those individuals will apply the information to execute their responsibilities. Use desktop tools such as spreadsheets or text documents to define preliminary information attributes, layout, and so on. Make sure that end users review, modify, and eventually sign off on these mock-ups. These will guide product configuration and process development and significantly reduce the amount of time and effort needed to create actual reports later.

DEPLOYING IMPROVEMENTS

Creating a Performance Baseline

As you prepare for deployment, it is key that you take time to establish a quantifiable baseline of your current operations. Otherwise, you will not have a point of comparison for measuring your results. You should have established specific goals for the outcomes you are expecting; to the extent possible, identify what the current state values are for these measures.

A good overall metric that will show the value of your improvements is to define your existing throughput. Identify how much work you are able to perform in terms of the different types of work that you deliver on a monthly or quarterly basis, for example, the number of projects completed, service requests responded to, and so on. Also measure your number of inbound requests by type and the amount of work you have in backlog. If you are reporting time (or as soon as you begin), measure how much average effort you are consuming per type of deliverable. Trend these values as you continue to deploy improvements.

Conducting Pilots

When implementing portfolio management improvements in large organizations, you may want to incorporate a pilot deployment to verify capabilities. The term pilot is often a misnomer, because a true pilot is a preliminary test deployment that ends. More often than not, what is actually undertaken is a "limited production deployment" to a small group in advance of rolling out changes to the full population of users.

Whether you conduct an actual pilot or use an initial team of pathfinders, the goal is the same: conduct a controlled and limited implementation to verify that the change is yielding the actual results desired under near-operational conditions. We consciously used the term "desired" rather than "designed" because early use will often uncover that the design of the improvement needs some adjustment.

The key to conducting a successful pilot is to manage its duration to an agreed period; usually a few weeks is ample time to determine if there are major concerns or whether the change is generally performing as planned. Unless serious flaws are uncovered, it is more important to make minor adjustments while you keep deployment momentum moving forward than it is to create a delay in an effort to make everything perfect.

Deploying a change in an operating organization is a bit like changing the lug nuts on a rotating tire, but it is best to effect the change as quickly as possible and get through the sometimes chaotic transition process. We have a Texas-inspired term to describe that period when a change is partially implemented—it's "straddling a barbed-wire fence." Being on one side or the other is OK, but having one part of an organization functioning differently from the other is an awkward and uncomfortable position to be in for any length of time.

Fostering Acceptance

Garnering organizational acceptance of operational changes depends on:

- Communicating the reasons for the change well in advance
- Making sure that the change is functionally effective
- Adequately preparing the staff for new functions and expectations

We spent some time discussing the personal and organizational effects of change in chapter 3. When deploying portfolio management improvements, each change needs to be proactively managed specific to how it impacts each affected group. We have touched on the first two items listed earlier; adequately preparing the organization to accept the change requires that you first recognize its full effects.

One of the more common implementation errors that we see is failure to prepare the staff for all aspects of a change. For example, providing software training for a new application is most effective when it is put in context with how it will enable them to perform new or revised processes. If you are asking the organization to do something new or different, you should position it relative to what was previously being done.

It is also important that the people affected clearly understand any changes in expectations and the implications of not meeting those expectations. Whenever possible, discussions around expectations and accountability should be held by the direct manager, supported by senior management. Asking training instructors or the PMO to communicate such subjects reduces the potential that individuals will take them seriously, when compared to hearing about it from those who have the authority to establish expectations and hold people accountable. The organization is more likely to successfully assimilate change when you make communications and training personally relevant.

Bear in mind that significant changes may take a few weeks for those affected to adjust. Provide adequate *proactive* support during the transition period. A dedicated hotline to answer any questions is helpful, but it is a passive measure that relies on users to ask for help. Nothing compares with making sure that managers are frequently checking in with their staff. When managers are actively involved in effecting a change, it carries weight and sends a powerful message. Staff will immediately recognize that the success of the change is something that is important to "the boss," rather than it only being seen as something asked for by "someone else." Without direct management support, users often perceive changes as unimportant or optional.

By directly involving managers in the deployment process, you give them a chance to ensure that their staff members are using new processes and tools as intended within their specific work environment. It also makes them accessible to coach, get feedback, and to sometimes, just listen. If you find that frustrations are running high or few people need some additional training, you have the opportunity to respond with immediate support, rather than allowing issues to fester and jeopardize results.

While this level of involvement and preparation may seem like a lot of work, we can assure you that it is much easier than trying to recover a failed and distrusted initiative many months later.

MEASURING THE VALUE RECEIVED

We stressed the importance of defining performance objectives during the planning stage of your initiative, capturing a baseline of current performance, and including performance measurement capabilities as a part of your improvements. These three elements make it relatively easy to measure the actual performance that you are able to achieve.

Like any other process change, one of the challenges of your portfolio management initiative is having enough patience to allow the benefits to completely emerge. Even though new capabilities may be deployed, incremental improvements will take some time to fully mature. Bear in mind that the real value of portfolio management is in how it helps you manage change more effectively. Therefore, your new capabilities must be put into practice to facilitate future changes through their cycle before you will realize its full value in the form of bottom-line contributions. Defining short-term successes that align with the desires of the sponsor of the initiative buys you patience as the rest of the benefits continue to develop.

Even with that, each small improvement increases the overall efficiency of the organization and enhances your ability to make better decisions. We further discuss the return on investment of implementing portfolio management in the concluding chapter.

REFINING YOUR PORTFOLIO MANAGEMENT CAPABILITIES

Earlier we mentioned that you should not obsess over making your implementation initiatives perfect before deploying them. You will always be refining your capabilities to meet new needs. We have discussed how your organization is always moving and changing just due to the dynamic environment in which we live. Embracing the discipline of portfolio management will result in a significant increase in the overall operational maturity of your organization, which adds yet another new dimension of change.

We have had the benefit of watching many organizations grow their capabilities and competencies over several years, and we never cease to be impressed by how far they have been able to advance. What may seem to be unnecessary complexities to you at the onset will likely become the next necessity as your portfolio management skills improve. The challenge to your organization will be to recognize each new need as it arises and to continually refine your processes, tools, and expertise to keep moving the organization forward.

THE ROLE OF AN IMPLEMENTATION PARTNER

We have been directly involved in several dozen portfolio-management implementation initiatives and have had secondary involvement in hundreds of others. The discussion that follows sums up what one of us would share with the project team members regarding their role during a kick-off meeting. It offers you some idea of what you should expect from a consulting organization or technology vendor that you engage to support your portfolio management initiative.

"I will be your principal consultant for this initiative. I am like any other member of the project team in that I bring specialized knowledge and skills for you to use to meet the objectives that we share.

I will serve a few different roles during this effort. I will act as your expert on the technology that you have acquired from us. I will facilitate efforts to translate your functional needs into how we can best configure the product to support them. I will respond to any requests of our organization directly when I can. If I cannot, I will call on additional resources as needed to help you be successful. I will own and help expedite anything you need from us and will take the lead to resolve any issues that may arise. You must own your initiative.

I am not the leader of this project; I am here to support your project manager and sponsor, and to be your advocate within our organization. You hold all the power; I cannot make you or your organization do anything it does not want to do. You control the money, the schedule, and the vast majority of the resources for this project. For every hour of effort that we put into your initiative, your organization will put in fifty.

My most important responsibility is to help you be successful in any way I can. No one understands your organization better than you do, and no one understands our products and methods better than we do. We need each other if we are to share a mutual success.

As an adviser, I will share the experience and insights I have gained over the years as a practitioner and as a consultant on several similar implementations. I will offer suggestions, make recommendations, and provide advice. I will be thinking several weeks ahead of where we are on the project at any given time, and will ask questions to help keep you on track.

If I think you are heading down a path or making a decision that will significantly jeopardize your success, I will hold up my index finger like this and explain my concerns. If you continue forward in the same manner, I will hold up two fingers, and again, explain my misgivings. I will do this a total of three times, and I will also make sure your sponsor is aware of my concerns. After that, I will sleep well at night."

The underlying message behind this story is that whether you are engaging a large consulting firm to help you with defining and structuring a global initiative, or working with a technology vendor to implement an application, you should approach it as a true partnership. The role of a consultant is to "lead the horse to water." Ultimately, it is up to you to decide whether to drink. No one can come into your organization for any amount of money and "make your problems go away," mainly because those problems are not theirs to fix, they are yours. Focus on getting mutual agreement about respective roles and responsibilities, hold your partner accountable to doing his or her part, and accept ownership for your own situation.

KEY POINTS IN THIS CHAPTER

☑ Implementing portfolio management is about changing how the organization works together.

☑ We recommend that you set a goal to establish a consistent degree of capability across all of the functions within the portfolio ecosystem through a series of iterative improvements.

☑ Our implementation approach leverages the concepts and practices we have described in this book.

☑ The first step is to conduct a series of assessments from a number of different perspectives, including

- a general operational assessment,
- an organizational assessment,
- a functional assessment, and
- a technological assessment.

☑ You can use the portfolio process map to conduct a functional assessment and identify specific opportunities to improve or use industry standards such as CMMi or OPM3.

☑ Based on the result of your assessments, identify the objectives, strategies, and investment options for your portfolio management initiative.

☑ Prioritize and sequence your approach to make targeted changes within specific functional areas and then build on the results of each improvement.

☑ Leverage a PMO to help manage your initiative and align the changes that need to occur with different aspects of your environment, including

- Vision and leadership
- Organizational commitment
- Information
- Skills and knowledge
- Processes
- Supporting technology

☑ Baseline your current state performance prior to implementing improvements so that you have a point of measurement to determine the value you are receiving.

☑ Ensure that your managers are actively involved in the process of assimilating changes by providing support to their staff, listening to feedback, setting expectations, and holding individuals accountable.

☑ Portfolio management helps you manage future cycles of change more effectively; be patient as the bottom-line value of your improvements fully mature.

☑ Approach the use of consulting organizations and technology vendors as a true partnership, with a clear understanding of how responsibilities are divided between your organization and supporting partners.

CHAPTER 20
SUMMARY

INEVITABLE CHANGE

WE STARTED THIS BOOK by making the case that change is relentless, constant, and inevitable. Change events are coming at an ever-increasing rate to impact our personal lives, our families, and our professional lives. Change *is* the only constant in today's world.

Change has transformed our organizations and how we serve our customers. Today, we are just as likely to create products and services from knowledge and information as from mortar and bricks. And our partners and competitors are as likely to come from around the globe as around the block.

Many organizations have not institutionalized their ability to manage change. They hang on to the outdated belief that the status quo is the norm and change is a one-time event. Our premise is that you will control change or it will control you. You will either get ahead of change to use it as a positive force, or you will be forced to react to it.

Portfolio management offers the tools and techniques to help you tame change. With portfolio management you can

- unify your organization,
- sharpen your strategies, and
- create measurable value.

PORTFOLIOS DRIVE DECISIONS

The core to managing change events is to understand them. You can then make good decisions about how to use your capacities to the benefit of your organization. Portfolio management helps you organize information about people, money, work, and deliverables, which is what influences your decisions about change.

You probably already have a great deal of this information in some form, but it is probably dispersed through the organization and may not be structured very well. It may be divided across a number of functional silos and in different databases and application systems. Portfolio management gives you the means to put your information to work. Portfolio tools and techniques provide a way for your organization to collect, analyze, and act on your information as a shared asset.

THE PORTFOLIO ECOSYSTEM

Chapter 1 introduced the concept of the portfolio ecosystem. In essence, this ecosystem allows us to realize that a change event transforms as it moves through its continuum. In the same way that water changes its state from a gas to a liquid to a solid, change transforms into opportunity, work, and value.

Throughout the book we have steadily added to the basic idea of the portfolio ecosystem as it was first introduced to build a complete picture of the cycle of change as shown in figure 20-1. Change events impact the ecosystem on a continual basis. We rely on processes as a framework for our decision making and performance measures to give us feedback. They are shown on the outer circle of figure 20-1.

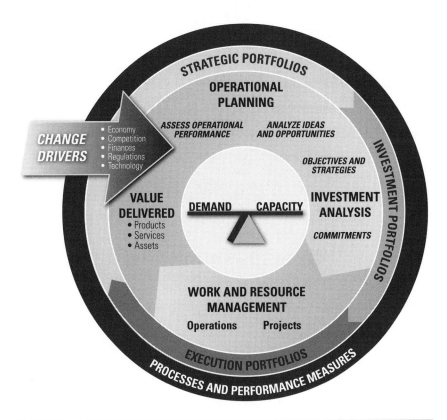

Figure 20-1: The Portfolio Ecosystem

We build portfolios to group information for decision making. We have used three types of portfolios—strategic, investment, and execution. Strategic portfolios guide our operational planning, which allows us to assess operational performance, organize strategies, and analyze ideas and opportunities. Investment portfolios help us organize the investment alternatives and make investment decisions. Execution portfolios direct our projects and other work and facilitate tactical resource management.

Finally, the center core of figure 20-1 reflects the interaction of demand and capacity. The decisions you make about change events always take into account the relationship between demand and capacity with the goal of creating the maximum value for your organization.

The portfolio ecosystem gives us a method to introduce a series of steps as a unified and extremely powerful method to manage change. The steps include:

1. **Operational planning**
    - Assess current state performance.
    - Evaluate change events.
    - Make strategic decisions and set goals.
    - Analyze ideas and opportunities.

2. **Investment analysis**
    - Evaluate investment opportunities.
    - Commit people and money to work.

3. **Work and resource management**
    - Execute work and manage resources.
    - Confirm the value delivered.

Portfolio management offers the information, tools, and techniques to manage this overall life cycle. It offers a *chain of custody* for the information that you use to make decisions and an audit trail for performance measurement. Portfolio management is an indispensable enterprise skill set for modern organizations.

An essential shared organizational service in managing the change life cycle is the portfolio management office (PMO.) The PMO offers an excellent way to communicate and coordinate the life cycle of change events throughout your organization. Some organizations view it as offering the same type of shared services as finance and HR. Successful organizations will institutionalize how they manage the life cycle of change today and in the future.

PORTFOLIO MANAGEMENT RETURN ON INVESTMENT

Implementing portfolio management is a business process improvement initiative that is validated by measuring your return on the investment. For organizations that currently do not have a comprehensive approach and tool set for managing the life cycle of change events, the potential for increasing organizational efficiency is worth millions of dollars a year and can offer a return on investment in months. This is why.

Human resources are the critical raw material of knowledge worker environments. Technology Service Organizations are almost always in the position of having a relatively fixed resource capacity to meet an excess of demand. As a result, the ability of an organization to increase the throughput of deliverables provides direct savings, in the form of reduced need for external or supplementary staff, avoiding or deferring future staff increases, reducing the per capita cost per deliverable, and/or realizing the benefit of more deliverables sooner.

Our experience over the years has shown us that it is reasonable to expect increases of 15 to 35 percent in the ability of the organization to accomplish work by implementing portfolio management depending on your current culture, tools, and processes. Process and cultural changes are the heart of the improvements supported by automation and tools.

To put a nominal productivity increase of 20 percent in monetary terms, an assumed average fully burdened FTE annual cost of $100,000 means that the typical *annual recurring savings per 100 staff* is $2 million. If you have 1,000 knowledge workers, the annual value of a 20 percent improvement in throughput is $20 million. We have worked with some organizations with tens of thousands of workers, and the benefits have been in excess of $100 million per year.

If your organization already uses some portfolio management techniques and you would like to expand, you still could expect a 10 percent improvement in productivity. That is only 4 hours per week per worker focused on higher-productivity work. Even if you need to start small and grow your efforts over time, the math is still compelling.

The Innovation Multiplier

This calculation by itself does not fully reflect the potential bottom-line benefit. The ability of an organization to move forward by accomplishing work of high value to improve its overall business posture is defined by innovation. Even small gains in the amount of effort spent on operational work can be reinvested into initiatives that transform and expand the business to further multiply gains.

Using a nominal operational spend ratio in knowledge worker organizations of 25 percent on innovation and 75 percent on current state operations as an example, a mere 5 percent reduction in operational costs that is reallocated to innovation nets a 20 percent increase in the ability of the organization to innovate. Time and effort spent on maintaining the operational status quo is inherently limited in its net value to the business. Redirecting capacity to engage in more business innovation has an almost unlimited ability to contribute to the success of the enterprise.

Implementing and Maintaining Portfolio Management

While every organization is different, we have seen typical start-up costs of portfolio management tools and techniques averaging from 3 to 5 percent of what the organization spends annually on knowledge workers. That includes process design, training, automation, and building a portfolio management office. With the recurring maintenance cost after start up averaging 2 percent per year compared to a 20 percent improvement in throughput, *organizations can expect to realize a net return on their investment in portfolio management within months.*

The Source of Productivity Improvements

A unified approach to decision making using the portfolio management process framework enables several specific improvements that allow your organization to become more focused, proactive, and efficient:

1. Improving alignment between strategic intent and the work being performed increases organizational focus to "do the most important work first."

2. Making consistent, informed, and transparent decisions for resource utilization and financial spending improves business governance.

3. Establishing common priorities fosters a unified sense of purpose and improves collaboration.

4. Enhancing visibility into individual capacities versus assignments allows resources to be better directed using achievable goals. This allows managers to hold staff accountable to target objectives and better control how time is utilized.

5. Using a common real-time data source and business application to manage work and resources ensures that all staff members have the information they need to make decisions as they work and that they have access to all the necessary functions to revise and immediately communicate plan changes.

6. Understanding and visibility of how the organization really operates allows specific bottlenecks, roadblocks, or inefficiencies to be identified and corrected.

7. Improving its ability to identify and adjust to business dynamics that impact work plans allows the organization to be more responsive to change influences.

All these improvements result in a more-focused organization that is better able to manage and employ its people and its money. Accurate measurements of how effort is currently being applied lead to immediate improvements in staff utilization. With a direct tie between money and strategy, you have a better understanding of what is important to your organization.

In addition to the direct benefits inherent in these improvements, a common secondary benefit is lower staff turnover, especially in critical skill sets. By working more productively rather than longer hours, and by making better use of individual talents and skills directed to high value activities, workers feel more engaged and successful, and the organization gains the self-confidence that stems from operating in a methodical manner at visibly higher performance levels. Members of your organization become unified through your vision and leadership. They have a clear set of objectives and a commitment to accomplish them.

Portfolio management provides an essential compass to steer your company through the seas of unending change. In this book we have distilled our decades of experience into a practical summary of concepts to help your organization improve its performance. To continue the journey that you have started, visit us at www.tamingchange.com. We welcome you to the growing community of practitioners who have learned to prosper in these turbulent times by *Taming Change with Portfolio Management.*

INDEX

ABOUT THE AUTHORS

PAT DURBIN is Chief Executive Officer and Founder of Planview, the award-winning leader in portfolio management solutions. With more than 30 years of experience in business process design and automation, he has designed multiple global management systems including Planview Enterprise. Prior to founding Planview, he served as Vice President of Research and Development and Worldwide Marketing for Artemis International and has held various positions at Sun Oil and McDonnell Douglas. Pat has a BS in Aeronautics from Saint Louis University and an MBA from the University of Illinois.

TERRY DOERSCHER is the Chief Process Architect for Planview. With more than 27 years of experience as a practitioner and consultant, his focus is on innovating world-class management techniques aligned to modern business challenges. Terry is a trusted advisor to many customers, and is a frequently cited industry expert and speaker. He is the primary author of Planview PRISMS Best Practices, and drives the 'PMO 2.0' series of events and research. Prior to joining Planview, Terry served in a number of roles in the public utility industry, and received his formal engineering education in the US Navy Nuclear Power Program. Terry is a founding director of the Enterprise Management Association–International.